Yankee Teacher to the World

RALPH WALDO EMERSON was one of America's outstanding men of letters. He was a wise man, a poet and a wit, and when he spoke, thoughtful men and women throughout the world found inspiration in his words.

CALLED THE SAGE OF CONCORD, Emerson was born in Boston 150 years ago. He became the Pastor of that city's famous Second Church, and ended his ministry to become a writer and a philosopher. His productive period lasted over forty years, during which time he personified New England individualism and became the perfect spokesman for the America of his day.

EMERSON illuminated a thousand timeless themes with simplicity and taste. Whether he wrote of Nature or man's conscience, of self-reliance or of Democracy, he blended sound Yankee common-sense with penetrating insight into the heart of man. Here, selected with love and care by Eduard C. Lindeman, are the best-known of Emerson's essays, his poems and the brilliant capsules of wisdom from his *Journals*. Nowhere in American writings is there a keener perception or a more universal appeal.

EDUARD C. LINDEMAN, a founder of the modern American adult education movement, noted educator, philosopher, writer and one of Emerson's most articulate admirers, was born in Michigan in 1885. For twenty-two years he was Professor of Social Philosophy at the N. Y. School of Social Work, Columbia University. He had served as President of the Conference of Social Work and was chairman of the Committee on Academic Freedom of the American Civil Liberties Union. The author of many books, Dr. Lindeman edited *Emerson, The Basic Writings of America's Sage*. He died in 1953.

Other Mentor Books of Special Interest

BASIC SELECTIONS FROM

EMERSON

Essays, Poems & Apothegms

EDITED BY

EDUARD C. LINDEMAN

Published by

THE NEW AMERICAN LIBRARY

Published as a MENTOR BOOK
By Arrangement with Houghton Mifflin Company

FIRST PRINTING, JANUARY, 1954
SECOND PRINTING, FEBRUARY, 1958
THIRD PRINTING, SEPTEMBER, 1959

Library of Congress Catalog Card No. 54-6005

MENTOR BOOKS are published by
The New American Library of World Literature, Inc.
501 Madison Avenue, New York 22, New York

PRINTED IN THE UNITED STATES OF AMERICA

CONTENTS

INTRODUCTION

In 1947 I edited a volume of Emerson's essays which was published as a Mentor Book under the title *Emerson: The Basic Writings of America's Sage;* during the past five years that volume has passed through four rather large printings. It was not an orthodox or conventional selection. I purposely avoided the old familiar essays known to most Americans and proceeded to the selection of lesser known essays. These were chosen on the basis of contemporary relevancy. I wanted younger readers who might have overlooked Emerson to realize that he had something to say for our time and this generation.

My effort was only in part successful. Many readers wanted the old favorites in a small, inexpensive volume. The present collection is a response to these requests. Emerson enthusiasts will find in this volume a collection of the best known of Emerson's essays, a representative sample of his poetry, and selections from his *Journals*. Nothing needs to be said by way of introduction to the essays and the poems. These are firmly woven into the very fabric of American life and culture. Emerson is to American life what Shakespeare is to British and Goethe to German. He was our most completely expressed writer and philosopher. The *Journals* are, however, unique.

They were begun in his adolescence and continued almost to the end of his long life. These *Journals* were not in any ordinary sense diaries. He included very little of event, and hence one does not read Emerson's *Journals* for the purpose of recapturing the history of his time. His own description of the purpose of the *Journals* is perhaps as revealing as any. He advised scholars to keep a journal and in it to "pay so much honor to the visits of Truth to your mind as to record them." I have called these "visits of Truth" *apothegms,* which may be taken to mean short and pithy condensations of wisdom.

Readers who have not before "tasted" these "visits of Truth" will be surprised by their candor, enlightened by their depth of insight and delighted by their originality and beauty.

EDUARD C. LINDEMAN,

Professor of Social Philosophy, New York School of Social Work, Columbia University, and Advisory Editor on Mentor Books, until his death in April, 1953.

———————————

Acknowledgments:

The essays included in this volume were taken from the Riverside Edition printed in 1903. The poems appear in Volume IX of that edition, which is published by Houghton Mifflin Company.

The apothegms were selected from *Journals of Ralph Waldo Emerson,* edited by Edward Waldo Emerson and Waldo Emerson Forbes, published by Houghton Mifflin Company, 1909.

Part I

ESSAYS

Nature

There are days which occur in this climate, at almost any season of the year, wherein the world reaches its perfection; when the air, the heavenly bodies and the earth make a harmony, as if Nature would indulge her offspring; when, in these bleak upper sides of the planet, nothing is to desire that we have heard of the happiest latitudes, and we bask in the shining hours of Florida and Cuba; when everything that has life gives sign of satisfaction, and the cattle that lie on the ground seem to have great and tranquil thoughts. These halcyons may be looked for with a little more assurance in that pure October weather which we distinguish by the name of the Indian summer. The day, immeasurably long, sleeps over the broad hills and warm wide fields. To have lived through all its sunny hours, seems longevity enough. The solitary places do not seem quite lonely. At the gates of the forest, the surprised man of the world is forced to leave his city estimates of great and small, wise and foolish. The knapsack of custom falls off his back with the first step he takes into these precincts. Here is sanctity which shames our religions, and reality which discredits our heroes. Here we find Nature to be the circumstance which dwarfs every other circumstance, and judges like a god all men that come to her. We have crept out of our close and crowded houses into the night and morning, and we see what majestic beauties daily wrap us in their bosom. How willingly we would escape the barriers which render them comparatively impotent, escape the sophistication and second thought, and suffer nature to entrance us. The tempered light of the woods is like a perpetual morning, and is stimulating and heroic. The anciently-reported spells of these places creep on us. The stems of pines, hemlocks and oaks almost gleam like iron on the excited eye. The incommunicable trees begin to persuade us to live with them, and quit our life of solemn trifles. Here no history, or church, or state is interpolated on the divine sky and the immortal year. How easily we might walk onward into the opening landscape, absorbed by new pictures and by thoughts fast succeeding each other, until by degrees the recollection of home was crowded out of the mind, all memory obliterated by the tyranny of the present, and we were led in triumph by nature.

These enchantments are medicinal, they sober and heal us. These are plain pleasures, kindly and native to us. We come to our own, and make friends with matter, which the ambitious chatter of the schools would persuade us to despise. We never can part with it; the mind loves its old home: as water to our thirst, so is the rock, the ground, to our eyes and hands and feet. It is firm water; it is cold flame; what health, what affinity! Ever an old friend, ever like a dear friend and brother when we chat affectedly with strangers, comes in this honest face, and takes a grave liberty with us, and shames us out of our nonsense. Cities give not the human sense room enough. We go out daily and nightly to feed the eyes on the horizon, and require so much scope, just as we need water for our bath. There are all degrees of natural influence, from these quarantine powers of Nature, up to her dearest and gravest ministrations to the imagination and the soul. There is the bucket of cold water from the spring, the wood fire to which the chilled traveler rushes for safety—and there is the sublime moral of autumn and of noon. We nestle in Nature, and draw our living as parasites from her roots and grains, and we receive glances from the heavenly bodies, which call us to solitude and foretell the remotest future. The blue zenith is the point in which romance and reality meet. I think if we should be rapt away into all that and dream of heaven, and should converse with Gabriel and Uriel, the upper sky would be all that would remain of our furniture.

It seems as if the day was not wholly profane in which we have given heed to some natural object. The fall of snowflakes in a still air, preserving to each crystal its perfect form; the blowing of sleet over a wide sheet of water, and over plains; the waving rye field; the mimic waving of acres of houstonia, whose innumerable florets whiten and ripple before the eye; the reflections of trees and flowers in glassy lakes; the musical, steaming, odorous south wind, which converts all trees to wind harps; the crackling and spurting of hemlock in the flames, or of pine logs, which yield glory to the walls and faces in the sitting room—these are the music and pictures of the most ancient religion. My house stands in low land, with limited outlook, and on the skirt of the village. But I go with my friend to the shore of our little river, and with one stroke of the paddle I leave the village politics and personalities, yes, and the world of villages and personalities, behind, and pass into a delicate realm of sunset and moonlight, too bright almost for spotted man to enter without novitiate and probation. We penetrate bodily this incredible beauty; we dip our hands in this painted element; our eyes are bathed in these lights and forms. A holiday, a *villeggiatura*, a royal revel, the proudest, most heart-rejoicing festival that valor and beauty, power and taste, ever decked and enjoyed, establishes itself on the instant. These sunset clouds, these delicately emerging stars, with their private and ineffable glances, signify it and proffer it. I am taught the poorness of our invention, the ugliness of towns and palaces. Art and luxury have early learned that they must work as enhancement and sequel to this original beauty. I am overinstructed for my return. Henceforth I shall be hard to please. I cannot go back to toys. I am grown expensive and sophisticated. I can no longer live without elegance, but a countryman shall be my master of revels. He who knows the most; he who knows what sweets and virtues are in the ground, the waters, the plants, the heavens, and how to come at these enchantments—is the rich and royal man. Only as far as the masters of the world have called in nature in their aid, can they reach the height of magnificence. This is the meaning of their hanging gardens, villas, garden houses, islands, parks and preserves, to back their faulty personality with these strong accessories. I do not wonder that the landed interest should be invincible in the State with these dangerous auxiliaries. These bribe and invite; not kings, not palaces, not men, not women, but these tender and poetic stars, eloquent of secret promises. We heard what the rich man said, we knew of his villa, his grove, his wine and his company, but the provocation and point of the invitation came out of these beguiling stars. In their soft glances I see what men strove to realize in some Versailles, or Paphos, or Ctesiphon. Indeed, it is the magical lights of the horizon and the blue sky for the background which save all our works of art, which were otherwise baubles. When the rich tax the poor with servility and obsequiousness, they should consider the effect of men reputed to be the possessors of nature on imaginative minds. Ah! if the rich were rich as the poor fancy riches! A boy hears a military band play on the field at night, and he has kings and queens and famous chivalry palpably before him. He hears the echoes of a horn in a hill country, in the Notch Mountains, for example, which converts the mountains into an Aeolian harp—and this supernatural *tiralira* restores to him the Dorian mythology, Apollo, Diana, and all divine hunters and huntresses. Can a musical note be so loftly, so haughtily beautiful! To the poor young poet, thus fabulous is his picture of society; he is loyal; he respects the rich; they are rich for the sake of his imagination; how poor his fancy would be, if they were not rich! That they have some high-fenced grove which they call a park; that they live in larger and better-garnished saloons than he has visited, and go in coaches, keeping only the society of the elegant, to watering places and to distant cities—these make the groundwork from which he has delineated estates of romance, compared with which their actual possessions are shanties and paddocks. The muse herself betrays her son, and enhances the gifts of wealth and well-born beauty by a radiation out of the air, and clouds, and forests that skirt the road—a certain haughty favor, as if from patrician genii to patricians, a kind of aristocracy in nature, a prince of the power of the air.

The moral sensibility which makes Edens and Tempes so easily, may not always be found, but the material landscape is never far off. We can find these enchantments without visiting the Como Lake, or the Madeira Islands. We exaggerate the praises of local scenery. In every landscape the point of astonishment is the meeting of the sky and earth, and that is seen from the first hillock as well as from the top of the Alleghenies. The stars at night stoop down over the brownest, homeliest common with all the spiritual magnificence which they shed on the Campagna, or on the marble deserts of Egypt. The uprolled clouds and the colors of morning and evening will transfigure maples and alders. The difference between landscape and landscape is small, but there is great difference in the beholders. There is nothing so wonderful in any particular landscape as the necessity of being beautiful under which every landscape lies. Nature cannot be surprised in undress. Beauty breaks in everywhere.

But it is very easy to outrun the sympathy of readers on this topic which schoolmen called *natura naturata,* or nature passive. One can hardly speak directly of it without excess. It is as easy to broach in mixed companies what is called "the subject of religion." A susceptible person does not like to indulge his tastes in this kind without the apology of some trivial necessity: he goes to see a wood lot, or to look at the crops, or to fetch a plant or a mineral from a remote locality, or he carries a fowling piece or a fishing rod. I suppose this shame must have a good reason. A dilettantism in nature is barren and unworthy. The fop of fields is no better than his brother of Broadway. Men are naturally hunters and inquisitive of woodcraft, and I suppose that such a gazetteer as woodcutters and Indians should furnish facts for, would take place in the most sumptuous drawing rooms of all the "Wreaths" and "Flora's chaplets" of the bookshops; yet ordinarily, whether we are too clumsy for so subtle a topic, or from whatever cause, as soon as men begin to write on nature, they fall into euphuism. Frivolity is a most unfit tribute to Pan, who ought to be represented in the mythology as the most continent of gods. I would not be frivolous before the admirable reserve and prudence of time, yet I cannot renounce the right of returning often to this old topic. The multitude of false churches accredits the true religion. Literature, poetry, science are the homage of man to this unfathomed secret, concerning which no sane man can affect an indifference or incuriosity. Nature is loved by what is best in us. It is loved as the city of God, although, or rather because, there is no citizen. The sunset is unlike anything that is underneath it: it wants men. And the beauty of nature must always seem unreal and mocking, until the landscape has human figures that are as good as itself. If there were good men, there would never be this rapture in nature. If the king is in the palace, nobody looks at the walls. It is when he is gone, and the house is filled with grooms and gazers, that we turn from the people to find relief in the majestic men that are suggested by the pictures and the architecture. The critics who complain of the sickly separation of the beauty of nature from the thing to be done, must consider that our hunting of the picturesque is inseparable from our protest against false society. Man is fallen; nature is erect, and serves as a differential thermometer, detecting the presence or absence of the divine sentiment in man. By fault of our dullness and selfishness we are looking up to nature, but when we are convalescent, nature will look up to us. We see the foaming brook with compunction; if our own life flowed with the right energy, we should shame the brook. The stream of zeal sparkles with real fire, and not with the reflex rays of sun and moon. Nature may be as selfishly studied as trade. Astronomy to the selfish becomes astrology; psychology, mesmerism (with intent to show where our spoons are gone); and anatomy and physiology become phrenology and palmistry.

But taking timely warning, and leaving many things unsaid on this topic, let us not longer omit our homage to the Efficient Nature, *natura naturans*, the quick cause before which all forms flee as the driven snows; itself secret, its works driven before it in flocks and multitudes (as the ancients represented nature by Proteus, a shepherd) and in undescribable variety. It publishes itself in creatures, reaching from particles and spiculae through transformation on transformation to the highest symmetries, arriving at consummate results without a shock or a leap. A little heat, that is a little motion, is all that differences the bald, dazzling white and deadly cold poles of the earth from the prolific tropical climates. All changes pass without violence, by reason of the two cardinal conditions of boundless space and boundless time. Geology has initiated us into the secularity of nature, and taught us to disuse our dame-school measures, and exchange our Mosaic and Ptolemaic schemes for her large style. We know nothing rightly, for want of perspective. Now

we learn what patient periods must round themselves before
the rock is formed; then before the rock is broken, and the first
lichen race has disintegrated the thinnest external plate into
soil, and opened the door for the remote Flora, Fauna, Ceres
and Pomona to come in. How far off is the trilobite! how far
the quadruped! how inconceivably remote is man! All duly arrive, and then race after race of men. It is a long way from
granite to oyster; farther yet to Plato and the preaching of the
immortality of the soul. Yet all must come, as surely as the first
atom has two sides.

Motion or change and identity or rest are the first and second
secrets of Nature: Motion and Rest. The whole code of her
laws may be written on the thumbnail, or the signet of a ring.
The whirling bubble on the surface of a brook admits us to the
secret of the mechanics of the sky. Every shell on the beach is
a key to it. A little water made to rotate in a cup explains the
formation of the simpler shells; the addition of matter from
year to year arrives at last at the most complex forms; and yet
so poor is nature with all her craft, that from the beginning to
the end of the universe she has but one stuff—but one stuff
with its two ends to serve up all her dreamlike variety. Compound it how she will, star, sand, fire, water, tree, man, it is
still one stuff, and betrays the same properties.

Nature is always consistent, though she feigns to contravene
her own laws. She keeps her laws, and seems to transcend
them. She arms and equips an animal to find its place and living in the earth, and at the same time she arms and equips another animal to destroy it. Space exists to divide creatures; but
by clothing the sides of a bird with a few feathers she gives
him a petty omnipresence. The direction is forever onward, but
the artist still goes back for materials and begins again with
the first elements on the most advanced stage: otherwise all
goes to ruin. If we look at her work, we seem to catch a
glance of a system in transition. Plants are the young of the
world, vessels of health and vigor; but they grope ever upward towards consciousness; the trees are imperfect men, and
seem to bemoan their imprisonment, rooted in the ground. The
animal is the novice and probationer of a more advanced
order. The men, though young, having tasted the first drop
from the cup of thought, are already dissipated: the maples
and ferns are still uncorrupt; yet no doubt when they come to
consciousness they too will curse and swear. Flowers so strictly
belong to youth that we adult men soon come to feel that their
beautiful generations concern not us: we have had our day;
now let the children have theirs. The flowers jilt us, and we are
old bachelors with our ridiculous tenderness.

Things are so strictly related that, according to the skill of the eye, from any one object the parts and properties of any other may be predicted. If we had eyes to see it, a bit of stone from the city wall would certify us of the necessity that man must exist, as readily as the city. That identity makes us all one, and reduces to nothing great intervals on our customary scale. We talk of deviations from natural life, as if artificial life were not also natural. The smoothest curled courtier in the boudoirs of a palace has an animal nature, rude and aboriginal as a white bear, omnipotent of its own ends, and is directly related, there amid essences and billets-doux, to Himalaya mountain chains and the axis of the globe. If we consider how much we are nature's, we need not be superstitious about towns, as if that terrific or benefic force did not find us there also, and fashion cities. Nature, who made the mason, made the house. We may easily hear too much of rural influences. The cool disengaged air of natural objects makes them enviable to us, chafed and irritable creatures with red faces, and we think we shall be as grand as they if we camp out and eat roots; but let us be men instead of woodchucks and the oak and the elm shall gladly serve us, though we sit in chairs of ivory on carpets of silk.

This guiding identity runs through all the surprises and contrasts of the piece, and characterizes every law. Man carries the world in his head, the whole astronomy and chemistry suspended in a thought. Because the history of nature is charactered in his brain, therefore is he the prophet and discoverer of her secrets. Every known fact in natural science was divined by the presentiment of somebody, before it was actually verified. A man does not tie his shoe without recognizing laws which bind the farthest regions of nature: moon, plant, gas, crystal are concrete geometry and numbers. Common sense knows its own, and recognizes the fact at first sight in chemical experiment. The common sense of Franklin, Dalton, Davy and Black is the same common sense which made the arrangements which now it discovers.

If the identity expresses organized rest, the counteraction runs also into organization. The astronomers said, "Give us matter and a little motion and we will construct the universe. It it not enough that we should have matter, we must also have a single impulse, one shove to launch the mass and generate the harmony of the centrifugal and centripetal forces. Once heave the ball from the hand, and we can show how all this mighty order grew." — "A very unreasonable postulate," said the metaphysicians, "and a plain begging of the question. Could you not prevail to know the genesis of projection, as well as the continuation of it?" Nature, meanwhile, had not waited for the discussion, but, right or wrong, bestowed the impulse, and the balls rolled. It was no great affair, a mere push, but the astronomers were right in making much of it, for there is no end to the consequences of the act. That famous aboriginal push propagates itself through all the balls of the system, and through every atom of every ball; through all the races of creatures, and through the history and performances of every individual. Exaggeration is in the course of things. Nature sends no creature, no man, into the world without adding a small excess of his proper quality. Given the planet, it is still necessary to add the impulse; so to every creature nature added a little violence of direction in its proper path, a shove to put it on its way; in every instance a slight generosity, a drop too much. Without electricity the air would rot, and without this violence of direction which men and women have, without a spice of bigot and fanatic, no excitement, no efficiency. We aim above the mark to hit the mark. Every act hath some falsehood of exaggeration in it. And when now and then comes along some sad, sharp-eyed man, who sees how paltry a game is played, and refuses to play but blabs the secret—how then? Is the bird flown? Oh no, the wary Nature sends a new troop of fairer forms, of lordlier youths, with a little more excess of direction to hold them fast to their several aims; make them a little wrongheaded in that direction in which they are rightest, and on goes the game again with a new whirl, for a generation or two more. The child with his sweet pranks, the fool of his senses, commanded by every sight and sound, without any power to compare and rank his sensations, abandoned to a whistle or a painted chip, to a lead dragoon or a gingerbread dog, individualizing everything, generalizing nothing, delighted with every new thing, lies down at night overpowered by the fatigue which this day of continual pretty madness has incurred. But Nature has answered her purpose with the curly, dimpled lunatic. She has tasked every faculty, and has secured the symmetrical growth of the bodily frame by all these attitudes and exertions—an end of the first importance, which could not be trusted to any care less perfect than her own. This glitter, this opaline luster, plays round the top of every toy to his eye to insure his fidelity, and he is deceived to his good. We are made alive and kept alive by the same art. Let the Stoics say what they please, we do not eat for the good of living, but because the meat is savory and the appetite is keen. The vegetable life does not content itself with casting from the flower or the tree a single seed, but it fills the air and earth with a prodigality of seeds, that, if thousands perish, thousands may plant themselves; that hundreds may come up, that tens may live to maturity; that at least one may replace the parent. All things betray the same calculated profusion. The excess of fear with which the animal frame is hedged round, shrinking from cold, starting at sight of a snake or at a sudden noise, protects us, through a multitude of groundless alarms, from some one real danger at last. The lover seeks in marriage his private felicity and perfection, with no prospective end; and Nature hides in his happiness her own end, namely progeny, or the perpetuity of the race.

But the craft with which the world is made, runs also into the mind and character of men. No man is quite sane; each has a vein of folly in his composition, a slight determination of blood to the head, to make sure of holding him hard to some one point which nature had taken to heart. Great causes are never tried on their merits; but the cause is reduced to particulars to suit the size of the partisans, and the contention is ever hottest on minor matters. Not less remarkable is the overfaith of each man in the importance of what he has to do or say. The poet, the prophet, has a higher value for what he utters than any hearer, and therefore it gets spoken. The strong, self-complacent Luther declares with an emphasis not to be mistaken, that "God himself cannot do without wise men." Jacob Behmen and George Fox betray their egotism in the pertinacity of their controversial tracts, and James Naylor once suffered himself to be worshipped as the Christ. Each prophet comes presently to identify himself with his thought, and to esteem his hat and shoes sacred. However this may discredit such persons with the judicious, it helps them with the people, as it gives heat, pungency and publicity to their words. A similar experience is not infrequent in private life. Each young and ardent person writes a diary, in which, when the hours of prayer and penitence arrive, he inscribes his soul. The pages thus written are to him burning and fragrant; he reads them on his knees by midnight and by the morning star; he wets them with his tears; they are sacred; too good for the world, and hardly yet to be shown to the dearest friend. This is the man-child that is born to the soul, and her life still circulates in the babe. The umbilical cord has not yet been cut. After some time has elapsed, he begins to wish to admit his friend to this hallowed experience, and with firmness, yet with hesitation, exposes the pages to his eye. Will they not burn his eyes? The friend coldly turns them over, and passes from the writing to conversation, with easy transition, which strikes the other party with astonishment and vexation. He cannot suspect the writing itself. Days and nights of fervid life, of communion with angels of darkness and of light, have engraved their shadowy characters on that tear-stained book. He suspects the intelligence or the heart of his friend. Is there then no friend? He cannot yet credit that one may have impressive experience and yet may not know how to put his private fact into literature: and perhaps the discovery that wisdom has other tongues and ministers than we, that though we should hold our peace the truth would not the less be spoken, might check injuriously the flames of our zeal. A man can only speak so long as he does not feel his speech to be partial and inadequate. It is partial, but he does not see it to be so whilst he utters it. As soon as he is released from the instinctive and particular and sees its partiality, he shuts his mouth in disgust. For no man can write anything who does not think that what he writes is for the time the history of the world; or do anything well who does not esteem his work to be of importance. My work may be of none, but I must not think it of none, or I shall not do it with impunity.

In like manner, there is throughout nature something mocking, something that leads us on and on, but arrives nowhere; keeps no faith with us. All promise outruns the performance. We live in a system of approximations. Every end is prospective of some other end, which is also temporary; a round and final success nowhere. We are encamped in nature, not domesticated. Hunger and thirst lead us on to eat and to drink; but bread and wine, mix and cook them how you will, leave us hungry and thirsty, after the stomach is full. It is the same with all our arts and performances. Our music, our poetry, our language itself, are not satisfactions, but suggestions. The hunger for wealth, which reduces the planet to a garden, fools the eager pursuer. What is the end sought? Plainly to secure the ends of good sense and beauty from the intrusion of deformity or vulgarity of any kind. But with an operose method! What a train of means to secure a little conversation! This palace of brick and stone, these servants, this kitchen, these stables, horses and equipage, this bank stock and file of mortgages, trade to all the world, country house and cottage by the waterside, all for a little conversation, high, clear and spiritual! Could it not be had as well by beggars on the highway? No, all these things came from successive efforts of these beggars to remove friction from the wheels of life, and give opportunity. Conversation, character, were the avowed ends; wealth was good as it appeased the animal cravings, cured the smoky chimney, silenced the creaking door, brought friends together in a warm and quiet room, and kept the children and the dinner table in a different apartment. Thought, virtue, beauty were the ends; but it was known that men of thought and virtue sometimes had the headache, or wet feet, or could lose good time whilst the room was getting warm in winter days. Unluckily, in the exertions necessary to remove these inconveniences, the main attention has been diverted to this object; the old aims have been lost sight of, and to remove friction has come to be the end. That is the ridicule of rich men; and Boston, London, Vienna, and now the governments generally of the world, are cities and governments of the rich; and the masses are not men, but *poor men*, that is, men who would be rich; this is the ridicule of the class, that they arrive with pains and sweat and fury nowhere; when all is done, it is for nothing. They are like one who has interrupted the conversation of a company to make his speech, and now has forgotten what he went to say. The appearance strikes the eye everywhere of an aimless society, of aimless nations. Were the ends of nature so great and cogent as to exact this immense sacrifice of men?

Quite analogous to the deceits in life, there is, as might be expected, a similar effect on the eye from the face of external nature. There is in woods and waters a certain enticement and flattery, together with a failure to yield a present satisfaction. This disappointment is felt in every landscape. I have seen the softness and beauty of the summer clouds floating feathery overhead, enjoying, as it seemed, their height and privilege of motion, whilst yet they appeared not so much the drapery of this place and hour, as forelooking to some pavilions and gardens of festivity beyond. It is an odd jealousy, but the poet finds himself not near enough to his object. The pine tree, the river, the bank of flowers before him, does not seem to be nature. Nature is still elsewhere. This or this is but outskirt and a far-off reflection and echo of the triumph that has passed by and is now at its glancing splendor and heyday, perchance in the neighboring fields, or, if you stand in the field, then in the adjacent woods. The present object shall give you this sense of stillness that follows a pageant which has just gone by. What splendid distance, what recesses of ineffable pomp and loveliness in the sunset! But who can go where they are, or lay his hand or plant his foot thereon? Off they fall from the round world forever and ever. It is the same among the men and women as among the silent trees; always a referred existence, an absence, never a presence and satisfaction. Is it that beauty can never be grasped? in persons and in landscape is equally inaccessible? The accepted and betrothed lover has lost the wildest charm of his maiden in her acceptance of him. She was heaven whilst he pursued her as a star; she cannot be heaven if she stoops to such a one as he.

What shall we say of this omnipresent appearance of that first projectile impulse, of this flattery and balking of so many well-meaning creatures? Must we not suppose somewhere in the universe a slight treachery and derision? Are we not engaged to a serious resentment of this use that is made of us? Are we tickled trout, and fools of nature? One look at the face of heaven and earth lays all petulance at rest, and soothes us to wiser convictions. To the intelligent, nature converts itself into a vast promise, and will not be rashly explained. Her secret is untold. Many and many an Oedipus arrives; he has the whole mystery teeming in his brain. Alas! the same sorcery has spoiled his skill; no syllable can he shape on his lips. Her mighty orbit vaults like the fresh rainbow into the deep, but no archangel's wing was yet strong enough to follow it and report of the return of the curve. But it also appears that our actions are seconded and disposed to greater conclusions than we designed. We are escorted on every hand through life by spiritual agents, and a beneficent purpose lies in wait for us. We cannot bandy words with Nature, or deal with her as we deal with persons. If we measure our individual forces against hers we may easily feel as if we were the sport of an insuperable destiny. But if, instead of identifying ourselves with the work, we feel that the soul of the Workman streams through us, we shall find the peace of the morning dwelling first in our hearts, and the fathomless powers of gravity and chemistry, and, over them, of life, pre-existing within us in their highest form.

The uneasiness which the thought of our helplessness in the chain of causes occasions us, results from looking too much at one condition of nature, namely, Motion. But the drag is never taken from the wheel. Wherever the impulse exceeds, the Rest or Identity insinuates its compensation. All over the wide fields of earth grows the prunella or self-heal. After every foolish day we sleep off the fumes and furies of its hours; and though we are always engaged with particulars, and often enslaved to them, we bring with us to every experiment the innate universal laws. These, while they exist in the mind as ideas, stand around us in nature forever embodied, a present sanity to expose and cure the insanity of men. Our servitude to particulars betrays us into a hundred foolish expectations. We anticipate a new era from the invention of a locomotive, or a balloon; the new engine brings with it the old checks. They say that by electromagnetism your salad will be grown from the seed whilst your fowl is roasting for dinner; it is a symbol of our modern aims and endeavors, of our condensation and acceleration of objects—but nothing is gained; nature cannot be cheated;

man's life is but seventy salads long, grow they swift or grow they slow. In these checks and impossibilities, however, we find our advantage, not less than in the impulses. Let the victory fall where it will, we are on that side. And the knowledge that we traverse the whole scale of being, from the center to the poles of nature, and have some stake in every possibility, lends that sublime luster to death, which philosophy and religion have too outwardly and literally striven to express in the popular doctrine of the immortality of the soul. The reality is more excellent than the report. Here is no ruin, no discontinuity, no spent ball. The divine circulations never rest nor linger. Nature is the incarnation of a thought, and turns to a thought again, as ice becomes water and gas. The world is mind precipitated, and the volatile essence is forever escaping again into the state of free thought. Hence the virtue and pungency of the influence on the mind of natural objects, whether inorganic or organized. Man imprisoned, man crystallized, man vegetative, speaks to man impersonated. That power which does not respect quantity, which makes the whole and the particle its equal channel, delegates its smile to the morning, and distills its essence into every drop of rain. Every moment instructs, and every object; for wisdom is infused into every form. It has been poured into us as blood; it convulsed us as pain; it slid into us as pleasure; it enveloped us in dull, melancholy days, or in days of cheerful labor; we did not guess its essence until after a long time.

From *Essays: Second Series*
Volume III

Lecture on the Times

READ AT THE MASONIC TEMPLE, BOSTON,
DECEMBER 2, 1841

The Times, as we say—or the present aspects of our social state, the Laws, Divinity, Natural Science, Agriculture, Art, Trade, Letters, have their root in an invisible spiritual reality. To appear in these aspects, they must first exist, or have some necessary foundation. Besides all the small reasons we assign, there is a great reason for the existence of every extant fact; a reason which lies grand and immovable, often unsuspected, behind it in silence. The Times are the masquerade of the Eternities; trivial to the dull, tokens of noble and majestic agents to the wise; the receptacle in which the Past leaves its history; the quarry out of which the genius of today is building up the Future. The Times—the nations, manners, institutions, opinions, votes, are to be studied as omens, as sacred leaves, whereon a weighty sense is inscribed, if we have the wit and the love to search it out. Nature itself seems to propound to us this topic, and to invite us to explore the meaning of the conspicuous facts of the day. Everything that is popular, it has been said, deserves the attention of the philosopher: and this for the obvious reason, that although it may not be of any worth in itself, yet it characterizes the people.

Here is very good matter to be handled, if we are skillful; an abundance of important practical questions which it behooves us to understand. Let us examine the pretensions of the attacking and defending parties. Here is this great fact of Conservatism, entrenched in its immense redoubts, with Himalaya for its front, and Atlas for its flank, and Andes for its rear, and the Atlantic and Pacific seas for its ditches and trenches; which has planted its crosses, and crescents, and stars and stripes, and various signs and badges of possession, over every rood of the planet, and says, "I will hold fast; and to whom I will, will I give; and whom I will, will I exclude and starve": so says Conservatism; and all the children of men attack the colossus in their youth, and all, or all but a few, bow before it when they are old. A necessity not yet commanded, a negative imposed on the will of man by his condition, a deficiency in his force, is the foundation on which it rests. Let this side be fairly stated. Meantime, on the other part, arises Reform, and offers the sentiment of Love as an overmatch to this material might. I wish to consider well this affirmative side, which has a loftier port and reason than heretofore, which encroaches on the other every day, puts it out of countenance, out of reason, and out of temper, and leaves it nothing but silence and possession.

The fact of aristocracy, with its two weapons of wealth and manners, is as commanding a feature of the nineteenth century and the American republic as of old Rome, or modern England. The reason and influence of wealth, the aspect of philosophy and religion, and the tendencies which have acquired the name of Transcendentalism in Old and New England; the aspect of poetry, as the exponent and interpretation of these things; the fuller development and the freer play of Character as a social and political agent—these and other related topics will in turn come to be considered.

But the subject of the Times is not an abstract question. We talk of the world, but we mean a few men and women. If you speak of the age, you mean your own platoon of people, as Dante and Milton painted in colossal their platoons, and called them Heaven and Hell. In our idea of progress, we do not go out of this personal picture. We do not think the sky will be bluer, or honey sweeter, or our climate more temperate, but only that our relation to our fellows will be simpler and happier. What is the reason to be given for this extreme attraction, which *persons* have for us, but that they are the Age? they are the results of the Past; they are the heralds of the Future. They indicate—these witty, suffering, blushing, intimidating figures of the only race in which there are individuals or changes, how far on the Fate has gone, and what it drives at. As trees make scenery, and constitute the hospitality of the landscape, so persons are the world to persons—a cunning mystery by which the Great Desert of thoughts and of planets takes this engaging form, to bring, as it would seem, its meanings nearer to the mind. Thoughts walk and speak, and look with eyes at me, and transport me into new and magnificent scenes. These are the pungent instructors who thrill the heart of each of us, and make all other teaching formal and cold. How I follow them with aching heart, with pining desire! I count myself nothing before them. I would die for them with joy. They can do what they will with me. How they lash us with those tongues! How they make the tears start, make us blush and turn pale, and lap us in Elysium to soothing dreams and castles in the air! By tones of triumph, of dear love, by threats, by pride that freezes, these have the skill to make the world look bleak and inhospitable, or seem the nest of tenderness and joy. I do not wonder at the miracles wh.. ' poetry attributes to the music of Orpheus, when I remember what I have experienced from the varied notes of the human voice. They are an incalculable energy which countervails all other forces in nature, because they are the channel of supernatural powers. There is no interest or institution so poor and withered, but if a new strong man could be born into it, he would immediately redeem and replace it. A personal ascendency—that is the only fact much worth considering. I remember, some years ago, somebody shocked a circle of friends of order here in Boston, who supposed that our people were identified with their religious denominations, by declaring that an eloquent man—let him be of what sect soever—would be ordained at once in one of our metropolitan churches. To be sure he would; and not only in ours but in any church, mosque, or temple on the planet; but he must be eloquent, able to supplant our method and classification by the superior beauty of his own. Every fact we have was brought here by some person; and there is none that will not change and pass away before a person whose nature is broader than the person which the fact in question represents. And so I find the Age walking about in happy and hopeful natures, in strong eyes and pleasant thoughts, and think I read it nearer and truer so, than in the statute book, or in the investments of capital, which rather celebrate with mournful music the obsequies of the last age. In the brain of a fanatic; in the wild hope of a mountain boy, called by city boys very ignorant, because they do not know what his hope has certainly apprised him shall be; in the love-glance of a girl; in the hairsplitting conscientiousness of some eccentric person who has found some new scruple to embarrass himself and his neighbors withal is to be found that which shall constitute the times to come, more than in the now organized and accredited oracles. For whatever is affirmative and now advancing, contains it. I think that only is real which men love and rejoice in; not what they tolerate, but what they choose; what they embrace and avow, and not the things which chill, benumb, and terrify them.

And so why not draw for these times a portrait gallery? Let us paint the painters. Whilst the Daguerreotypist, with camera-obscura and silver plate, begins now to traverse the land, let us set up our Camera also, and let the sun paint the people. Let us paint the agitator, and the man of the old school, and the member of Congress, and the college professor, the formidable editor, the priest and reformer, the contemplative girl, and the fair aspirant for fashion and opportunities, the woman of the world who has tried and knows—let us examine how well she knows. Could we indicate the indicators, indicate those who most accurately represent every good and evil tendency of the general mind, in the just order which they take on this canvas of Time, so that all witnesses should recognize a spiritual law as each well-known form flitted for a moment across the wall, we should have a series of sketches which would report to the next ages the color and quality of ours.

Certainly I think if this were done there would be much to admire as well as to condemn; souls of as lofty a port as any in Greek or Roman fame might appear; men of great heart, of strong hand, and of persuasive speech; subtle thinkers, and men of wide sympathy, and an apprehension which looks over all history and everywhere recognizes its own. To be sure, there will be fragments and hints of men, more than enough: bloated promises, which end in nothing or little. And then truly great men, but with some defect in their composition which neutralizes their whole force. Here is a Damascus blade, such as you may search through nature in vain to parallel, laid up on the shelf in some village to rust and ruin. And how many seem not quite available for that idea which they represent? Now and then comes a bolder spirit, I should rather say, a more surrendered soul, more informed and led by God, which is much in advance of the rest, quite beyond their sympathy, but predicts what shall soon be the general fullness; as when we stand by the seashore, whilst the tide is coming in, a wave comes up the beach far higher than any foregoing one, and recedes; and for a long while none comes up to that mark; but after some time the whole sea is there and beyond it.

But we are not permitted to stand as spectators of the pageant which the times exhibit; we are parties also, and have a responsibility which is not to be declined. A little while this interval of wonder and comparison is permitted us, but to the end that we shall play a manly part. As the solar system moves forward in the heavens, certain stars open before us, and certain stars close up behind us; so is man's life. The reputations that were great and inaccessible change and tarnish. How great were once Lord Bacon's dimensions! he is now reduced almost to the middle height; and many another star has turned out to be a planet or an asteroid: only a few are the fixed stars which have no parallax, or none for us. The change and decline of old reputations are the gracious marks of our own growth. Slowly, like light of morning, it steals on us, the new fact, that we who were pupils or aspirants are now society: do compose a portion of that head and heart we are wont to think worthy of all reverence and heed. We are the representatives of religion and intellect, and stand in the light of Ideas, whose rays stream through us to those younger and more in the dark. What further relations we sustain, what new lodges we are entering, is now unknown. Today is a king in disguise. Today always looks mean to the thoughtless, in the face of an uniform experience that all good and great and happy actions are made up precisely of these blank todays. Let us not be so deceived. Let us unmask the king as he passes. Let us not inhabit times of wonderful and various promise without divining their tendency. Let us not see the foundations of nations, and of a new and better order of things, laid, with roving eyes, and an attention preoccupied with trifles.

The two omnipresent parties of History, the party of the Past and the party of the Future, divide society today as of old. Here is the innumerable multitude of those who accept the state and the church from the last generation, and stand on no argument but possession. They have reason also, and, as I think, better reason than is commonly stated. No Burke, no Metternich, has yet done full justice to the side of conservatism. But this class, however large, relying not on the intellect but on the instinct, blends itself with the brute forces of nature, is respectable only as nature is; but the individuals have no attraction for us. It is the dissenter, the theorist, the aspirant, who is quitting this ancient domain to embark on seas of adventure, who engages our interest. Omitting then for the present all notice of the stationary class, we shall find that the movement party divides itself into two classes, the actors, and the students.

The actors constitute that great army of martyrs who, at least in America, by their conscience and philanthropy, occupy the ground which Calvinism occupied in the last age, and compose the visible church of the existing generation. The present age will be marked by its harvest of projects for the reform of domestic, civil, literary, and ecclesiastical institutions The leaders of the crusades against War, Negro slavery, Usages of trade, Court and Custom-house Oaths, and so on to the agitators on the system of Education and the laws of Property, are the right successors of Luther, Knox, Robinson, Fox, Penn, Wesley, and Whitefield. They have the same virtues and vices; the same noble impulse, and the same bigotry. These movements are on all accounts important; they not only check the special abuses, but they educate the conscience and the intellect of the people. How can such a question as the Slave trade be agitated for forty years by all the Christian nations, without throwing great light on ethics into the general mind? The fury with which the slave trader defends every inch of his bloody deck and his howling auction platform, is a trumpet to alarm the ear of mankind, to wake the dull, and drive all neutrals to take sides and to listen to the argument and the verdict. The Temperance question, which rides the conversation of ten thousand circles, and is tacitly recalled at every public and at every private table, drawing with it all the curious ethics of the Pledge, of the Wine question, of the equity of the manufacture and the trade, is a gymnastic training to the casuistry and conscience of the time. Antimasonry had a deep right and wrong, which gradually emerged to sight out of the turbid controversy. The political questions touching the Banks; the Tariff; the limits of the executive power; the right of the constituent to instruct the representative; the treatment of the Indians; the Boundary wars; the Congress of nations; all are pregnant with ethical conclusions; and it is well if government and our social order can extricate themselves from these alembics and find themselves still government and social order. The student of history will hereafter compute the singular value of our endless discussion of questions to the mind of the period.

Whilst each of these aspirations and attempts of the people for the Better is magnified by the natural exaggeration of its advocates, until it excludes the others from sight, and repels discreet persons by the unfairness of the plea, the movements are in reality all parts of one movement. There is a perfect chain—see it, or see it not—of reforms emerging from the surrounding darkness, each cherishing some part of the general idea, and all must be seen in order to do justice to any one. Seen in this their natural connection, they are sublime. The conscience of the Age demonstrates itself in this effort to raise the life of man by putting it in harmony with his idea of the Beautiful and the Just. The history of reform is always identical, it is the comparison of the idea with the fact. Our modes of living are not agreeable to our imagination. We suspect they are unworthy. We arraign our daily employments. They appear to us unfit, unworthy of the faculties we spend on them. In conversation with a wise man, we find ourselves apologizing for our employments; we speak of them with shame. Nature, literature, science, childhood, appear to us beautiful; but not our daily work, not the ripe fruit and considered labors of man. This beauty which the fancy finds in everything else, certainly accuses the manner of life we lead. Why should it be hateful? Why should it contrast thus with all natural beauty? Why should it not be poetic, and invite and raise us? Is there a necessity that the works of man should be sordid? Perhaps not. Out of this fair Idea in the mind springs the effort at the Perfect. It is the interior testimony to a fairer possibility of life and manners which agitates society every day with the offer of some new amendment. If we would make more strict inquiry concerning its origin, we find ourselves rapidly approaching the inner boundaries of thought, that term where speech becomes silence, and science conscience. For the origin of all reform is in that mysterious fountain of the moral sentiment in man, which, amidst the natural, ever contains the supernatural for men. That is new and creative. That is alive. That alone can make a man other than he is. Here or nowhere resides unbounded energy, unbounded power.

The new voices in the wilderness crying "Repent" have revived a hope, which had well-nigh perished out of the world, that the thoughts of the mind may yet, in distant age, in some happy hour, be executed by the hands. That is the hope, of which all other hopes are parts. For some ages, these ideas have been consigned to the poet and musical composer, to the prayers and the sermons of churches; but the thought that they can ever have any footing in real life, seems long since to have been exploded by all judicious persons. Milton, in his best

tract, describes a relation between religion and the daily occupations, which is true until this time.

"A wealthy man, addicted to his pleasure and to his profits,
finds religion to be a traffic so entangled, and of so many pid-
dling accounts, that of all mysteries he cannot skill to keep a
stock going upon that trade. What should he do? Fain he would
have the name to be religious; fain he would bear up with his
neighbors in that. What does he therefore, but resolve to give
over toiling, and to find himself out some factor, to whose care
and credit he may commit the whole managing of his religious
affairs; some divine of note and estimation that must be. To
him he adheres, resigns the whole warehouse of his religion,
with all the locks and keys, into his custody; and indeed makes
the very person of that man his religion; esteems his associat-
ing with him a sufficient evidence and commendatory of his
own piety. So that a man may say his religion is now no more
within himself, but is become a dividual movable, and goes
and comes near him, according as that good man frequents
the house. He entertains him, gives him gifts, feasts him, lodges
him; his religion comes home at night, prays, is liberally
supped, and sumptuously laid to sleep; rises, is saluted, and
after the malmsey, or some well-spiced brewage, and better
breakfasted than he whose morning appetite would have gladly fed on green figs between Bethany and Jerusalem, his religion walks abroad at eight, and leaves his kind entertainer in
the shop, trading all day without his religion."

This picture would serve for our times. Religion was not invited to eat or drink or sleep with us, or to make us divide an
estate, but was a holiday guest. Such omissions judge the
church; as the compromise made with the slaveholder, not
much noticed at first, every day appears more flagrant mischief to the American constitution. But now the purists are
looking into all these matters. The more intelligent are growing
uneasy on the subject of Marriage. They wish to see the character represented also in that covenant. There shall be nothing
brutal in it, but it shall honor the man and the woman, as
much as the most diffusive and universal action. Grimly the
same spirit looks into the law of Property, and accuses men of
driving a trade in the great boundless providence which had
given the air, the water, and the land to men, to use and not to
fence in and monopolize. It casts its eye on Trade, and Day
Labor, and so it goes up and down, paving the earth with eyes,
destroying privacy and making thorough lights. Is all this for
nothing? Do you suppose that the reforms which are preparing
will be as superficial as those we know?

By the books it reads and translates, judge what books it will presently print. A great deal of the profoundest thinking of antiquity, which had become as good as obsolete for us, is now reappearing in extracts and allusions, and in twenty years will get all printed anew. See how daring is the reading, the speculation, the experimenting of the time. If now some genius shall arise who could unite these scattered rays! And always such a genius does embody the ideas of each time. Here is great variety and richness of mysticism, each part of which now only disgusts whilst it forms the sole thought of some poor Perfectionist or "Comer out," yet when it shall be taken up as the garniture of some profound and all-reconciling thinker, will appear the rich and appropriate decoration of his robes.

These reforms are our contemporaries; they are ourselves; our own light, and sight, and conscience; they only name the relation which subsists between us and the vicious institutions which they go to rectify. They are the simplest statements of man in these matters; the plain right and wrong. I cannot choose but allow and honor them. The impulse is good, and the theory; the practice is less beautiful. The Reformers affirm the inward life, but they do not trust it, but use outward and vulgar means. They do not rely on precisely that strength which wins me to their cause; not on love, not on a principle, but on men, on multitudes, on circumstances, on money, on party; that is, on fear, on wrath, and pride. The love which lifted men to the sight of these better ends was the true and best distinction of this time, the disposition to trust a principle more than a material force. I think *that* the soul of reform; the conviction that not sensualism, not slavery, not war, not imprisonment, not even government, are needed—but in lieu of them all, reliance on the sentiment of man, which will work best the more it is trusted; not reliance on numbers, but, contrariwise, distrust of numbers and the feeling that then are we strongest when most private and alone. The young men who have been vexing society for these last years with regenerative methods seem to have made this mistake; they all exaggerated some special means, and all failed to see that the Reform of Reforms must be accomplished without means.

The Reforms have their high origin in an ideal justice, but they do not retain the purity of an idea. They are quickly organized in some low, inadequate form, and present no more poetic image to the mind than the evil tradition which they reprobated. They mix the fire of the moral sentiment with personal and party heats, with measureless exaggerations, and the blindness that prefers some darling measure to justice and truth. Those who are urging with most ardor what are called the greatest benefits of mankind, are narrow, self-pleasing, con-

ceited men, and affect us as the insane do. They bite us, and
we run mad also. I think the work of the reformer as innocent
as other work that is done around him; but when I have seen
it near, I do not like it better. It is done in the same way, it is
done profanely, not piously; by management, by tactics and
clamor. It is a buzz in the ear. I cannot feel any pleasure in
sacrifices which display to me such partiality of character. We
do not want action, but men; not a chemical drop of water, but
rain; the spirit that sheds and showers actions, countless, endless actions. You have on some occasion played a bold part.
You have set your heart and face against society when you
thought it wrong, and returned it frown for frown. Excellent:
now can you afford to forget it, reckoning all your action no
more than the passing of your hand through the air, or a little
breath of your mouth? The world leaves no track in space, and
the greatest action of man no mark in the vast idea. To the
youth diffident of his ability and full of compunction at his un-
profitable existence, the temptation is always great to lend
himself to public movements, and as one of a party accomplish
what he cannot hope to effect alone. But he must resist the
degradation of a man to a measure. I must get with truth,
though I should never come to act, as you call it, with effect. I
must consent to inaction. A patience which is grand; a brave
and cold neglect of the offices which prudence exacts, so it be
done in a deep upper piety; a consent to solitude and inaction
which proceeds out of an unwillingness to violate character, is
the century which makes the gem. Whilst therefore I desire to
express the respect and joy I feel before this sublime connection of reforms now in their infancy around us, I urge the more
earnestly the paramount duties of self-reliance. I cannot find
language of sufficient energy to convey my sense of the sacredness of private integrity. All men, all things, the state, the
church, yea, the friends of the heart are phantasms and un-
re___ ___ide the sanctuary of the heart. With so much awe, with
_ much fear, let it be respected.

The great majority of men, unable to judge of any principle
until its light falls on a fact, are not aware of the evil that is
around them until they see it in some gross form, as in a class
of intemperate men, or slaveholders, or soldiers, or fraudulent
persons. Then they are greatly moved; and magnifying the importance of that wrong, they fancy that if that abuse were redressed all would go well, and they fill the land with clamor to
correct it. Hence the missionary, and other religious efforts. If
every island and every house had a Bible, if every child was
brought into the Sunday School, would the wounds of the
world heal, and man be upright?

But the man of ideas, accounting the circumstance nothing, judges of the commonwealth from the state of his own mind. "If," he says, "I am selfish, then is there slavery, or the effort to establish it, wherever I go. But if I am just, then is there no slavery, let the laws say what they will. For if I treat all men as gods, how to me can there be any such thing as a slave?" But how frivolous is your war against circumstances. This denouncing philanthropist is himself a slaveholder in every word and look. Does he free me? Does he cheer me? He is the state of Georgia, or Alabama, with their sanguinary slave laws, walking here on our northeastern shores. We are all thankful he has no more political power, as we are fond of liberty ourselves. I am afraid our virtue is a little geographical. I am not mortified by our vice; that is obduracy; it colors and palters, it curses and swears, and I can see to the end of it; but I own our virtue makes me ashamed; so sour and narrow, so thin and blind, virtue so vicelike. Then again, how trivial seem the contests of the abolitionist, whilst he aims merely at the circumstances of the slave. Give the slave the least elevation of religious sentiment, and he is no slave; you are the slave; he not only in his humility feels his superiority, feels that much deplored condition of his to be a fading trifle, but he makes you feel it too. He is the master. The exaggeration which our young people make of his wrongs, characterizes themselves. What are no trifles to them, they naturally think are no trifles to Pompey.

We say then that the reforming movement is sacred in its origin; in its management and details, timid and profane. These benefactors hope to raise man by improving his circumstances: by combination of that which is dead they hope to make something alive. In vain. By new infusions alone of the spirit by which he is made and directed, can he be remade and reinforced. The sad Pestalozzi, who shared with all ardent spirits the hope of Europe on the outbreak of the French Revolution, after witnessing its sequel, recorded his conviction that "the amelioration of outward circumstances will be the effect but can never be the means of mental and moral improvement." Quitting now the class of actors, let us turn to see how it stands with the other class of which we spoke, namely, the students.

A new disease has fallen on the life of man. Every Age, like every human body, has its own distemper. Other times have had war, or famine, or a barbarism, domestic or bordering, as their antagonism. Our forefathers walked in the world, and went to their graves tormented with the fear of Sin and the terror of the Day of Judgment. These terrors have lost their force, and our torment is Unbelief, the Uncertainty as to what we ought to do; the distrust of the value of what we do, and the distrust that the Necessity (which we all at least believe in) is fair and beneficent. Our Religion assumes the negative form of rejection. Out of love of the true, we repudiate the false; and the Religion is an abolishing criticism. A great perplexity hangs like a cloud on the brow of all cultivated persons, a certain imbecility in the best spirits, which distinguishes the period. We do not find the same trait in the Arabian, in the Hebrew, in Greek, Roman, Norman, English periods; no, but in other men a natural firmness. The men did not see beyond the need of the hour. They planted their foot strong, and doubted nothing. We mistrust every step we take. We find it the worst thing about time that we know not what to do with it. We are so sharp-sighted that we can neither work nor think, neither read Plato nor not read him.

Then there is what is called a too intellectual tendency. Can there be too much intellect? We have never met with any such excess. But the criticism which is leveled at the laws and manners, ends in thought, without causing a new method of life. The genius of the day does not incline to a deed, but to a beholding. It is not that men do not wish to act; they pine to be employed, but are paralyzed by the uncertainty what they should do. The inadequacy of the work to the faculties is the painful perception which keeps them still. This happens to the best. Then, talents bring their usual temptations, and the current literature and poetry with perverse ingenuity draw us away from life to solitude and meditation. This could well be borne, if it were great and involuntary; if the men were ravished by their thought, and hurried into ascetic extravagances. Society could then manage to release their shoulder from its wheel and grant them for a time this privilege of sabbath. But they are not so. Thinking, which was a rage, is become an art. The thinker gives me results, and never invites me to be present with him at his invocation of truth, and to enjoy with him its proceeding into his mind.

So little action amidst such audacious and yet sincere profession, that we begin to doubt if that great revolution in the art of war, which has made it a game of posts instead of a game of battles, has not operated on Reform; whether this be not also a war of posts, a paper blockade, in which each party is to display the utmost resources of his spirit and belief, and no conflict occur, but the world shall take that course which the demonstration of the truth shall indicate.

But we must pay for being too intellectual, as they call it. People are not as lighthearted for it. I think men never loved

life less. I question if care and doubt ever wrote their names so
legibly on the faces of any population. This *Ennui*, for which
we Saxons had no name, this word of France, has got a terrific
significance. It shortens life, and bereaves the day of its light.
Old age begins in the nursery, and before the young American
is put into jacket and trousers, he says, "I want something
which I never saw before"; and "I wish I was not I." I have
seen the same gloom on the brow even of those adventurers
from the intellectual class who had dived deepest and with
most success into active life. I have seen the authentic sign of
anxiety and perplexity on the greatest forehead of the State.
The canker worms have crawled to the topmost bough of the
wild elm, and swing down from that. Is there less oxygen in
the atmosphere? What has checked in this age the animal spirits
which gave to our forefathers their bounding pulse?

But have a little patience with this melancholy humor. Their
unbelief arises out of a greater Belief; their inaction out of a
scorn of inadequate action. By the side of these men, the hot
agitators have a certain cheap and ridiculous air; they even
look smaller than the others. Of the two, I own I like the spec-
ulators best. They have some piety which looks with faith to a
fair Future, unprofaned by rash and unequal attempts to realize
it. And truly we shall find much to console us, when we consider the cause of their uneasiness. It is the love of greatness, it
is the need of harmony, the contrast of the dwarfish Actual
with the exorbitant Idea. No man can compare the idea and
aspirations of the innovators of the present day with those of
former periods, without feeling how great and high this criticism is. The revolutions that impend over society are not now
from ambition and rapacity, from impatience of one or another form of government, but from new modes of thinking,
which shall recompose society after a new order, which shall
animate labor by love and science, which shall destroy the
value of many kinds of property and replace all property within the dominion of reason and equity. There was never so great
a thought laboring in the breasts of men as now. It almost
seems as if what was aforetime spoken fabulously and hiero-
glyphically, was now spoken plainly, the doctrine, namely, of
the indwelling of the Creator in man. The spiritualist wishes
this only, that the spiritual principle should be suffered to
demonstrate itself to the end, in all possible applications to the
state of man, without the admission of anything unspiritual,
that is, anything positive, dogmatic, or personal. The excellence of this class consists in this, that they have believed; that,
affirming the need of new and higher modes of living and action, they have abstained from the recommendation of low

methods. Their fault is that they have stopped at the intellectual perception; that their will is not yet inspired from the Fountain of Love. But whose fault is this? and what a fault, and to what inquiry does it lead! We have come to that which is the spring of all power, of beauty and virtue, of art and poetry; and who shall tell us according to what law its inspirations and its informations are given or withholden?

I do not wish to be guilty of the narrowness and pedantry of inferring the tendency and genius of the Age from a few and insufficient facts or persons. Every age has a thousand sides and signs and tendencies, and it is only when surveyed from inferior points of view that great varieties of character appear. Our time too is full of activity and performance. Is there not something comprehensive in the grasp of a society which to great mechanical invention and the best institutions of property adds the most daring theories; which explores the subtlest and most universal problems? At the manifest risk of repeating what every other Age has thought of itself, we might say we think the Genius of this Age more philosophical than any other has been, righter in its aims, truer, with less fear, less fable, less mixture of any sort.

But turn it how we will, as we ponder this meaning of the times, every new thought drives us to the deep fact that the Time is the child of the Eternity. The main interest which any aspects of the Times can have for us, is the great spirit which gazes through them, the light which they can shed on the wonderful questions, What we are? and Whither we tend? We do not wish to be deceived. How we drift, like white sail across the wild ocean, now bright on the wave, now darkling in the trough of the sea—but from what port did we sail? Who knows? Or to what port are we bound? Who knows? There is no one to tell us but such poor weather-tossed mariners as ourselves, whom we speak as we pass, or who have hoisted some signal, or floated to us some letter in a bottle from far. But what know they more than we? They also found themselves on this wondrous sea. No; from the older sailors, nothing. Over all their speaking trumpets, the gray sea and the loud winds answer, Not to us; not in Time. Where then but in Ourselves, where but in that Thought through which we communicate with absolute nature, and are made aware that whilst we shed the dust of which we are built, grain by grain, till it is all gone, the law which clothes us with humanity remains anew? where but in the intuitions which are vouchsafed us from within, shall we learn the Truth? Faithless, faithless, we fancy that with the dust we depart and are not, and do not know that the law and the perception of the law are at last one; that only as

much as the law enters us, becomes us, we are living men—
immortal with the immortality of this law. Underneath all these
appearances lies that which is, that which lives, that which
causes. This ever renewing generation of appearances rests
on a reality, and a reality that is alive.

To a true scholar the attraction of the aspects of nature, the
departments of life, and the passages of his experiences is simply the information they yield him of this supreme nature
which lurks within all. That reality, that causing force is moral.
The Moral Sentiment is but its other name. It makes by its
presence or absence right and wrong, beauty and ugliness,
genius or depravation. As the granite comes to the surface and
towers into the highest mountains, and, if we dig down, we
find it below the superficial strata, so in all the details of our
domestic or civil life is hidden the elemental reality, which
ever and anon comes to the surface, and forms the grand men,
who are the leaders and examples, rather than the companions,
of the race. The granite is curiously concealed under a thousand formations and surfaces, under fertile soils, and grasses,
and flowers, under well-manured, arable fields, and large towns
and cities, and it makes the foundation of these, and is always
indicating its presence by slight but sure signs. So is it with the
Life of our life; so close does that also hide. I read it in glad
and in weeping eyes; I read it in the pride and in the humility
of people; it is recognized in every bargain and in every com-
plaisance, in every criticism, and in all praise; it is voted for at
elections; it wins the cause with juries; it rides the stormy eloquence of the senate, sole victor; histories are written on it,
holidays decreed to it; statues, tombs, churches, built to its
honor; yet men seem to fear and to shun it when it comes
barely to view in our immediate neighborhood.

For that reality let us stand; that let us serve, and for that
speak. Only so far as *that* shines through them are these times
or any times worth consideration. I wish to speak of politics,
education, business, and religion around us without ceremony
or false deference. You will absolve me from the charge of
flippancy, or malignity, or the desire to say smart things at the
expense of whomsoever, when you see that reality is all we
prize, and that we are bound on our entrance into nature to
speak for that. Let it not be recorded in our own memories
that in this moment of the Eternity, when we who were named
by our names flitted across the light, we were afraid of any
fact, or disgraced the fair Day by a pusillanimous preference
of our bread to our freedom. What is the scholar, what is the
man, *for*, but for hospitality to every new thought of his time?
Have you leisure, power, property, friends? You shall be the

asylum and patron of every new thought, every unproven opinion, every untried project which proceeds out of good will and honest seeking. All the newspapers, all the tongues of today will of course at first defame what is noble; but you who hold not of today, not of the times, but of the Everlasting, are to stand for it: and the highest compliment man ever receives from heaven is the sending to him its disguised and discredited angels.

From *Nature Addresses and Lectures*
Volume I

Character

LECTURE BEFORE THE PARKER FRATERNITY, BOSTON, 1864

Morals respects what men call goodness, that which all men agree to honor as justice, truth-speaking, good will and good works. Morals respects the source or motive in this action. It is the science of substances, not of shows. It is the *what*, and not the *how*. It is that which all men profess to regard, and by their real respect for which they recommend themselves to each other.

There is this eternal advantage to morals, that, in the question between truth and goodness, the moral cause of the world lies behind all else in the mind. It was for good, it is to good, that all works. Surely it is not to prove or show the truth of things—that s___ d_ a little cold and scholastic—no, it is for benefit, that _____. As we say in our modern politics, catching at last the language of morals, that the object of the State is the greatest good for the greatest number—so, the reason we must give for the existence of the world is, that it is for the benefit of all being.

Morals implies freedom and will. The will constitutes the man. He has his life in Nature, like a beast: but choice is born in him; here is he that chooses; here is the Declaration of Independence, the July Fourth, of zoology and astronomy. He chooses—as the rest of the creation does not. But will, pure and perceiving, is not willfulness. When a man, through stubbornness, insists to do this or that, something absurd or whimsical, only because he will, he is weak, he blows with his lips against the tempest, he dams the incoming ocean with his cane. It were an unspeakable calamity if anyone should think he had the right to impose a private will on others. That is the part of a striker, an assassin. All violence, all that is dreary and repels, is not power but the absence of power.

Morals is the direction of the will on universal ends. He is immoral who is acting to any private end. He is moral—we say it with Marcus Aurelius and with Kant—whose aim or motive may become a universal rule, binding on all intelligent beings; and with Vauven argues, "the mercenary sacrifice of the public good to a private interest is the eternal stamp of vice."

All the virtues are special directions of this motive; justice is the application of this good of the whole to the affairs of each one; courage is contempt of danger in the determination to see this good of the whole enacted; love is delight in the preference of that benefit redounding to another over the securing of our own share; humility is a sentiment of our insignificance when the benefit of the universe is considered.

If from these external statements we seek to come a little nearer to the fact, our first experiences in moral, as in intellectual, nature, force us to discriminate a universal mind, identical in all men. Certain biases, talents, executive skills, are special to each individual; but the high, contemplative, all-commanding vision, the sense of Right and Wrong, is alike to all. Its attributes are self-existence, eternity, intuition and command. It is the mind of the mind. We belong to it, not it to us. It is in all men, and constitutes them men. In bad men it is dormant, as health is in men entranced or drunken; but, however inoperative, it exists underneath whatever vices and errors. The extreme simplicity of this intuition embarrasses every attempt at analysis. We can only mark, one by one, the perfections which it combines in every act. It admits of no appeal, looks to no superior essence. It is the reason of things.

The antagonist nature is the individual, formed into a finite body of exact dimensions, with appetites which take from everybody else what they appropriate to themselves, and would enlist the entire spiritual faculty of the individual, if it were possible, in catering for them. On the perpetual conflict between the dictate of this universal mind and the wishes and interests of the individual, the moral discipline of life is built. The one craves a private benefit, which the other requires him to renounce out of respect to the absolute good. Every hour puts the individual in a position where his wishes aim at something which the sentiment of duty forbids him to seek. He that speaks the truth executes no private function of an individual will, but the world utters a sound by his lips. He who doth a just action seeth therein nothing of his own, but an inconceivable nobleness attaches to it, because it is a dictate of the general mind. We have no idea of power so simple and so entire as this. It is the basis of thought, it is the basis of being. Compare all that we call ourselves, all our private and personal venture in the world, with this deep of moral nature in which we lie, and our private good becomes an impertinence, and we take part with hasty shame against ourselves.

> *High instincts, before which our mortal Nature*
> *Did tremble like a guilty Thing surprised:*
> . . . .
> *Which, be they what they may,*
> *Are yet the fountain light of all our day,*
> *Are yet a master light of all our seeing;*
> *Uphold us, cherish, and have power to make*
> *Our noisy years seem moments in the being*
> *Of the eternal Silence: truths that wake*
> *To perish never.*

The moral element invites man to great enlargements, to find his satisfaction, not in particulars or events, but in the purpose and tendency; not in bread, but in his right to his bread; not in much corn or wool, but in its communication.

Not by adding, then, does the moral sentiment help us; no, but in quite another manner. It puts us in place. It centers, it concentrates us. It puts us at the heart of Nature, where we belong, in the cabinet of science and of causes, there where all the wires terminate which hold the world in magnetic unity, and so converts us into universal beings.

This wonderful sentiment, which endears itself as it is obeyed, seems to be the fountain of intellect; for no talent gives the impression of sanity, if wanting this; nay, it absorbs everything into itself. Truth, Power, Goodness, Beauty, are its varied names—faces of one substance, the heart of all. Before it, what are persons, prophets, or seraphim but its passing agents, momentary rays of its light?

The moral sentiment is alone omnipotent. There is no labor or sacrifice to which it will not bring a man, and which it will not make easy. Thus there is no man who will bargain to sell his life, say at the end of a year, for a million or ten millions of gold dollars in hand, or for any temporary pleasures, or for any rank, as of peer or prince; but many a man does not hesitate to lay down his life for the sake of a truth, or in the cause of his country, or to save his son or his friend. And under the action of this sentiment of the Right, his heart and mind expand above himself, and above Nature.

> *Though Love repine, and Reason chafe,*
> *There came a voice without reply,*
> *'T is man's perdition to be safe,*
> *When for the truth he ought to die.*

Such is the difference of the action of the heart within and of the sense without. One is enthusiasm, and the other more or less amounts of horsepower.

Devout men, in the endeavor to express their convictions, have used different images to suggest this latent force; as, the light, the seed, the Spirit, the Holy Ghost, the Comforter, the Demon, the still, small voice, etc.—all indicating its power and its latency. It is serenely above all mediation. In all ages, to all men, it saith, *I am*; and he who hears it feels the impiety of wandering from this revelation to any record or to any rival. The poor Jews of the wilderness cried: "Let not the Lord speak to us; let Moses speak to us." But the simple and sincere soul makes the contrary prayer: "Let no intruder come between thee and me; deal THOU with me; let me know it is thy will, and I ask no more." The excellence of Jesus, and of every true teacher, is, that he affirms the Divinity in him and in us— not thrusts himself between it and us. It would instantly indispose us to any person claiming to speak for the Author of Nature, the setting forth any fact or law which he did not find in our consciousness. We should say with Heraclitus: "Come into this smoky cabinet; God is here also: approve yourself to him."

We affirm that in all men is this majestic perception and command; that it is the presence of the Eternal in each perishing man; that it distances and degrades all statements of whatever saints, heroes, poets, as obscure and confused stammerings before its silent revelation. *They* report the truth. *It* is the truth. When I think of Reason, of Truth, of Virtue, I cannot conceive them as lodged in your soul and lodged in my soul, but that you and I and all souls are lodged in that; and I may easily speak of that adorable nature, there where only I behold it in my dim experiences, in such terms as shall seem to the frivolous, who dare not fathom their consciousness, as profane. How is a man a man? How can he exist to weave relations of joy and virtue with other souls, but because he is inviolable, anchored at the center of Truth and Being? In the ever-returning hour of reflection, he says: "I stand here glad at heart of all the sympathies I can awaken and share, clothing myself with them as with a garment of shelter and beauty, and yet knowing that it is not in the power of all who surround me to take from me the smallest thread I call mine. If all things are taken away, I have still all things in my relation to the Eternal."

We pretend not to define the way of its access to the private heart. It passes understanding. There was a time when Christianity existed in one child. But if the child had been killed by Herod, would the element have been lost? God sends his message, if not by one, then quite as well by another. When the Master of the Universe has ends to fulfill, he impresses his will on the structure of minds.

The Divine Mind imparts itself to the single person: his whole duty is to this rule and teaching. The aid which others give us is like that of the mother to the child—temporary, gestative, a short period of lactation, a nurse's or a governess's care; but on his arrival at a certain maturity, it ceases, and would be hurtful and ridiculous if prolonged. Slowly the body comes to the use of its organs; slowly the soul unfolds itself in the new man. It is partial at first, and honors only some one or some few truths. In its companions it sees other truths honored, and successively finds their foundation also in itself. Then it cuts the cord, and no longer believes "because of thy saying," but because it has recognized them in itself.

The Divine Mind imparts itself to the single person: but it is also true that men act powerfully on us. There are men who astonish and delight, men who instruct and guide. Some men's words I remember so well that I must often use them to express my thought. Yes, because I perceive that we have heard the same truth, but they have heard it better. That is only to say, there is degree and gradation throughout Nature; and the Deity does not break his firm laws in respect to imparting truth, more than in imparting material heat and light. Men appear from time to time who receive with more purity and fullness these high communications. But it is only as fast as this hearing from another is authorized by its consent with his own, that it is pure and safe to each; and all receiving from abroad must be controlled by this immense reservation.

It happens now and then, in the ages, that a soul is born which has no weakness of self, which offers no impediment to the Divine Spirit, which comes down into Nature as if only for the benefit of souls, and all its thoughts and perceptions of things as they are, without any infirmity of earth. Such souls are as the apparition of gods among men, and simply by their presence pass judgment on them. Men are forced by their own self-respect to give them a certain attention. Evil men shrink and pay involuntary homage by hiding or apologizing for their action.

When a man is born with a profound moral sentiment, preferring truth, justice and the serving of all men to any honors or any gain, men readily feel the superiority. They who deal with him are elevated with joy and hope; he lights up the house or the landscape in which he stands. His actions are poetic and miraculous in their eyes. In his presence, or within his influence, everyone believes in the immortality of the soul. They feel that the invisible world sympathizes with him. The Arabians delight in expressing the sympathy of the unseen world with holy men.

> *When Omar prayed and loved,*
> *Where Syrian waters roll,*
> *Aloft the ninth heaven glowed and moved*
> *To the tread of the jubilant soul.*

A chief event of life is the day in which we have encountered a mind that startled us by its large scope. I am in the habit of thinking—not, I hope, out of a partial experience, but confirmed by what I notice in many lives—that to every serious mind Providence sends from time to time five or six or seven teachers who are of the first importance to him in the lessons they have to impart. The highest of these not so much gives particular knowledge, as they elevate by sentiment and by their habitual grandeur of view.

Great men serve us as insurrections do in bad governments. The world would run into endless routine, and forms incrust forms, till the life was gone. But the perpetual supply of new genius shocks us with thrills of life, and recalls us to principles. Lucifer's wager in the old drama was, "There is no steadfast man on earth." He is very rare. "A man is already of consequence in the world when it is known that we can implicitly rely on him." She how one noble person dwarfs a whole nation of underlings. This steadfastness we indicate when we praise character.

Character denotes habitual self-possession, habitual regard to interior and constitutional motives, a balance not to be overset or easily disturbed by outward events and opinion, and by implication points to the source of right motive. We sometimes employ the word to express the strong and consistent will of men of mixed motive, but, when used with emphasis, it points to what no events can change, that is, a will built on the reason of things. Such souls do not come in troops: oftenest appear solitary, like a general without his command, because those who can understand and uphold such appear rarely, not many, perhaps not one, in a generation. And the memory and tradition of such a leader is preserved in some strange way by those who only half understand him, until a true disciple comes, who apprehends and interprets every word.

The sentiment never stops in pure vision, but will be enacted. It affirms not only its truth, but its supremacy. It is not only insight, as science, as fancy, as imagination is; or an entertainment, as friendship and poetry are; but it is a sovereign rule: and the acts which it suggests—as when it impels a man to go forth and impart it to other men, or sets him on some asceticism or some practice of self-examination to hold him to obedience, or some zest to unite men to abate some nuisance, or establish some reform or charity which it commands—are the homage we render to this sentiment, as compared with the lower regard we pay to other thoughts: and the private or social practices we establish in its honor we call religion.

The sentiment, of course, is the judge and measure of every expression of it—measures Judaism, Stoicism, Christianity, Buddhism, or whatever philanthropy, or politics, or saint, or seer pretends to speak in its name. The religions we call false were once true. They also were affirmations of the conscience correcting the evil customs of their times. The populace drag down the gods to their own level, and give them their egotism; whilst in Nature is none at all, God keeping out of sight, and known only as pure law, though resistless. Châteaubriand said, with some irreverence of phrase, If God made man in his image, man has paid him well back. "*Si Dieu a fait l'homme à son image, l'homme l'a bien rendu.*" Every nation is degraded by the goblins it worships instead of this Deity. The Dionysia and Saturnalia of Greece and Rome, the human sacrifice of the Druids, the Sradda of Hindus, the Purgatory, the Indulgences, and the Inquisition of Popery, the vindictive mythology of Calvinism, are examples of this perversion.

Every particular instruction is speedily embodied in a ritual, is accommodated to humble and gross minds, and corrupted. The moral sentiment is the perpetual critic on these forms, thundering its protest, sometimes in earnest and lofty rebuke; but sometimes also it is the source, in natures less pure, of sneers and flippant jokes of common people, who feel that the forms and dogmas are not true for them, though they do not see where the error lies.

The religion of one age is the literary entertainment of the next. We use in our idlest poetry and discourse the words Jove,

Neptune, Mercury, as mere colors, and can hardly believe that they had to the lively Greek the anxious meaning which, in our towns, is given and received in churches when our religious names are used: and we read with surprise the horror of Athens when, one morning, the statues of Mercury in the temples were found broken, and the like consternation was in the city as if, in Boston, all the Orthodox churches should be burned in one night.

The greatest dominion will be to the deepest thought. The establishment of Christianity in the world does not rest on any miracle but the miracle of being the broadest and most humane doctrine. Christianity was once a schism and protest against the impieties of the time, which had originally been protests against earlier impieties, but had lost their truth. Varnhagen von Ense, writing in Prussia in 1848, says: "The Gospels belong to the most aggressive writings. No leaf thereof could attain the liberty of being printed (in Berlin) today. What Mirabeaus, Rousseaus, Diderots, Fichtes, Heines, and many other heretic, one can detect therein!"

But before it was yet a national religion it was alloyed, and, in the hands of hot Africans, of luxurious Byzantines, of fierce Gauls, its creeds were tainted with their barbarism. In Holland, in England, in Scotland, it felt the national narrowness. How unlike our habitual turn of thought was that of the last century in this country! Our ancestors spoke continually of angels and archangels with the same good faith as they would have spoken of their own parents or their late minister. Now the words pale, are rhetoric, and all credence is gone. Our horizon is not far, say one generation, or thirty years: we all see so much. The older see two generations, or sixty years. But what has been running on through three horizons, or ninety years, looks to all the world like a law of Nature, and 't is an impiety to doubt. Thus, 't is incredible to us, if we look into the religious books of our grandfathers, how they held themselves in such a pinfold. But why not? As far as they could see, through two or three horizons, nothing but ministers and ministers. Calvinism was one and the same thing in Geneva, in Scotland, in Old and New England. If there was a wedding, they had a sermon; if a funeral, then a sermon; if a war, or smallpox, or a comet, or cankerworms, or a deacon died—still a sermon: Nature was a pulpit; the churchwarden or tithingman was a petty persecutor; the presbytery, a tyrant; and in many a house in country places the poor children found seven sabbaths in a week. Fifty or a hundred years ago, prayers were said, morning and evening, in all families; grace was said at table; an exact observance of the Sunday was kept in the houses of laymen as of clergymen. And one sees with some pain the disuse of rites so charged with humanity and aspiration. But it by no means follows, because those offices are much disused, that the men and women are irreligious; certainly not that they have less integrity or sentiment, but only, let us hope, that they see that they can omit the form without loss of real ground; perhaps that they find some violence, some cramping of their freedom of thought, in the constant recurrence of the form.

So of the changed position and manners of the clergy. They have dropped, with the sacerdotal garb and manners of the last century, many doctrines and practices once esteemed indispensable to their order. But the distinctions of the true clergymen are not less decisive. Men ask now, "Is he serious? Is he a sincere man, who lives as he teaches? Is he a benefactor?" So far the religion is now where it should be. Persons are discriminated as honest, as having public and universal regards, or otherwise—are discriminated according to their aims, and not by these ritualities.

The changes are inevitable; the new age cannot see with the eyes of the last. But the change is in what is superficial; the principles are immortal, and the rally on the principle must arrive as people become intellectual. I consider theology to be the rhetoric of morals. The mind of this age has fallen away from theology to morals. I conceive it an advance. I suspect, that, when the theology was most florid and dogmatic, it was the barbarism of the people, and that, in that very time, the best men also fell away from theology, and rested in morals. I think that all the dogmas rest on morals, and that it is only a question of youth or maturity, of more or less fancy in the recipient; that the stern determination to do justly, to speak the truth, to be chaste and humble, was substantially the same, whether under a self-respect, or under a vo.. .iade on the . ·ɐs at the shrine of Madonna.

vʌhen once Selden had said that the priests seemed to him to be baptizing their own fingers, the rite of baptism was getting late in the world. Or when once it is perceived that the English missionaries in India put obstacles in the way of schools (as is alleged)—do not wish to enlighten but to Christianize the Hindus—it is seen at once how wide of Christ is English Christianity.

Mankind at large always resemble frivolous children: they are impatient of thought, and wish to be amused. Truth is too simple for us; we do not like those who unmask our illusions. Fontenelle said: "If the Deity should lay bare to the eyes of men the secret system of Nature, the causes by which all the astronomic results are affected, and they finding no magic, no mystic numbers, no fatalities, but the greatest simplicity, I am persuaded they would not be able to suppress a feeling of mortification, and would exclaim, with disappointment, 'Is that all?' " And so we paint over the barrenness of ethics with the quaint grotesques of theology.

We boast the triumph of Christianity over Paganism, meaning the victory of the spirit over the senses; but Paganism hides itself in the uniform of the Church. Paganism has only taken the oath of allegiance, taken the cross, but is Paganism still, outvotes the true men by millions of majority, carries the bag, spends the treasure, writes the tracts, elects the minister, and persecutes the true believer.

There is a certain secular progress of opinion, which, in civil countries, reaches everybody. One service which this age has rendered is, to make life and wisdom of every past man accessible and available to all. Socrates and Marcus Aurelius are allowed to be saints; Mahomet is no longer accursed; Voltaire is no longer a scarecrow; Spinoza has come to be revered. "The time will come," says Varnhagen von Ense, "when we shall treat the jokes and sallies against the myths and church-rituals of Christianity—say the sarcasms of Voltaire, Frederick the Great, and D'Alembert—good-naturedly and without offense: since, at the bottom, those men mean honestly, their polemics proceed out of a religious striving, and what Christ meant and willed is in essence more with them than with their opponents, who only wear and misrepresent the *name* of Christ. . . . Voltaire was an apostle of Christian ideas; only the names were hostile to him, and he never knew it otherwise. He was like the son of the vinedresser in the Gospel, who said No, and went; the other said Yea, and went not. These men preached the true God—Him whom men serve by justice and uprightness; but they called themselves atheists."

When the highest conceptions, the lessons of religion, are imported, the nation is not culminating, has not genius, but is servile. A true nation loves its vernacular tongue. A completed nation will not impart its religion. Duty grows everywhere, like children, like grass; and we need not go to Europe or to Asia to learn it. I am not sure that the English religion is not all quoted. Even the Jeremy Taylors, Fullers, George Herberts, steeped, all of them, in Church traditions, are only using their fine fancy to emblazon their memory. 'T is Judaea, not England, which is the ground. So with the mordant Calvinism of Scotland and America. But this quoting distances and disables them: since with every repeater something of creative force is lost, as we feel when we go back to each original moralist. Pythagoras, Socrates, the Stoics, the Hindu, Behmen, George

Fox—these speak originally; and how many sentences and books we owe to unknown authors—to writers who were not careful to set down name or date or titles or cities or postmarks in these illuminations!

We, in our turn, want power to drive the ponderous State. The constitution and law in America must be written on ethical principles, so that the entire power of the spiritual world can be enlisted to hold the loyalty of the citizen, and to repel every enemy as by force of Nature. The laws of old empires stood on the religious convictions. Now that their religions are outgrown, the empires lack strength. Romanism in Europe does not represent the real opinion of enlightened men. The Lutheran Church does not represent in Germany the opinions of the universities. In England, the gentlemen, the journals, and now, at last, churchmen and bishops, have fallen away from the Anglican Church. And in America, where are no legal ties to churches, the looseness appears dangerous.

Our religion has got on as far as Unitarianism. But all the forms grow pale. The walls of the temple are wasted and thin, and, at last, only a film of whitewash, because the mind of our culture has already left our liturgies behind. "Every age," says Varnhagen, "has another sieve for the religious tradition, and will sift it out again. Something is continually lost by this treatment, which posterity cannot recover."

But it is a capital truth that Nature, moral as well as material, is always equal to herself. Ideas always generate enthusiasm. The creed, the legend, forms of worship, swiftly decay. Morals is the incorruptible essence, very heedless in its richness of any past teacher or witness, heedless of their lives and fortunes. It does not ask whether you are wrong or right in your anecdotes of them; but it is all in all how you stand to your own tribunal.

The lines of the religious sects are very shifting; their platforms unstable; the whole science of theology of great uncertainty, and resting very much on the opinions of who may chance to be the leading doctors of Oxford or Edinburgh, of Princeton or Cambridge, today. No man can tell what religious revolutions await us in the next years; and the education in the divinity colleges may well hesitate and vary. But the science of ethics has no mutation; and whoever feels any love or skill for ethical studies may safely lay out all his strength and genius in working in that mine. The pulpit may shake, but this platform will not. All the victories of religion belong to the moral sentiment. Some poor soul beheld the Law blazing through such impediments as he had, and yielded himself to humility and joy. What was gained by being told that it was justification by faith?

The Church, in its ardor for beloved persons, clings to the miraculous, in the vulgar sense, which has even an immoral tendency, as one sees in Greek, Indian and Catholic legends, which are used to gloze every crime. The soul, penetrated with the beatitude which pours into it on all sides, asks no interpositions, no new laws—the old are good enough for it—finds in every cart path of labor ways to heaven, and the humblest lot exalted. Men will learn to put back the emphasis peremptorily on pure morals, always the same, not subject to doubtful interpretation, with no sale of indulgences, no massacre of heretics, no female slaves, no disfranchisement of woman, no stigma on race; to make morals the absolute test, and so uncover and drive out the false religions. There is no vice that has not skulked behind them. It is only yesterday that our American churches, so long silent on Slavery, and notoriously hostile to the Abolitionist, wheeled into line for Emancipation.

I am far from accepting the opinion that the revelations of the moral sentiment are insufficient, as if it furnished a rule only, and not the spirit by which the rule is animated. For I include in these, of course, the history of Jesus, as well as those of every divine soul which in any place or time delivered any grand lesson to humanity; and I find in the eminent experiences in all times a substantial agreement. The sentiment itself teaches unity of source, and disowns every superiority other than of deeper truth. Jesus has immense claims on the gratitude of mankind, and knew how to guard the integrity of his brother's soul from himself also; but, in his disciples, admiration of him runs away with their reverence for the human soul, and they hamper us with limitations of person and text. Every exaggeration of these is a violation of the soul's right, and inclines the manly reader to lay down the New Testament, to take up the Pagan philosophers. It is not that the Upanishads or the Maxims of Antoninus are better, but that they do not invade his freedom; because they are only suggestions, whilst the other adds the inadmissible claim of positive authority—of an external command, where command cannot be. This is the secret of the mischievous result that, in every period of intellectual expansion, the Church ceases to draw into its clergy those who best belong there, the largest and freest minds, and that in its most liberal forms, when such minds enter it, they are coldly received, and find themselves out of place. This charm in the Pagan moralists, of suggestion, the charm of poetry, of mere truth (easily disengaged from their historical accidents which nobody wishes to force on us), the New Testa-

ment loses by its connection with a church. Mankind cannot
long suffer this loss, and the office of this age is to put all these
writings on the eternal footing of equality of origin in the
instincts of the human mind. It is certain that each inspired
master will gain instantly by the separation from the idolatry
of ages.

To their great honor, the simple and free minds among our
clergy have not resisted the voice of Nature and the advanced
perceptions of the mind; and every church divides itself into
a liberal and expectant class, on one side, and an unwilling
and conservative class on the other. As it stands with us now,
a few clergymen, with a more theological cast of mind, retain
the traditions, but they carry them quietly. In general discourse,
they are never obtruded. If the clergyman should travel in
France, in England, in Italy, he might leave them locked up
in the same closet with his "occasional sermons" at home, and,
if he did not return, would never think to send for them. The
orthodox clergymen hold a little firmer to theirs, as Calvinism
has a more tenacious vitality; but that is doomed also, and
will only die last; for Calvinism rushes to be Unitarianism, as
Unitarianism rushes to be pure Theism.

But the inspirations are never withdrawn. In the worst times,
men of organic virtue are born—men and women of native
integrity and indifferently in high and low conditions. There
will always be a class of imaginative youths, whom poetry,
whom the love of beauty, lead to the adoration of the moral
sentiment, and these will provide it with new historic forms and
songs. Religion is as inexpugnable as the use of lamps, or of
wells, or of chimneys. The Sunday is the core of our civilization, dedicated to thought and reverence. It invites to the
noblest solitude and the noblest society, to whatever means and
aids of spiritual refreshment. Men may well come together to
kindle each other to virtuous living. Confucius said, "If in the
morning I hear of the right way, and in the evening die, I can
be happy."

The churches already indicate the new spirit in adding to
the perennial office of teaching, beneficent activities—as in
creating hospitals, ragged schools, offices of employment for
the poor, appointing almoners to the helpless, guardians of
foundlings and orphans. The power that in other times inspired
crusades, or the colonization of New England, or the modern
revivals, flies to the help of the deaf-mute and the blind, to the
education of the sailor and the vagabond boy, to the reform of
convicts and harlots—as the war created the Hilton Head and
Charleston missions, the Sanitary Commission, the nurses and
teachers at Washington.

In the present tendency of our society, in the new importance of the individual, when thrones are crumbling and presidents and governors are forced every moment to remember their constituencies; when counties and towns are resisting centralization, and the individual voter his party—society is threatened with actual granulation, religious as well as political. How many people are there in Boston? Some two hundred thousand. Well, then so many sects. Of course each poor soul loses all his old stays; no bishop watches him, no confessor reports that he has neglected the confessional, no class leader admonishes him of absences, no fagot, no penance, no fine, no rebuke. Is not this wrong? is not this dangerous? 'T is not wrong, but the law of growth. It is not dangerous, any more than the mother's withdrawing her hands from the tottering babe, at his first walk across the nursery floor: the child fears and cries, but achieves the feat, instantly tries it again, and never wishes to be assisted more. And this infant soul must learn to walk alone. At first he is forlorn, homeless; but this rude stripping him of all support drives him inward, and he finds himself unhurt; he finds himself face to face with the majestic Presence, reads the original of the Ten Commandments, the original of Gospels and Epistles; nay, his narrow chapel expands to the blue cathedral of the sky, where he

> *Looks in and sees each blissful deity,*
> *Where he before the thunderous throne doth lie.*

To nations or to individuals the progress of opinion is not a loss of moral restraint, but simply a change from coarser to finer checks. No evil can come from reform which a deeper thought will not correct. If there is any tendency in national expansion to form character, religion will not be a loser. There is a fear that pure truth, pure morals, will not make a religion for the affections. Whenever the sublimities of character shall be incarnated in a man, we may rely that awe and love and insatiable curiosity will follow his steps. Character is the habit of action from the permanent vision of truth. It carries a superiority to all the accidents of life. It compels right relation to every other man—domesticates itself with strangers and enemies. "But I, father," says the wise Prahlada, in the Vishnu Purana, "know neither friends nor foes, for I behold Kesava in all beings as in my own soul." It confers perpetual insight. It sees that a man's friends and his foes are of his own household, of his own person. What would it avail me, if I could destroy my enemies? There would be as many tomorrow. That which I hate and fear is really in myself, and no knife is long enough to reach to its heart. Confucius said one day to Ke Kang: "Sir, in carrying on your government, why should you use killing at all? Let your evinced desires be for what is good, and the people will be good. The grass must bend, when the wind blows across it." Ke Kang, distressed about the number of thieves in the state, inquired of Confucius how to do away with them. Confucius said, "If you, sir, were not covetous, although you should reward them to do it, they would not steal."

Its methods are subtle, it works without means. It indulges no enmity against any, knowing, with Prahlada, that "the suppression of malignant feeling is itself a reward." The more reason, the less government. In a sensible family, nobody ever hears the words "shall" and "shan't"; nobody commands, and nobody obeys, but all conspire and joyfully co-operate. Take off the roofs of hundreds of happy houses, and you shall see this order without ruler, and the like in every intelligent and moral society. Command is exceptional, and marks some break in the link of reason; as the electricity goes round the world without a spark or a sound, until there is a break in the wire or the water chain. Swedenborg said that, "in the spiritual world, when one wishes to rule, or despises others, he is thrust out of doors." Goethe, in discussing the characters in Wilhelm Meister, maintained his belief that "pure loveliness and right good will are the highest manly prerogatives, before which all energetic heroism, with its luster and renown, must recede." In perfect accord with this, Henry James affirms, that "to give the feminine element in life its hard-earned but eternal supremacy over the masculine has been the secret inspiration of all past history."

There is no end to the sufficiency of character. It can afford to wait; it can do without what is called success; it cannot but succeed. To a well-principled man existence is victory. He defends himself against failure in his main design by making every inch of the road to it pleasant. There is no trifle, and no obscurity to him: he feels the immensity of the chain whose last link he holds in his hand, and is led by it. Having nothing, this spirit hath all. It asks, with Marcus Aurelius, "What matter by whom the good is done?" It extols humility—by every self-abasement lifted higher in the scale of being. It makes no stipulations for earthly felicity—does not ask, in the absoluteness of its trust, even for the assurance of continued life.

Self-Reliance

I read the other day some verses written by an eminent painter which were original and not conventional. The soul always hears an admonition in such lines, let the subject be what it may. The sentiment they instill is of more value than any thought they may contain. To believe your own thought, to believe that what is true for you in your private heart is true for all men—that is genius. Speak your latent conviction, and it shall be the universal sense; for the inmost in due time becomes the outmost, and our first thought is rendered back to us by the trumpets of the Last Judgment. Familiar as the voice of the mind is to each, the highest merit we ascribe to Moses, Plato and Milton is that they set at naught books and traditions, and spoke not what men, but what *they* thought. A man should learn to detect and watch that gleam of light which flashes across his mind from within more than the luster of the firmament of bards and sages. Yet he dismisses without notice his thought, because it is his. In every work of genius we recognize our own rejected thoughts; they come back to us with a certain alienated majesty. Great works of art have no more affecting lesson for us than this. They teach us to abide by our spontaneous impression with good-humored inflexibility the most when the whole cry of voices is on the other side. Else tomorrow a stranger will say with masterly good sense precisely what we have thought and felt all the time, and we shall be forced to take with shame our own opinion from another.

There is a time in every man's education when he arrives at the conviction that envy is ignorance; that imitation is suicide; that he must take himself for better for worse as his portion; that though the wide universe is full of good, no kernel of nourishing corn can come to him but through his toil bestowed on that plot of ground which is given to him to till. The power which resides in him is new in nature, and none but he knows what that is which he can do, nor does he know until he has tried. Not for nothing one face, one character, one fact, makes much impression on him, and another none. This sculpture in the memory is not without pre-established harmony. The eye was placed where one ray should fall, that it might testify of that particular ray. We but half express ourselves, and are ashamed of that divine idea which each of us represents. It may be safely trusted as proportionate and of good issues, so it be faithfully imparted, but God will not have his work made manifest by cowards. A man is relieved and gay when he has put his heart into his work and done his best; but what he has said or done otherwise shall give him no peace. It is a deliverance which does not deliver. In the attempt his genius deserts him; no muse befriends; no invention, no hope.

Trust thyself: every heart vibrates to that iron string. Accept the place the divine providence has found for you, the society of your contemporaries, the connection of events. Great men have always done so, and confided themselves childlike to the genius of their age, betraying their perception that the absolutely trustworthy was seated at their heart, working through their hands, predominating in all their being. And we are now men, and must accept in the highest mind the same transcendent destiny; and not minors and invalids in a protected corner, not cowards fleeing before a revolution, but guides, redeemers and benefactors, obeying the Almighty effort and advancing on Chaos and the Dark.

What pretty oracles nature yields us on this text in the face and behavior of children, babes, and even brutes! That divided and rebel mind, that distrust of a sentiment because our arithmetic has computed the strength and means opposed to our purpose, these have not. Their mind being whole, their eye is as yet unconquered, and when we look in their faces we are disconcerted. Infancy conforms to nobody; all conform to it; so that one babe commonly makes four or five out of the adults who prattle and play to it. So God has armed youth and puberty and manhood no less with its own piquancy and charm, and made it enviable and gracious and its claims not to be put by, if it will stand by itself. Do not think the youth has no force, because he cannot speak to you and me. Hark! in the next room his voice is sufficiently clear and emphatic. It seems he knows how to speak to his contemporaries. Bashful or bold then, he will know how to make us seniors very unnecessary.

The nonchalance of boys who are sure of a dinner, and would disdain as much as a lord to do or say aught to conciliate one, is the healthy attitude of human nature. A boy is in the parlor what the pit is in the playhouse; independent, irresponsible, looking out from his corner on such people and facts as pass by, he tries and sentences them on their merits, in the swift, summary way of boys, as good, bad, interesting, silly, eloquent, troublesome. He cumbers himself never about consequences, about interests: he gives an independent, genuine verdict. You must court him; he does not court you. But the man is as it were clapped into jail by his consciousness. As soon as he has once acted or spoken with *éclat* he is a committed person, watched by the sympathy or the hatred of hundreds, whose affections must now enter into his account. There is no Lethe for this. Ah, that he could pass again into his neutrality! Who can thus avoid all pledges and, have observed, observe again from the same unaffected, unbiased, unbribable, unaffrighted innocence—must always be formidable. He would utter opinions on all passing affairs, which being seen to be not private but necessary, would sink like darts into the ear of men and put them in fear.

These are the voices which we hear in solitude, but they grow faint and inaudible as we enter into the world. Society everywhere is in conspiracy against the manhood of every one of its members. Society is a joint-stock company, in which the members agree, for the better securing of his bread to each shareholder, to surrender the liberty and culture of the eater. The virtue in most request is conformity. Self-reliance is its aversion. It loves not realities and creators, but names and customs.

Whoso would be a man, must be a nonconformist. He who would gather immortal palms must not be hindered by the name of goodness, but must explore if it be goodness. Nothing is at last sacred but the integrity of your own mind. Absolve you to yourself, and you shall have the suffrage of the world. I remember an answer which when quite young I was prompted to make to a valued adviser who was wont to importune me with the dear old doctrines of the church. On my saying, "What have I to do with the sacredness of traditions, if I live wholly from within?" my friend suggested—"But these impulses may be from below, not from above." I replied, "They do not seem to me to be such; but if I am the Devil's child, I will live then from the Devil." No law can be sacred to me but that of my nature. Good and bad are but names very readily transferable to that or this; the only right is what is after my constitution; the only wrong what is against it. A man is to carry himself in the presence of all opposition as if everything were titular and ephemeral but he. I am ashamed to think how easily we capitulate to badges and names, to large societies and dead institutions. Every decent and well-spoken individual affects and sways me more than is right. I ought to go upright and vital, and speak the rude truth in all ways. If malice and vanity wear the coat of philanthropy, shall that pass? If an angry bigot assumes this bountiful cause of Abolition, and comes to me with his last news from Barbados, why should I not say to him, "Go love thy infant; love thy woodchopper; be good-natured and modest; have that grace; and never varnish your hard, uncharitable ambition with this incredible tenderness for black folk a thousand miles off. Thy love afar is spite at home." Rough and graceless would be such greeting, but truth is handsomer than the affectation of love. Your goodness must have some edge to it—else it is none. The doctrine of hatred must be preached, as the counteraction of the doctrine of love, when that pules and whines. I shun father and mother and wife and brother when my genius calls me. I would write on the lintels of the doorpost, *Whim*. I hope it is somewhat better than whim at last, but we cannot spend the day in explanation. Expect me not to show cause why I seek or why I exclude company. Then again, do not tell me, as a good man did today, of my obligation to put all poor men in good situations. Are they *my* poor? I tell thee, thou foolish philanthropist, that I grudge the dollar, the dime, the cent I give to such men as do not belong to me and to whom I do not belong. There is a class of persons to whom by all spiritual affinity I am bought and sold; for them I will go to prison if need be; but your miscellaneous popular charities; the education at college of fools; the building of meeting-houses to the vain end to which many now stand; alms to sots, and the thousandfold Relief Societies—though I confess with shame I sometimes succumb and give the dollar, it is a wicked dollar, which by and by I shall have the manhood to withhold.

Virtues are, in the popular estimate, rather the exception than the rule. There is the man *and* his virtues. Men do what is called a good action, as some piece of courage or charity, much as they would pay a fine in expiation of daily nonappearance on parade. Their works are done as an apology or extenuation of their living in the world—as invalids and the insane pay a high board. Their virtues are penances. I do not wish to expiate, but to live. My life is for itself and not for a spectacle. I much prefer that it should be of a lower strain, so it be genuine and equal, than that it should be glittering and unsteady. I wish it to be sound and sweet, and not to need diet and bleeding. I ask primary evidence that you are a man, and refuse this appeal from the man to his actions. I know that for myself it makes no difference whether I do or forbear those actions which are reckoned excellent. I cannot consent to pay for a privilege where I have intrinsic right. Few and mean as my gifts may be, I actually am, and do not need for my own assurance or the assurance of my fellows any secondary testimony.

What I must do is all that concerns me, not what the people think. This rule, equally arduous in actual and in intellectual life, may serve for the whole distinction between greatness and meanness. It is the harder because you will always find those who think they know what is your duty better than you know it. It is easy in the world to live after the world's opinion; it is easy in solitude to live after our own; but the great man is he who in the midst of the crowd keeps with perfect sweetness the independence of solitude.

The objection to conforming to usages that have become dead to you is that it scatters your force. It loses your time and blurs the impression of your character. If you maintain a dead church, contribute to a dead Bible-society, vote with a great party either for the government or against it, spread your table like base housekeepers—under all these screens I have difficulty to detect the precise man you are: and of course so much force is withdrawn from your proper life. But do your work, and I shall know you. Do your work, and you shall reinforce yourself. A man must consider what a blindman's-buff is this game of conformity. If I know your sect I anticipate your argument. I hear a preacher announce for his text and topic the expediency of one of the institutions of his church. Do I not know beforehand that not possibly can he say a new and spontaneous word? Do I not know that with all this ostentation of examining the grounds of the institution he will do no such thing? Do I not know that he is pledged to himself not to look but at one side, the permitted side, not as a man, but as a parish minister? He is a retained attorney, and these airs of the bench are the emptiest affectation. Well, most men have bound their eyes with one or another handkerchief, and attached themselves to some one of these communities of opinion. This conformity makes them not false in a few particulars, authors of a few lies, but false in all particulars. Their every truth is not quite true. Their two is not the real two, their four not the real four; so that every word they say chagrins us and we know not where to begin to set them right. Meantime nature is not slow to equip us in the prison-uniform of the party to which we adhere. We come to wear one cut of face and figure, and acquire by degrees the gentlest asinine expression. There is a mortifying experience in particular, which does not fail to wreak itself also in the general history; I mean "the foolish face of praise," the forced smile which we put on in company where we do not feel at ease, in answer to conversation which does not interest us. The muscles, not spontaneously moved but moved by a low usurping willfulness, grow tight about the outline of the face, with the most disagreeable sensation.

For nonconformity the world whips you with its displeasure. And therefore a man must know how to estimate a sour face. The bystanders look askance on him in the public street or in the friend's parlor. If this aversion had its origin in contempt and resistance like his own he might well go home with a sad countenance; but the sour faces of the multitude, like their sweet faces, have no deep cause, but are put on and off as the wind blows and a newspaper directs. Yet is the discontent of the multitude more formidable than that of the senate and the college. It is easy enough for a firm man who knows the world to brook the rage of the cultivated classes. Their rage is decorous and prudent, for they are timid, as being very vulnerable themselves. But when to their feminine rage the indignation of the people is added, when the ignorant and the poor are aroused, when the unintelligent brute force that lies at the bottom of society is made to growl and mow, it needs the habit of magnanimity and religion to treat it godlike as a trifle of no concernment.

The other terror that scares us from self-trust is our consistency; a reverence for our past act or word because the eyes of others have no other data for computing our orbit than our past acts, and we are loth to disappoint them.

But why should you keep your head over your shoulder? Why drag about this corpse of your memory, lest you contradict somewhat you have stated in this or that public place? Suppose you should contradict yourself; what then? It seems to be a rule of wisdom never to rely on your memory, but to bring the past for judgment into the thousand-eyed present, and live ever in a new day. In your metaphysics you have denied personality to the Deity, yet when the devout motions of the soul come, yield to them heart and life, though they should clothe God with shape and color. Leave your theory, as Joseph his coat in the hand of the harlot, and flee.

A foolish consistency is the hobgoblin of little minds, adored by little statesmen and philosophers and divines. With consistency a great soul has simply nothing to do. He may as well concern himself with his shadow on the wall. Speak what you think now in hard words and tomorrow speak what tomorrow thinks in hard words again, though it contradict everything you said today. —"Ah, so you shall be sure to be misunderstood."—Is it so bad then to be misunderstood? Pythagoras was misunderstood, and Socrates, and Jesus, and Luther, and Copernicus, and Galileo, and Newton, and every pure and wise spirit that ever took flesh. To be great is to be misunderstood.

I suppose no man can violate his nature. All the sallies of his will are rounded in by the law of his being, as the inequalities of Andes and Himmaleh are insignificant in the curve of the sphere. Nor does it matter how you gauge and try him. A character is like an acrostic or Alexandrian stanza—read it forward, backward, or across, it still spells the same thing. In this pleasing contrite wood-life which God allows me, let me record day by day my honest thought without prospect or retrospect, and, I cannot doubt, it will be found symmetrical, though I mean it not and see it not. My book should smell of pines and resound with the hum of insects. The swallow over my window should interweave that thread or straw he carries in his bill into my web also. We pass for what we are. Character teaches above our wills. Men imagine that they communicate their virtue or vice only by overt actions, and do not see that virtue or vice emit a breath every moment.

There will be an agreement in whatever variety of actions, so they be each honest and natural in their hour. For of one will, the actions will be harmonious, however unlike they seem. These varieties are lost sight of at a little distance, at a little height of thought. One tendency unites them all. The voyage of the best ship is a zigzag line of a hundred tacks. See the line from a sufficient distance, and it straightens itself to the average tendency. Your genuine action will explain itself and will explain your other genuine actions. Your conformity explains nothing. Act singly, and what you have already done singly will justify you now. Greatness appeals to the future. If I can be firm enough today to do right and scorn eyes, I must have done so much right before as to defend me now. Be it how it will, do right now. Always scorn appearances and you always may. The force of character is cumulative. All the foregone days of virtue work their health into this. What makes the majesty of the heroes of the senate and the field, which so fills the imagination? The consciousness of a train of great days and victories behind. They shed a united light on the advancing actor. He is attended as by a visible escort of angels. That is it which throws thunder into Chatham's voice, and dignity into Washington's port, and America into Adams's eye. Honor is venerable to us because it is no ephemera. It is always ancient virtue. We worship it today because it is not of today. We love it and pay it homage because it is not a trap for our love and homage, but is self-dependent, self-derived, and therefore of an old immaculate pedigree, even if shown in a young person.

I hope in these days we have heard the last of conformity and consistency. Let the words be gazetted and ridiculous henceforward. Instead of the gong for dinner, let us hear a whistle from the Spartan fife. Let us never bow and apologize more. A great man is coming to eat at my house. I do not wish to please him; I wish that he should wish to please me. I will stand here for humanity, and though I would make it kind, I would make it true. Let us affront and reprimand the smooth mediocrity and squalid contentment of the times, and hurl in the face of custom and trade and office, the fact which is the upshot of all history, that there is a great responsible Thinker and Actor working wherever a man works; that a true man belongs to no other time or place, but is the center of things. Where he is, there is nature. He measures you and all men and all events. Ordinarily, everybody in society reminds us of somewhat else, or of some other person. Character, reality, reminds you of nothing else; it takes place of the whole creation. The man must be so much that he must make all circumstances indifferent. Every true man is a cause, a country and an age; requires infinite spaces and numbers and time fully to accomplish his design—and posterity seem to follow his steps as a train of clients. A man Caesar is born, and for ages after we have a Roman Empire. Christ is born, and millions of minds so grow and cleave to his genius that he is confounded with virtue and the possible of man. An institution is the lengthened shadow of one man; as, Monachism, of the Hermit Antony; the Reformation, of Luther; Quakerism, of Fox; Methodism, of Wesley; Abolition, of Clarkson. Scipio, Milton called "the height of Rome"; and all history resolves itself very easily into the biography of a few stout and earnest persons.

Let a man then know his worth, and keep things under his feet. Let him not peep or steal, or skulk up and down with the air of a charity-boy, a bastard, or an interloper in the world which exists for him. But the man in the street, finding no worth in himself which corresponds to the force which built a tower or sculptured a marble god, feels poor when he looks on these. To him a palace, a statue, or a costly book have an alien and forbidding air, much like a gay equipage, and seem to say like that, "Who are you, Sir?" Yet they all are his, suitors for his notice, petitioners to his faculties that they will come out and take possession. The picture waits for my verdict; it is not to command me, but I am to settle its claims to praise. That popular fable of the sot who was picked up dead-drunk in the street, carried to the duke's house, washed and dressed and laid in the duke's bed, and, on his waking, treated with all obsequious ceremony like the duke, and assured that he had been insane, owes its popularity to the fact that it symbolizes so well the state of man, who is in the world a sort of sot, but now and then wakes up, exercises his reason and finds himself a true prince.

Our reading is mendicant and sycophantic. In history our imagination plays us false. Kingdom and lordship, power and estate, are a gaudier vocabulary than private John and Edward in a small house and common day's work; but the things of life are the same to both; the sum total of both is the same. Why all this deference to Alfred and Scanderbeg and Gustavus? Suppose they were virtuous; did they wear out virtue? As great a stake depends on your private act today as followed their public and renowned steps. When private men shall act with original views, the luster will be transferred from the actions of kings to those of gentlemen.

The world has been instructed by its kings, who have so magnetized the eyes of nations. It has been taught by this colossal symbol the mutual reverence that is due from man to man. The joyful loyalty with which men have everywhere suffered the king, the noble, or the great proprietor to walk among them by a law of his own, make his own scale of men and things and reverse theirs, pay for benefits not with money but with honor, and represent the law in his person, was the hieroglyphic by which they obscurely signified their consciousness of their own right and comeliness, the right of every man.

The magnetism which all original action exerts is explained when we inquire the reason of self-trust. Who is the Trustee? What is the aboriginal Self, on which a universal reliance may be grounded? What is the nature and baffling star, without parallax, without which shoots a ray of beauty even actions, if the least mark of independen leads us to that source, at once the esse and of life, which we call Spontaneity this primary wisdom as Intuition, whils tuitions. In that deep force, the last fac cannot go, all things find their commo of being which in calm hours rises, we soul, is not diverse from things, from time, from man, but one with them a from the same source whence their life We first share the life by which things them as appearances in nature and for their cause. Here is the fountain of Here are the lungs of that inspiration wl and which cannot be denied without in lie in the lap of immense intelligence, which makes us receivers of its truth and organs of its activity. When we discern justice, when we discern truth, we do nothing of ourselves, but allow a passage to its beams. If we ask whence this comes, if we seek to pry into the soul that causes, all philosophy is at fault. Its presence or its absence is all we can affirm. Every man discriminates between the voluntary acts of his mind and his involuntary perceptions, and knows that to his involuntary perceptions a perfect faith is due. He may err in the expression of them, but he knows that these things are so, like day and night, not to be disputed. My willful actions and acquisitions are but roving—the idlest reverie, the faintest native emotion, command my curiosity and respect. Thoughtless people contradict as readily the statement of perceptions as of opinions, or rather much more readily; for they do not distinguish between perception and notion. They fancy that I choose to see this or that thing. But perception is not whimsical, but fatal. If I see a trait, my children will see it after me, and in course of time all mankind—although it may chance that no one has seen it before me. For my perception of it is as much a fact as the sun.

The relations of the soul to the divine spirit are so pure that it is profane to seek to interpose helps. It must be that when God speaketh he should communicate, not one thing, but all things; should fill the world with his voice; should scatter forth light, nature, time, souls, from the center of the present thought; and new date and new create the whole. Whenever a mind is simple and receives a divine wisdom, old things pass away—means, teachers, texts, temples fall; it lives now, and absorbs past and future into the present hour. All things are made sacred by relation to it—one as much as another. All things are dissolved to their center by their cause, and in the universal miracle petty and particular miracles disappear. If therefore a man claims to know and speak of God and carries you backward to the phraseology of some old moldered nation in another country, in another world, believe him not. Is the acorn better than the oak which is its fullness and completion? Is the parent better than the child into whom he has cast his ripened being? Whence then this worship of the past? The centuries are conspirators against the sanity and authority of the soul. Time and space are but physiological colors which the eye makes, but the soul is light: where it is, is day; where it was, is night; and history is an impertinence and an injury if it be anything more than a cheerful apologue or parable of my being and becoming.

Man is timid and apologetic; he is no longer upright; he dares not to say "I think," "I am," but quotes some saint or sage. He is ashamed before the blade of grass or the blowing rose. These roses under my window make no reference to former roses or to better ones; they are for what they are; they exist with God today. There is no time to them. There is simply the rose; it is perfect in every moment of its existence. Before a leaf-bud has burst, its whole life acts; in the full-blown flower there is no more; in the leafless root there is no less. Its nature is satisfied and it satisfies nature in all moments alike. But man postpones or remembers; he does not live in the present, but with reverted eye laments the past, or, heedless of the riches that surround him, stands on tiptoe to foresee the future. He cannot be happy and strong until he too lives with nature in the present, above time.

This should be plain enough. Yet see what strong intellects dare not yet hear God himself unless he speak the phraseology of I know not what David, or Jeremiah, or Paul. We shall not always set so great a price on a few texts, on a few lives. We are like children who repeat by rote the sentences of grandames and tutors, and, as they grow older, of the men of talents and character they chance to see—painfully recollecting the exact words they spoke; afterwards, when they come into the point of view which those had who uttered these sayings, they understand them and are willing to let the words go; for at any time they can use words as good when occasion comes. If we live truly, we shall see truly. It is as easy for the strong man to be strong as it is for the weak to be weak. When we have new perception, we shall gladly disburden the memory of its hoarded treasures as old rubbish. When a man lives with God, his voice shall be as sweet as the murmur of the brook and the rustle of the corn.

And now at last the highest truth on this subject remains unsaid; probably cannot be said; for all that we say is the far-off remembering of the intuition. That thought by what I can now nearest approach to say it, is this. When good is near you, when you have life in yourself, it is not by any known or accustomed way; you shall not discern the footprints of any other; you shall not see the face of man; you shall not hear any name—the way, the thought, the good, shall be wholly strange and new. It shall exclude example and experience. You take the way from man, not to man. All persons that ever existed are its forgotten ministers. Fear and hope are alike beneath it. There is somewhat low even in hope. In the hour of vision there is nothing that can be called gratitude, nor properly joy. The soul raised over passion beholds identity and eternal causation, perceives the self-existence of Truth and Right, and calms itself with knowing that all things go well. Vast spaces of nature, the Atlantic Ocean, the South Sea; long intervals of time, years, centuries, are of no account. This which I think and feel underlay every former state of life and circumstances, as it does underlie my present, and what is called life and what is called death.

Life only avails, not the having lived. Power ceases in the

instant of repose; it resides in the moment of transition from a past to a new state, in the shooting of the gulf, in the darting to an aim. This one fact the world hates; that the soul *becomes*; for that forever degrades the past, turns all riches to poverty, all reputation to a shame, confounds the saint with the rogue, shoves Jesus and Judas equally aside. Why then do we prate of self-reliance? Inasmuch as the soul is present there will be power not confident but agent. To talk of reliance is a poor external way of speaking. Speak rather of that which relies because it works and is. Who has more obedience than I masters me, though he should not raise his finger. Round him I must revolve by the gravitation of spirits. We fancy it rhetoric when we speak of eminent virtue. We do not yet see that virtue is Height, and that a man or a company of men, plastic and permeable to principles, by the law of nature must overpower and ride all cities, nations, kings, rich men, poets, who are not.

This is the ultimate fact which we so quickly reach on this, as on every topic, the resolution of all into the ever-blessed ONE. Self-existence is the attribute of the Supreme Cause, and it constitutes the measure of good by the degree in which it enters into all lower forms. All things real are so by so much virtue as they contain. Commerce, husbandry, hunting, whaling, war, eloquence, personal weight, are somewhat, and engage my respect as examples of its presence and impure action. I see the same law working in nature for conservation and growth. Power is, in nature, the essential measure of right. Nature suffers nothing to remain in her kingdoms which cannot help itself. The genesis and maturation of a planet, its poise and orbit, the bended tree recovering itself from the strong wind, the vital resources of every animal and vegetable, are demonstrations of the self-sufficing and therefore self-relying soul.

Thus all concentrates: let us not rove; let us sit at home with the cause. Let us stun and astonish the intruding rabble of men and books and institutions by a simple declaration of the divine fact. Bid the invad`_____ __ `the shoes from off their feet, for God is here within. Let our simplicity judge them, and our docility to our own law demonstrate the poverty of nature and fortune beside our native riches.

But now we are a mob. Man does not stand in awe of man, nor is his genius admonished to stay at home, to put itself in communication with the internal ocean, but it goes abroad to beg a cup of water of the urns of other men. We must go alone. I like the silent church before the service begins better than any preaching. How far off, how cool, how chaste the persons look, begirt each one with a precinct or sanctuary! So let us always sit. Why should we assume the faults of our friend, or wife, or father, or child, because they sit around our heart, or are said to have the same blood? All men have my blood and I all men's. Not for that will I adopt their petulance or folly, even to the extent of being ashamed of it. But your isolation must not be mechanical, but spiritual, that is, must be elevation. At times the whole world seems to be in conspiracy to importune you with emphatic trifles. Friend, client, child, sickness, fear, want, charity, all knock at once at thy closet door and say—"Come out unto us." But keep thy state; come not into their confusion. The power men possess to annoy me I give them by a weak curiosity. No man can come near me but through my act. "What we love that we have, but by desire we bereave ourselves of the love."

If we cannot at once rise to the sanctities of obedience and faith, let us at least resist our temptations; let us enter into the state of war and wake Thor and Woden, courage and constancy, in our Saxon breasts. This is to be done in our smooth times by speaking the truth. Check this lying hospitality and lying affection. Live no longer to the expectation of these deceived and deceiving people with whom we converse. Say to them, "O father, O mother, O wife, O brother, O friend, I have lived with you after appearances hitherto. Henceforward I am the truth's. Be it known unto you that henceforward I obey no law less than the eternal law. I will have no covenants but proximities. I shall endeavor to nourish my parents, to support my family, to be the chaste husband of one wife—but these relations I must fill after a new and unprecedented way. I appeal from your customs. I must be myself. I cannot break myself any longer for you, or you. If you can love me for what I am, we shall be the appier. If you cannot, I will still seek to deserve that you should. I will not hide my tastes or aversions. I will so trust that what is deep is holy, that I will do strongly before the sun and moon whatever inly rejoices me and the heart appoints. If you are noble, I will love you; if you are not, I will not hurt you and myself by hypocritical attentions. If you are true, but not in the same truth with me, cleave to your companions; I will seek my own. I do this not selfishly but humbly and truly. It is alike your interest, and mine, and all men's, however long we have dwelt in lies, to live in truth. Does this sound harsh today? You will soon love what is dictated by your nature as well as mine, and if we follow the truth it will bring us out safe at last." But so may you give these friends pain. Yes, but I cannot sell my liberty and my power, to save their sensibility. Besides, all persons have their moments of reason, when they look out into the region of absolute truth; then will they justify me and do the same thing.

The populace think that your rejection of popular standards is a rejection of all standard, and mere antinomianism; and the bold sensualist will use the name of philosophy to gild his crimes. But the law of consciousness abides. There are two confessionals, in one or the other of which we must be shriven. You may fulfill your round of duties by clearing yourself in the *direct*, or in the *reflex* way. Consider whether you have satisfied your relations to father, mother, cousin, neighbor, town, cat and dog—whether any of these can upbraid you. But I may also neglect this reflex standard and absolve me to myself. I have my own stern claims and perfect circle. It denies the name of duty to many offices that are called duties. But if I can discharge its debts it enables me to dispense with the popular code. If anyone imagines that this law is lax, let him keep its commandments one day.

And truly it demands something godlike in him who has cast off the common motives of humanity and has ventured to trust himself for a taskmaster. High be his heart, faithful his will, clear his sight, that he may in good earnest be doctrine, society, law, to himself, that a simple purpose may be to him as strong as iron necessity is to others!

If any man consider the present aspects of what is called by distinction *society*, he will see the need of these ethics. The sinew and heart of man seem to be drawn out, and we are become timorous, desponding whimperers. We are afraid of truth, afraid of fortune, afraid of death, and afraid of each other. Our age yields no great and perfect persons. We want men and women who shall renovate life and our social state, but we see that most natures are insolvent, cannot satisfy their own wants, have an ambition out of all proportion to their practical force and do lean and beg day and night continually. Our housekeeping is mendicant, our arts, our occupations, our marriages, our religion we have not chosen, but society has chosen for us. We are parlor soldiers. We shun the rugged battle of fate, where strength is born.

If our young men miscarry in their first enterprises they lose all heart. If the young merchant fails, men say he is *ruined*. If the finest genius studies at one of our colleges and is not installed in an office within one year afterwards in the cities or suburbs of Boston or New York, it seems to his friends and to himself that he is right in being disheartened and in complaining the rest of his life. A sturdy farm lad from New Hampshire or Vermont, who in turn tries all the professions, who *teams it, farms it, peddles,* keeps a school, preaches, edits a newspaper, goes to Congress, buys a township, and so forth, in successive years, and always like a cat falls on his feet, is worth a hundred of these city dolls. He walks abreast with his days and feels no shame in not "studying a profession," for he does not postpone his life, but lives already. He has not one chance, but a hundred chances. Let a Stoic open the resources of man and tell men they are not leaning willows, but can and must detach themselves; that with the exercise of self-trust, new powers shall appear; that a man is the word made flesh, born to shed healing to the nations; that he should be ashamed of our compassion, and that the moment he acts from himself, tossing the laws, the books, idolatries and customs out of the window, we pity him no more but thank and revere him—and that teacher shall restore the life of man to splendor and make his name dear to all history.

It is easy to see that a greater self-reliance must work a revolution in all the offices and relations of men; in their religion; in their education; in their pursuits; their modes of living; their association; in their property; in their speculative views.

1. In what prayers do men allow themselves! That which they call a holy office is not so much as brave and manly. Prayer looks abroad and asks for some foreign addition to come through some foreign virtue, and loses itself in endless mazes of natural and supernatural, and mediatorial and miraculous. Prayer that craves a particular commodity, anything less than all good, is vicious. Prayer is the contemplation of the facts of life from the highest point of view. It is the soliloquy of a beholding and jubilant soul. It is the spirit of God pronouncing his works good. But prayer as a means to effect a private end is meanness and theft. It supposes dualism and not unity in nature and conciousness. As soon as the man is at one with God, he will not beg. He will then see prayer in all action. The prayer of the farmer kneeling in his field to weed it, the prayer of the rower kneeling with the stroke of his oar, are true prayers heard throughout nature, though for cheap ends. Caratach, in Fletcher's "Bonduca," when admonished to inquire the mind of the god Audate, replies,

> *His hidden meaning lies in our endeavors;*
> *Our valors are our best gods.*

Another sort of false prayers are our regrets. Discontent is the want of self-reliance; it is infirmity of will. Regret calamities if you can thereby help the sufferer; if not, attend your own work and already the evil begins to be repaired. Our sympathy is just as base. We come to them who weep foolishly and sit down and cry for company, instead of imparting to them truth and health in rough electric shocks, putting them once more in communication with their own reason. The secret of fortune is joy in our hands. Welcome evermore to gods and men is the self-helping man. For him all doors are flung wide; him all tongues greet, all honors crown, all eyes follow with desire. Our love goes out to him and embraces him because he did not need it. We solicitously and apologetically caress and celebrate him because he held on his way and scorned our disapprobation. The gods love him because men hated him. "To the persevering mortal," said Zoroaster, "the blessed Immortals are swift."

As men's prayers are a disease of the will, so are their creeds a disease of the intellect. They say with those foolish Israelites, "Let not God speak to us, lest we die. Speak thou, speak any man with us, and we will obey." Everywhere I am hindered of meeting God in my brother, because he has shut his own temple doors and recites fables merely of his brother's, or his brother's brother's God. Every new mind is a new classification. If it prove a mind of uncommon activity and power, a Locke, a Lavoisier, a Hutton, a Bentham, a Fourier, it imposes its classification on other men, and lo! a new system. In proportion to the depth of the thought, and so to the number of the objects it touches and brings within reach of the pupil, is his complacency. But chiefly is this apparent in creeds and churches, which are also classifications of some powerful mind acting on the elemental thought of duty and man's relation to the Highest. Such is Calvinism, Quakerism, Swedenborgism. The pupil takes the same delight in subordinating everything to the new terminology as a girl who has just learned botany in seeing a new earth and new seasons thereby. It will happen for a time that the pupil will find his intellectual power has grown by the study of his master's mind. But in all unbalanced minds the classification is idolized, passes for the end and not for a speedily exhaustible means, so that the walls of the system blend to their eye in the remote horizon with the walls of the universe; the luminaries of heaven seem to them hung on the arch their master built. They cannot imagine how you aliens have any right to see—how you can see; "It must be somehow that you stole the light from us." They do not yet perceive that light, unsystematic, indomitable, will break into any cabin, even into theirs. Let them chirp awhile and call it their own. If they are honest and do well, presently their neat new pinfold will be too strait and low, will crack, will lean, will rot and vanish, and the immortal light, all young and joyful, million-orbed, million-colored, will beam over the universe as on the first morning.

2. It is for want of self-culture that the superstition of Traveling, whose idols are Italy, England, Egypt, retains its fascination for all educated Americans. They who made England, Italy or Greece venerable in the imagination, did so by sticking fast where they were, like an axis of the earth. In manly hours we feel that duty is our place. The soul is no traveler; the wise man stays at home, and when his necessities, his duties, on any occasion call him from his house, or into foreign lands, he is at home still and shall make men sensible by the expression of his countenance that he goes, the missionary of wisdom and virtue, and visits cities and men like a sovereign and not like an interloper or a valet.

I have no churlish objection to the circumnavigation of the globe for the purpose of art, of study, and benevolence, so that the man is first domesticated, or does not go abroad with the hope of finding somewhat greater than he knows. He who travels to be amused, or to get somewhat which he does not carry, travels away from himself, and grows old even in youth among old things. In Thebes, in Palmyra, his will and mind have become old and dilapidated as they. He carries ruins to ruins.

Traveling is a fool's paradise. Our first journeys discover to us the indifference of places. At home I dream that at Naples, at Rome, I can be intoxicated with beauty and lose my sadness. I pack my trunk, embrace my friends, embark on the sea and at last wake up in Naples, and there beside me is the stern fact, the sad self, unrelenting, identical, that I fled from. I seek the Vatican and the palaces. I affect to be intoxicated with sights and suggestions, but I am not intoxicated. My giant goes with me wherever I go.

3. But the rage of traveling is a symptom of a deeper unsoundness affecting the whole intellectual action. The intellect is vagabond, and our system of education fosters restlessness. Our minds travel when our bodies are forced to stay at home. We imitate; and what is imitation but the traveling of the mind? Our houses are built with foreign taste; our shelves are garnished with foreign ornaments; our opinions, our tastes, our faculties, lean, and follow the Past and the Distant. The soul created the arts wherever they have flourished. It was in his own mind that the artist sought his model. It was an application of his own thought to the thing to be done and the conditions to be observed. And why need we copy the Doric or the Gothic model? Beauty, convenience, grandeur of thought and quaint expression are as near to us as to any, and if the

American artist will study with hope and love the precise thing to be done by him, considering the climate, the soil, the length of the day, the wants of the people, the habit and form of the government, he will create a house in which all these will find themselves fitted, and taste and sentiment will be satisfied also.

Insist on yourself; never imitate. Your own gift you can present every moment with the cumulative force of a whole life's cultivation; but of the adopted talent of another you have only an extemporaneous half possession. That which each can do best none but his Maker can teach him. No man yet knows what it is, nor can, till that person has exhibited it. Where is the master who could have taught Shakespeare? Where is the master who could have instructed Franklin, or Washington, or Bacon, or Newton? Every great man is a unique. The Scipionism of Scipio is precisely that part he could not borrow. Shakespeare will never be made by the study of Shakespeare. Do that which is assigned you, and you cannot hope too much or dare too much. There is at this moment for you an utterance brave and grand as that of the colossal chisel of Phidias, or trowel of the Egyptians, or the pen of Moses or Dante, but different from all these. Not possibly will the soul, all rich, all eloquent, with thousand-cloven tongue, deign to repeat itself; but if you can hear what these patriarchs say, surely you can reply to them in the same pitch of voice; for the ear and the tongue are two organs of one nature. Abide in the simple and noble regions of thy life, obey thy heart, and thou shalt reproduce the Foreworld again.

4. As our Religion, our Education, our Art look abroad, so does our spirit of society. All men plume themselves on the improvement of society, and no man improves.

Society never advances. It recedes as fast on one side as it gains on the other. It undergoes continual changes; it is barbarous, it is civilized, it is christianized, it is rich, it is scientific; but this change is not amelioration. For everything that is given something is taken. Society acquires new arts and loses old instincts. What a contrast between the well-clad, reading, writing, thinking American, with a watch, a pencil and a bill of exchange in his pocket, and the naked New Zealander, whose property is a club, a spear, a mat and an undivided twentieth of a shed to sleep under! But compare the health of the two men and you shall see that the white man has lost his aboriginal strength. If the traveler tell us truly, strike the savage with a broadaxe and in a day or two the flesh shall unite and heal as if you struck the blow into soft pitch, and the same blow shall send the white to his grave.

The civilized man has built a coach, but has lost the use of his feet. He is supported on crutches, but lacks so much support of muscle. He has a fine Geneva watch, but he fails of the skill to tell the hour by the sun. A Greenwich nautical almanac he has, and so being sure of the information when he wants it, the man in the street does not know a star in the sky. The solstice he does not observe; the equinox he knows as little; and the whole bright calendar of the year is without a dial in his mind. His notebooks impair his memory; his libraries overload his wit; the insurance office increases the number of accidents; and it may be a question whether machinery does not encumber; whether we have not lost by refinement some energy, by a Christianity, entrenched in establishments and forms, some vigor of wild virtue. For every Stoic was a Stoic; but in Christendom where is the Christian?

There is no more deviation in the moral standard than in the standard of height or bulk. No greater men are now than ever were. A singular equality may be observed between the great men of the first and of the last ages; nor can all the science, art, religion, and philosophy of the nineteenth century avail to educate greater men than Plutarch's heroes, three or four and twenty centuries ago. Not in time is the race progressive. Phocion, Socrates, Anaxagoras, Diogenes, are great men, but they leave no class. He who is really of their class will not be called by their name, but will be his own man, and in his turn the founder of a sect. The arts and inventions of each period are only its costume and do not invigorate men. The harm of the improved machinery may compensate its good. Hudson and Behring accomplished so much in their fishing boats as to astonish Parry and Franklin, whose equipment exhausted the resources of science and art. Galileo, with an opera glass, discovered a more splendid series of celestial phenomena than any one since. Columbus found the New World in an undecked boat. It is curious to see the periodical disuse and perishing of means and machinery which were introduced with loud laudation a few years or centuries before. The great genius returns to essential man. We reckoned the improvements of the art of war among the triumphs of science, and yet Napoleon conquered Europe by the bivouac, which consisted of falling back on naked valor and disencumbering it of all aids. The Emperor held it impossible to make a perfect army, says Las Casas, "without abolishing our arms, magazines, commissaries and carriages, until, in imitation of the Roman custom, the soldier should receive his supply of corn, grind it in his hand mill and bake his bread himself."

Society is a wave. The wave moves onward, but the water of which it is composed does not. The same particle does not rise from the valley to the ridge. Its unity is only phenomenal. The persons who make up a nation today, next year die, and their experience dies with them.

And so the reliance on Property, including the reliance on governments which protect it, is the want of self-reliance. Men have looked away from themselves and at things so long that they have come to esteem the religious, learned, and civil institutions as guards of property, and they deprecate assaults on these, because they feel them to be assaults on property. They measure their esteem of each other by what each has, and not by what each is. But a cultivated man becomes ashamed of his property, out of new respect for his nature. Especially he hates what he has if he sees that it is accidental—came to him by inheritance, or gift, or crime; then he feels that it is not having; it does not belong to him, has no root in him and merely lies there because no revolution or no robber takes it away. But that which a man is, does always by necessity acquire; and what the man acquires is living property, which does not wait the beck of rulers, or mobs, or revolutions, or fire, or storm, or bankruptcies, but perpetually renews itself wherever the man breathes. "Thy lot or portion of life," said the Caliph Ali, "is seeking after thee; therefore be at rest from seeking after it." Our dependence on these foreign goods leads us to our slavish respect for numbers. The political parties meet in numerous conventions; the greater the concourse and with each new uproar of an announcement, The Delegation from Essex! The Democrats from New Hampshire! The Whigs of Maine! the young patriot feels himself stronger than before by a new thousand of eyes and arms. In like manner the reformers summon conventions and vote and resolve in multitude. Not so, O friends! will the God deign to enter and inhabit you, but by a method precisely the reverse. It is only as a man puts off all foreign support and stands alone that I see him to be strong and to prevail. He is weaker by every recruit to his banner. Is not a man better than a town? Ask nothing of men, and, in the endless mutation, thy only firm column must presently appear the upholder of all that surrounds thee. He who knows that power is inborn, that he is weak because he has looked for good out of him and elsewhere, and, so perceiving, throws himself unhesitatingly on his thought, instantly rights himself, stands in the erect position, commands his limbs, works miracles; just as a man who stands on his feet is stronger than a man who stands on his head.

So use all that is called Fortune. Most men gamble with her, and gain all, and lose all, as her wheel rolls. But do thou leave as unlawful these winnings, and deal with Cause and Effect, the chancellors of God. In the Will work and acquire, and thou hast chained the wheel of Chance, and shall sit hereafter out of fear from her rotations. A political victory, a rise of rents, the recovery of your sick or the return of your absent friend, or some other favorable event, raises your spirits, and you think good days are preparing for you. Do not believe it. Nothing can bring you peace but yourself. Nothing can bring you peace but the triumph of principles.

From *Essays: First Series*
Volume II

Compensation

Ever since I was a boy I have wished to write a discourse on Compensation; for it seemed to me when very young that on this subject life was ahead of theology and the people knew more than the preachers taught. The documents too from which the doctrine is to be drawn, charmed my fancy by their endless variety, and lay always before me, even in sleep; for they are the tools in our hands, the bread in our basket, the transactions of the street, the farm and the dwelling-house; greetings, relations, debts and credits, the influence of character, the nature and endowment of all men. It seemed to me also that in it might be shown men a ray of divinity, the present action of the soul of this world, clean from all vestige of tradition; and so the heart of man might be bathed by an inundation of eternal love, conversing with that which he knows was always and always must be, because it really is now. It appeared moreover that if this doctrine could be stated in terms with any resemblance to those bright intuitions in which this truth is sometimes revealed to us, it would be a star in many dark hours and crooked passages in our journey, that would not suffer us to lose our way.

I was lately confirmed in these desires by hearing a sermon at church. The preacher, a man esteemed for his orthodoxy, unfolded in the ordinary manner the doctrine of the Last Judgment. He assumed that judgment is not executed in this world; that the wicked are successful; that the good are miserable; and then urged from reason and from Scripture a compensation to be made to both parties in the next life. No offense appeared to be taken by the congregation at this doctrine. As far as I could observe when the meeting broke up they separated without remark on the sermon.

Yet what was the import of this teaching? What did the preacher mean by saying that the good are miserable in the present life? Was it that houses and lands, offices, wine, horses, dress, luxury are had by unprincipled men, whilst the saints are poor and despised; and that a compensation is to be made to these last hereafter, by giving them the like gratifications another day—bank stock and doubloons, venison and champagne? This must be the compensation intended; for what else? Is it that they are to have leave to pray and praise? to love and serve men? Why, that they can do now. The legitimate inference the disciple would draw was, "We are to have *such* a good time as the sinners have now"; or, to push it to its extreme import, "You sin now, we shall sin by and by; we would sin now, if we could; not being successful we expect our revenge tomorrow."

The fallacy lay in the immense concession that the bad are successful; that justice is not done now. The blindness of the preacher consisted in deferring to the base estimate of the market of what constitutes a manly success, instead of confronting and convicting the world from the truth; announcing the presence of the soul; the omnipotence of the will; and so establishing the standard of good and ill, of success and falsehood.

I find a similar base tone in the popular religious works of the day and the same doctrines assumed by the literary men when occasionally they treat the related topics. I think that our popular theology has gained in decorum, and not in principle, over the superstitions it has displaced. But men are better than their theology. Their daily life gives it the lie. Every ingenuous and aspiring soul leaves the doctrine behind him in his own experience, and all men feel sometimes the falsehood which they cannot demonstrate. For men are wiser than they know. That which they hear in schools and pulpits without afterthought, if said in conversation would probably be questioned in silence. If a man dogmatize in a mixed company on Providence and the divine laws, he is answered by a silence which conveys well enough to an observer the dissatisfaction of the hearer, but his incapacity to make his own statement.

I shall attempt in this and the following chapter to record some facts that indicate the path of the law of Compensation; happy beyond my expectation if I shall truly draw the smallest arc of this circle.

Polarity, or action and reaction, we meet in every part of nature; in darkness and light; in heat and cold; in the ebb and flow of waters; in male and female; in the inspiration and expiration of plants and animals; in the equation of quantity and quality in the fluids of the animal body; in the systole and diastole of the heart; in the undulations of fluids and of sound; in the centrifugal and centripetal gravity; in electricity, galvanism and chemical affinity. Superinduce magnetism at one end of a needle, the opposite magnetism takes place at the other end. If the south attracts, the north repels. To empty here, you must condense there. An inevitable dualism bisects nature, so that each thing is a half, and suggests another thing to make it whole; as, spirit, matter; man, woman; odd, even; subjective, objective; in, out; upper, under; motion, rest; yea, nay.

Whilst the world is thus dual, so is every one of its parts. The entire system of things gets represented in every particle. There is somewhat that resembles the ebb and flow of the sea, day and night, man and woman, in a single needle of the pine, in a kernel of corn, in each individual of every animal tribe. The reaction, so grand in the elements, is repeated within these small boundaries. For example, in the animal kingdom the physiologist has observed that no creatures are favorites, but a certain compensation balances every gift and every defect. A surplusage given to one part is paid out of a reduction from another part of the same creature. If the head and neck are enlarged, the trunk and extremities are cut short.

The theory of the mechanic forces is another example. What we gain in power is lost in time, and the converse. The periodic or compensating errors of the planets is another instance. The influences of climate and soil in political history is another. The cold climate invigorates. The barren soil does not breed fevers, crocodiles, tigers or scorpions.

The same dualism underlies the nature and condition of man. Every excess causes a defect; every defect an excess. Every sweet hath its sour; every evil its good. Every faculty which is a receiver of pleasure has an equal penalty put on its abuse. It is to answer for its moderation with its life. For every grain of wit there is a grain of folly. For everything you have missed, you have gained something else; and for everything you gain, you lose something. If riches increase, they are increased that use them. If the gatherer gathers too much, Nature takes out of the man what she puts into his chest; swells the estate, but kills the owner. Nature hates monopolies and exceptions. The waves of the sea do not more speedily seek a level from their loftiest tossing than the varieties of condition tend to equalize themselves. There is always some leveling circumstance that puts down the overbearing, the strong, the rich, the fortunate, substantially on the same ground with all others. Is a man too strong and fierce for society and by temper and position a bad citizen—a morose ruffian, with a dash of the pirate in him? Nature sends him a troop of pretty sons and daughters who are getting along in the dame's classes at the village school, and love and fear for them smooths his grim scowl to courtesy. Thus she contrives to intenerate the granite and feldspar, takes the boar out and puts the lamb in and keeps her balance true.

The farmer imagines power and place are fine things. But the President has paid dear for his White House. It has commonly cost him all his peace, and the best of his manly attributes. To preserve for a short time so conspicuous an appearance before the world, he is content to eat dust before the real masters who stand erect behind the throne. Or do men desire the more substantial and permanent grandeur of genius? Neither has this an immunity. He who by force of will or of thought is great and overlooks thousands, has the charges of that eminence. With every influx of light comes new danger. Has he light? he must bear witness to the light, and always outrun that sympathy which gives him such keen satisfaction, by his fidelity to new revelations of the incessant soul. He must hate father and mother, wife and child. Has he all that the world loves and admires and covets? he must cast behind him their admiration and afflict them by faithfulness to his truth and become a byword and a hissing.

This law writes the laws of cities and nations. It is in vain to build or plot or combine against it. Things refuse to be mismanaged long. *Res nolunt diu male administrari.* Though no checks to a new evil appear, the checks exist, and will appear. If the government is cruel, the governor's life is not safe. If you tax too high, the revenue will yield nothing. If you make the criminal code sanguinary, juries will not convict. If the law is too mild, private vengeance comes in. If the government is a terrific democracy, the pressure is resisted by an overcharge of energy in the citizen, and life glows with a fiercer flame. The true life and satisfactions of man seem to elude the utmost rigors or felicities of condition and to establish themselves with great indifference under all varieties of circumstances. Under all governments the influence of character remains the same—in Turkey and in New England about alike. Under the primeval despots of Egypt, history honestly confesses that man must have been as free as culture could make him.

These appearances indicate the fact that the universe is

represented in every one of its particles. Everything in nature contains all the powers of nature. Everything is made of one hidden stuff; as the naturalist sees one type under every metamorphosis, and regards a horse as a running man, a fish as a swimming man, a bird as a flying man, a tree as a rooted man. Each new form repeats not only the main character of the type, but part for part all the details, all the aims, furtherances, hindrances, energies and whole system of every other. Every occupation, trade, art, transaction, is a compend of the world and a correlative of every other. Each one is an entire emblem of human life; of its good and ill, its trials, its enemies, its course and its end. And each one must somehow accommodate the whole man and recite all his destiny.

The world globes itself in a drop of dew. The microscope cannot find the animalcule which is less perfect for being little. Eyes, ears, taste, smell, motion, resistance, appetite and organs of reproduction that take hold on eternity—all find room to consist in the small creature. So do we put our life into every act. The true doctrine of omnipresence is that God reappears with all his parts in every moss and cobweb. The value of the universe contrives to throw itself into every point. If the good is there, so is the evil; if the affinity, so the repulsion; if the force, so the limitation.

Thus is the universe alive. All things are moral. That soul which within us is a sentiment, outside of us is a law. We feel its inspiration; but there in history we can see its fatal strength. "It is in the world, and the world was made by it." Justice is not postponed. A perfect equity adjusts its balance in all parts of life. Ἀεὶ γὰρ εὖ πίπτουσιν οἱ Διὸς κύβοι — The dice of God are always loaded. The world looks like a multiplication table, or a mathematical equation, which, turn it how you will, balances itself. Take what figure you will, its exact value, nor more nor less, still returns to you. Every secret is told, every crime is punished, every virtue rewarded, every wrong redressed, in silence and certainty. What we call retribution is the universal necessity by which the whole appears wherever a part appears. If you see smoke, there must be fire. If you see a hand or a limb, you know that the trunk to which it belongs is there behind.

Every act rewards itself, or in other words integrates itself, in a twofold manner; first in the thing, or in real nature; and secondly in the circumstance, or in apparent nature. Men call the circumstance the retribution. The causal retribution is in the thing and is seen by the understanding; it is inseparable from the thing, but is often spread over a long time and so does not become distinct until after many years. The specific stripes may follow late after the offense, but they follow because they accompany it. Crime and punishment grow out of one stem. Punishment is a fruit that unsuspected ripens within the flower of the pleasure which concealed it. Cause and effect, means and ends, seed and fruit, cannot be severed; for the effect already blooms in the cause, the end pre-exists in the means, the fruit in the seed.

Whilst thus the world will be whole and refuses to be disparted, we seek to act partially, to sunder, to appropriate; for example—to gratify the senses we sever the pleasure of the sense from the needs of the character. The ingenuity of man has always been dedicated to the solution of one problem—how to detach the sensual sweet, the sensual strong, the sensual bright, etc., from the moral sweet, the moral deep, the moral fair; that is, again, to contrive to cut clean off this upper surface so thin as to leave it bottomless; to get a *one end,* without an *other end.* The soul says, "Eat"; the body would feast. The soul says, "The man and woman shall be one flesh and one soul"; the body would join the flesh only. The soul says, "Have dominion over all things to the ends of virtue"; the body would have the power over things to its own ends.

The soul strives amain to live and work through all things. It would be the only fact. All things shall be added unto it—power, pleasure, knowledge, beauty. The particular man aims to be somebody; to set up for himself; to truck and higgle for a private good; and, in particulars, to ride that he may ride; to dress that he may be dressed; to eat that he may eat; and to govern, that he may be seen. Men seek to be great; they would have offices, wealth, power and fame. They think that to be great is to possess one side of nature, the sweet, without the other side, the bitter.

This dividing and detaching is steadily counteracted. Up to this day it must be owned no projector has had the smallest success. The parted water reunites behind our hand. Pleasure is taken out of pleasant things, profit out of profitable things, power out of strong things, as soon as we seek to separate them from the whole. We can no more halve things and get the sensual good, by itself, than we can get an inside that shall have no outside, or a light without a shadow. "Drive out Nature with a fork, she comes running back."

Life invests itself with inevitable conditions, which the unwise seek to dodge, which one and another brags that he does not know, that they do not touch him—but the brag is on the lips, the conditions are in his soul. If he escapes them in one part they attack him in another more vital part. If he has escaped them in form and in the appearance, it is because he has resisted his life and fled from himself, and the retribution is so much death. So signal is the failure of all attempts to make this separation of the good from the tax, that the experiment would not be tried—since to try it is to be mad— but for the circumstance that when the disease begins in the will, of rebellion and separation, the intellect is at once infected, so that the man ceases to see God whole in each object, but is able to see the sensual allurement of an object and not see the sensual hurt; he sees the mermaid's head but not the dragon's tail, and thinks he can cut off that which he would have from that which he would not have. "How secret art thou who dwellest in the highest heavens in silence, O thou only great God, sprinkling with an unwearied providence certain penal blindnesses upon such as have unbridled desires!"

The human soul is true to these facts in the painting of fable, of history, of law, of proverbs, of conversation. It finds a tongue in literature unawares. Thus the Greeks called Jupiter, Supreme Mind; but having traditionally ascribed to him many base actions, they involuntarily made amends to reason by tying up the hands of so bad a god. He is made as helpless as a king of England. Prometheus knows one secret which Jove must bargain for; Minerva, another. He cannot get his own thunders; Minerva keeps the key of them:

> *Of all the gods, I only know the keys*
> *That ope the solid doors within whose vaults*
> *His thunders sleep.*

A plain confession of the in-working of the All and of its moral aim. The Indian mythology ends in the same ethics; and it would seem impossible for any fable to be invented and get any currency which was not moral. Aurora forgot to ask youth for her lover, and though Tithonus is immortal, he is old. Achilles is not quite invulnerable; the sacred waters did not wash the heel by which Thetis held him. Siegfried, in the Nibelungen, is not quite immortal, for a leaf fell on his back whilst he was bathing in the dragon's blood, and that spot which it covered is mortal. And so it must be. There is a crack in everything God has made. It would seem there is always this vindictive circumstance stealing in at unawares even into the wild poesy in which the human fancy attempted to make bold holiday and to shake itself free of the old laws— this backstroke, this kick of the gun, certifying that the law is fatal; that in nature nothing can be given, all things are sold.

This is that ancient doctrine of Nemesis, who keeps watch in the universe and lets no offense go unchastised. The Furies, they said, are attendants on justice, and if the sun in heaven should transgress his path they would punish him. The poets related that stone walls and iron swords and leathern thongs had an occult sympathy with the wrongs of their owners; that the belt which Ajax gave Hector dragged the Trojan hero over the field at the wheels of the car of Achilles, and the sword which Hector gave Ajax was that on whose point Ajax fell. They recorded that when the Thasians erected a statue to Theagenes, a victor in the games, one of his rivals went to it by night and endeavored to throw it down by repeated blows, until at last he moved it from its pedestal and was crushed to death beneath its fall.

This voice of fable has in it somewhat divine. It came from thought above the will of the writer. That is the best part of each writer which has nothing private in it; that which he does not know; that which flowed out of his constitution and not from his too active invention; that which in the study of a single artist you might not easily find, but in the study of many you would abstract as the spirit of them all. Phidias it is not, but the work of man in that early Hellenic world that I would know. The name and circumstances of Phidias, however convenient for history, embarrass when we come to the highest criticism. We are to see that which man was tending to do in a given period, and was hindered, or, if you will, modified in doing, by the interfering volitions of Phidias, or Dante, or Shakespeare, the organ whereby man at the moment wrought.

Still more striking is the expression of this fact in the proverbs of all nations, which are always the literature of reason, or the statements of an absolute truth without qualification. Proverbs, like the sacred books of each nation, are the sanctuary of the intuitions. That which the droning world, chained to appearances, will not allow the realist to say in his own words, it will suffer him to say in proverbs without contradiction. And this law of laws, which the pulpit, the senate and the college deny, is hourly preached in all markets and workshops by flights of proverbs, whose teaching is as true and as omnipresent as that of birds and flies.

All things are double, one against another.—Tit for tat; an eye for an eye; a tooth for a tooth; blood for blood; measure for measure; love for love.—Give, and it shall be given you.— He that watereth shall be watered himself.—What will you have? quoth God; pay for it and take it.—Nothing venture, nothing have.—Thou shalt be paid exactly for what thou hast

done, no more, no less.—Who doth not work shall not eat.—
Harm watch, harm catch.—Curses always recoil on the head
of him who imprecates them.—If you put a chain around the
neck of a slave, the other end fastens itself around your own.
—Bad counsel confounds the adviser.—The Devil is an ass.

It is thus written, because it is thus in life. Our action is
overmastered and characterized above our will by the law of
nature. We aim at a petty end quite aside from the public good,
but our act arranges itself by irresistible magnetism in a line
with the poles of the world.

A man cannot speak but he judges himself. With his will or
against his will he draws his portrait to the eye of his companions by every word. Every opinion reacts on him who utters
it. It is a thread-ball thrown at a mark, but the other end remains in the thrower's bag. Or rather it is a harpoon hurled at
the whale, unwinding, as it flies, a coil of cord in the boat, and,
if the harpoon is not good, or not well thrown, it will go nigh
to cut the steersman in twain or to sink the boat.

You cannot do wrong without suffering wrong. "No man
had ever a point of pride that was not injurious to him," said
Burke. The exclusive in fashionable life does not see that he
excludes himself from enjoyment, in the attempt to appropriate it. The exclusionist in religion does not see that he shuts
the door of heaven on himself, in striving to shut out others.
Treat men as pawns and ninepins and you shall suffer as well
as they. If you leave out their heart, you shall lose your own.
The senses would make things of all persons; of women, of
children, of the poor. The vulgar proverb, "I will get it from
his purse or get it from his skin," is sound philosophy.

All infractions of love and equity in our social relations are
speedily punished. They are punished by fear. Whilst I stand
in simple relations to my fellow man, I have no displeasure in
meeting him. We meet as water meets water, or as two currents
of air mix, with perfect diffusion and interpenetration of nature. But as soon as there is any departure from simplicity and
attempt at halfness, or good for me that is not good for him,
my neighbor feels the wrong; he shrinks from me as far as I
have shrunk from him; his eyes no longer seek mine; there is
war between us; there is hate in him and fear in me.

All the old abuses in society, universal and particular, all
unjust accumulations of property and power, are avenged in
the same manner. Fear is an instructor of great sagacity and
the herald of all revolutions. One thing he teaches, that there
is rottenness where he appears. He is a carrion crow, and
though you see not well what he hovers for, there is death
somewhere. Our property is timid, our laws are timid, our

cultivated classes are timid. Fear for ages had boded and mowed and gibbered over government and property. The obscene bird is not there for nothing. He indicates great wrongs which must be revised.

Of the like nature is that expectation of change which instantly follows the suspension of our voluntary activity. The terror of cloudless noon, the emerald of Polycrates, the awe of prosperity, the instinct which leads every generous soul to impose on itself tasks of a noble asceticism and vicarious virtue, are the tremblings of the balance of justice through the heart and mind of man.

Experienced men of the world know very well that it is best to pay scot and lot as they go along, and that a man often pays dear for a small frugality. The borrower runs in his own debt. Has a man gained anything who has received a hundred favors and rendered none? Has he gained by borrowing, through indolence or cunning, his neighbor's wares, or horses, or money? There arises on the deed the instant acknowledgment of benefit on the one part and of debt on the other; that is, of superiority and inferiority. The transaction remains in the memory of himself and his neighbors; and every new transaction alters according to its nature their relation to each other. He may soon come to see that he had better have broken his own bones than to have ridden in his neighbor's coach, and that "the highest price he can pay for a thing is to ask for it."

A wise man will extend this lesson to all parts of life, and know that it is the part of prudence to face every claimant and pay every just demand on your time, your talents, or your heart. Always pay; for first or last you must pay your entire debt. Persons and events may stand for a time between you and justice, but it is only a postponement. You must pay at last your own debt. If you are wise you will dread a prosperity which only loads you with more. Benefit is the end of nature. But for every benefit which you receive, a tax is levied. He is great who confers the most benefits. He is base—and that is the one base thing in the universe—to receive favors and render none. In the order of nature we cannot render benefits to those from whom we receive them, or only seldom. But the benefit we receive must be rendered again, line for line, deed for deed, cent for cent, to somebody. Beware of too much good staying in your hand. It will fast corrupt and worm worms. Pay it away quickly in some sort.

Labor is watched over by the same pitiless laws. Cheapest, say the prudent, is the dearest labor. What we buy in a broom, a mat, a wagon, a knife, is some application of good sense to a common want. It is best to pay in your land a skillful gardener, or to buy good sense applied to gardening; in your sailor, good sense applied to navigation; in the house, good sense applied to cooking, sewing, serving; in your agent, good sense applied to accounts and affairs. So do you multiply your presence, or spread yourself throughout your estate. But because of the dual constitution of things, in labor as in life there can be no cheating. The thief steals from himself. The swindler swindles himself. For the real price of labor is knowledge and virtue, whereof wealth and credit are signs. These signs, like paper money, may be counterfeited or stolen, but that which they represent, namely, knowledge and virtue, cannot be counterfeited or stolen. These ends of labor cannot be answered but by real exertions of the mind, and in obedience to pure motives. The cheat, the defaulter, the gambler, cannot extort the knowledge of material and moral nature which his honest care and pains yield to the operative. The law of nature is, Do the thing, and you shall have the power; but they who do not the thing have not the power.

Human labor, through all its forms, from the sharpening of a stake to the construction of a city or an epic, is one immense illustration of the perfect compensation of the universe. The absolute balance of Give and Take, the doctrine that everything has its price—and if that price is not paid, not that thing but something else is obtained, and that it is impossible to get anything without its price—is not less sublime in the columns of a ledger than in the budgets of states, in the laws of light and darkness, in all the action and reaction of nature. I cannot doubt that the high laws which each man sees implicated in those processes with which he is conversant, the stern ethics which sparkle on his chisel edge, which are measured out by his plumb and foot rule, which stand as manifest in the footing of the shop bill as in the history of a state—do recommend to him his trade, and though seldom named, exalt his business to his imagination.

The league between virtue and nature engages all things to assume a hostile front to vice. The beautiful laws and substances of the world persecute and whip the traitor. He finds that things are arranged for truth and benefit, but there is no den in the wide world to hide a rogue. Commit a crime, and the earth is made of glass. Commit a crime, and it seems as if a coat of snow fell on the ground, such as reveals in the woods the track of every partridge and fox and squirrel and mole. You cannot recall the spoken word, you cannot wipe out the foot track, you cannot draw up the ladder, so as to leave no inlet or clew. Some damning circumstance always transpires.

The laws and substances of nature—water, snow, wind, gravitation—become penalties to the thief.

On the other hand the law holds with equal sureness for all right action. Love, and you shall be loved. All love is mathematically just, as much as the two sides of an algebraic equation. The good man has absolute good, which like fire turns everything to its own nature, so that you cannot do him any harm; but as the royal armies sent against Napoleon, when he approached cast down their colors and from enemies became friends, so disasters of all kinds, as sickness, offense, poverty, prove benefactors:

> *Winds blow and waters roll*
> *Strength to the brave and power and deity,*
> *Yet in themselves are nothing.*

The good are befriended even by weakness and defect. As no man had ever a point of pride that was not injurious to him, so no man had ever a defect that was not somewhere made useful to him. The stag in the fable admired his horns and blamed his feet, but when the hunter came, his feet saved him, and afterwards, caught in the thicket, his horns destroyed him. Every man in his lifetime needs to thank his faults. As no man thoroughly understands a truth until he has contended against it, so no man has a thorough acquaintance with the hindrances or talents of men until he has suffered from the one and seen the triumph of the other over his own want of the same. Has he a defect of temper that unfits him to live in society? Thereby he is driven to entertain himself alone and acquire habits of self-help; and thus, like the wounded oyster, he mends his shell with pearl.

Our strength grows out of our weakness. The indignation which arms itself with secret forces does not awaken until we are pricked and stung and sorely assailed. A great man is always willing to be little. Whilst he sits on the cushion of advantages, he goes to sleep. When he is pushed, tormented, defeated, he has a chance to learn something; he has been put on his wits, on his manhood; he has gained facts; learns his ignorance; is cured of the insanity of conceit; has got moderation and real skill. The wise man throws himself on the side of his assailants. It is more his interest than it is theirs to find his weak point. The wound cicatrizes and falls off from him like a dead skin, and when they would triumph, lo! he has passed on invulnerable. Blame is safer than praise. I hate to be defended in a newspaper. As long as all that is said is said against me, I feel a certain assurance of success. But as soon as honeyed

words of praise are spoken for me I feel as one that lies unprotected before his enemies. In general, every evil to which
we do not succumb is a benefactor. As the Sandwich Islander
believes that the strength and valor of the enemy he kills passes
into himself, so we gain the strength of the temptation we resist.

The same guards which protect us from disaster, defect and
enmity, defend us, if we will, from selfishness and fraud. Bolts
and bars are not the best of our institutions, nor is shrewdness
in trade a mark of wisdom. Men suffer all their life long under the foolish superstition that they can be cheated. But it is as
impossible for a man to be cheated by anyone but himself, as
for a thing to be and not to be at the same time. There is a
third silent party to all our bargains. The nature and soul of
things takes on itself the guaranty of the fulfillment of every
contract, so that honest service cannot come to loss. If you
serve an ungrateful master, serve him the more. Put God in
your debt. Every stroke shall be repaid. The longer the pay-
ment is *withholden,* the better for you; for compound interest
on compound interest is the rate and usage of this exchequer.

The history of persecution is a history of endeavors to cheat
nature, to make water run up hill, to twist a rope of sand. It
makes no difference whether the actors be many or one, a
tyrant or a mob. A mob is a society of bodies voluntarily be-
reaving themselves of reason and traversing its work. The mob
is man voluntarily descending to the nature of the beast. Its
fit hour of activity is night. Its actions are insane, like its whole
constitution. It persecutes a principle; it would whip a right;
it would tar and feather justice, by inflicting fire and outrage
upon the houses and persons of those who have these. It resembles the prank of boys, who run with fire engines to put
out the ruddy aurora streaming to the stars. The inviolate
spirit turns their spite against the wrongdoers. The martyr
cannot be dishonored. Every lash inflicted is a tongue of fame;
every prison a more illustrious abode; every burned book or
house enlightens the world; every suppressed or expunged
word reverberates through the earth from side to side. Hours
of sanity and consideration are always arriving to communities, as to individuals, when the truth is seen and the martyrs
are justified.

Thus do all things preach the indifferency of circumstances.
The man is all. Everything has two sides, a good and an evil.
Every advantage has its tax. I learn to be content. But the doctrine of compensation is not the doctrine of indifferency. The
thoughtless say, on hearing these representations—What boots
it to do well? there is one event to good and evil; if I gain any

good I must pay for it; if I lose any good I gain some other; all actions are indifferent.

There is a deeper fact in the soul than compensation, to wit, its own nature. The soul is not a compensation, but a life. The soul *is*. Under all this running sea of circumstances, whose waters ebb and flow with perfect balance, lies the aboriginal abyss of real Being. Essence, or God, is not a relation or a part, but the whole. Being is the vast affirmative, excluding negation, self-balanced, and swallowing up all relations, parts and times within itself. Nature, truth, virtue, are the influx from thence. Vice is the absence or departure of the same. Nothing, Falsehood, may indeed stand as the great Night or shade on which as a background the living universe paints itself forth, but no fact is begotten by it; it cannot work, for it is not. It cannot work any good; it cannot work any harm. It is harm inasmuch as it is worse not to be than to be.

We feel defrauded of the retribution due to evil acts, because the criminal adheres to his vice and contumacy and does not come to a crisis or judgment anywhere in visible nature. There is no stunning confutation of his nonsense before men and angels. Has he therefore outwitted the law? Inasmuch as he carries the malignity and the lie with him he so far decreases from nature. In some manner there will be a demonstration of the wrong to the understanding also; but, should we not see it, this deadly deduction makes square the eternal account.

Neither can it be said, on the other hand, that the gain of rectitude must be bought by any loss. There is no penalty to virtue; no penalty to wisdom; they are proper additions of being. In a virtuous action I properly *am*; in a virtuous act I add to the world; I plant into deserts conquered from Chaos and Nothing and see the darkness receding on the limits of the horizon. There can be no excess to love, none to knowledge, none to beauty, when these attributes are considered in the purest sense. The soul refuses limits, and always affirms an Optimism, never a Pessimism.

His life is a progress, and not a station. His instinct is trust. Our instinct uses "more" and "less" in application to man, of the *presence of the soul,* and not of its absence; the brave man is greater than the coward; the true, the benevolent, the wise, is more a man and not less, than the fool and knave. There is no tax on the good of virtue, for that is the incoming of God himself, or absolute existence, without any comparative. Material good has its tax, and if it came without desert or sweat, has no root in me, and the next wind will blow it away. But all the good of nature is the soul's, and may be had if paid for in nature's lawful coin, that is, by labor which the heart and the head allow. I no longer wish to meet a good I do not earn, for example to find a pot of buried gold, knowing that it brings with it new burdens. I do not wish more external goods— neither possessions, nor honors, nor powers, nor persons. The gain is apparent; the tax is certain. But there is no tax on the knowledge that the compensation exists and that it is not desirable to dig up treasure. Herein I rejoice with a serene eternal peace. I contract the boundaries of possible mischief. I learn the wisdom of St. Bernard— "Nothing can work me damage except myself; the harm that I sustain I carry about with me, and never am a real sufferer but by my own fault."

In the nature of the soul is the compensation for the inequalities of condition. The radical tragedy of nature seems to be the distinction of More and Less. How can Less not feel the pain; how not feel indignation or malevolence towards More? Look at those who have less faculty, and one feels sad and knows not well what to make of it. He almost shuns their eye; he fears they will upbraid God. What should they do? It seems a great injustice. But see the facts nearly and these mountainous inequalities vanish. Love reduces them as the sun melts the iceberg in the sea. The heart and soul of all men being one, this bitterness of *His* and *Mine* ceases. His is mine. I am my brother and my brother is me. If I feel overshadowed and outdone by great neighbors, I can yet love; I can still receive; and he that loveth maketh his own the grandeur he loves. Thereby I make the discovery that my brother is my guardian, acting for me with the friendliest designs, and the estate I so admired and envied is my own. It is the nature of the soul to appropriate all things. Jesus and Shakespeare are fragments of the soul, and by love I conquer and incorporate them in my own conscious domain. His virtue—is not that mine? His wit—if it cannot be made mine, it is not wit.

Such also is the natural history of calamity. The changes which break up at short intervals the prosperity of men are advertisements of a nature whose law is growth. Every soul is by this intrinsic necessity quitting its whole system of things, its friends and home and laws and faith, as the shellfish crawls out of its beautiful but stony case, because it no longer admits of its growth, and slowly forms a new house. In proportion to the vigor of the individual these revolutions are frequent, until in some happier mind they are incessant and all worldly relations hang very loosely about him, becoming as it were a transparent fluid membrane through which the living form is seen, and not, as in most men, an indurated heterogeneous fabric of many dates and of no settled character, in which man is imprisoned. Then there can be enlargement, and the man of today scarcely recognizes the man of yesterday. And such should be the outward biography of man in time, a putting off of dead circumstances day by day, as he renews his raiment day by day. But to us, in our lapsed estate, resting, not advancing, resisting, not co-operating with the divine expansion, this growth comes by shocks.

We cannot part with our friends. We cannot let our angels go. We do not see that they only go out that archangels may come in. We are idolaters of the old. We do not believe in the riches of the soul, in its proper eternity and omnipresence. We do not believe there is any force in today to rival or re-create that beautiful yesterday. We linger in the ruins of the old tent where once we had bread and shelter and organs, nor believe that the spirit can feed, cover, and nerve us again. We cannot again find aught so dear, so sweet, so graceful. But we sit and weep in vain. The voice of the Almighty saith, "Up and onward for evermore!" We cannot stay amid the ruins. Neither will we rely on the new; and so we walk ever with reverted eyes, like those monsters who look backwards.

And yet the compensations of calamity are made apparent to the understanding also, after long intervals of time. A fever, a mutilation, a cruel disappointment, a loss of wealth, a loss of friends seems at the moment unpaid loss, and unpayable. But the sure years reveal the deep remedial force that underlies all facts. The death of a dear friend, wife, brother, lover, which seemed nothing but privation, somewhat later assumes the aspect of a guide or genius; for it commonly operates revolutions in our way of life, terminates an epoch of infancy or of youth which was waiting to be closed, breaks up a wonted occupation, or a household, or style of living, and allows the formation of new ones more friendly to the growth of character. It permits or constrains the formation of new acquaintances and the reception of new influences that prove of the first importance to the next years; and the man or woman who would have remained a sunny garden flower, with no room for its roots and too much sunshine for its head, by the falling of the walls and the neglect of the gardener is made the banyan of the forest, yielding shade and fruit to wide neighborhoods of men.

From *Essays: First Series*
Volume II

The Sovereignty of Ethics

Since the discovery of Oersted that galvanism and electricity and magnetism are only forms of one and the same force, and convertible each into the other, we have continually suggested to us a larger generalization: that each of the great departments of Nature—chemistry, vegetation, the animal life—exhibits the same laws on a different plane; that the intellectual and moral worlds are analogous to the material. There is a kind of latent omniscience not only in every man, but in every particle. That convertibility we so admire in plants and animal structures, whereby the repairs and the ulterior uses are subserved, when one part is wounded or deficient, by another; this self-help and self-creation proceed from the same original power which works remotely in grandest and meanest structures by the same design—works in a lobster or a mite-worm as a wise man would if imprisoned in that poor form. 'T is the effort of God, of the Supreme Intellect, in the extremest frontier of his universe.

As this unity exists in the organization of insect, beast and bird, still ascending to man, and from lower type of man to the highest yet attained, so it does not less declare itself in the spirit or intelligence of the brute. In ignorant ages it was common to vaunt the human superiority by underrating the instinct of other animals; but a better discernment finds that the difference is only of less and more. Experiment shows that the bird and the dog reason as the hunter does, that all the animals show the same good sense in their humble walk that the man who is their enemy or friend does; and, if it be in smaller measure, yet it is not diminished, as his often is, by freak and folly. St. Pierre says of the animals that a moral sentiment seems to have determined their physical organization.

I see the unity of thought and of morals running through all animated Nature; there is no difference of quality, but only of more and less. The animal who is wholly kept down in Nature has no anxieties. By yielding, as he must do, to it, he is enlarged and reaches his highest point. The poor grub, in the hole of a tree, by yielding itself to Nature, goes blameless through its low part and is rewarded at last, casts its filthy hull, expands into a beautiful form with rainbow wings, and makes a part of the summer day. The Greeks called it Psyche, a manifest emblem of the soul. The man down in Nature occupies himself in guarding, in feeding, in warming and multiplying his body, and, as long as he knows no more, we justify him; but presently a mystic change is wrought, a new perception opens, and he is made a citizen of the world of souls: he feels what is called duty; he is aware that he owes a higher allegiance to do and live as a good member of this universe. In the measure in which he has this sense he is a man, rises to the universal life. The high intellect is absolutely at one with moral nature. A thought is embosomed in a sentiment, and the attempt to detach and blazon the thought is like a show of cut flowers. The moral is the measure of health, and in the voice of Genius I hear invariably the moral tone, even when it is disowned in words; health, melody and a wider horizon belong to moral sensibility. The finer the sense of justice, the better poet. The believer says to the skeptic:

> *One avenue was shaded from thine eyes*
> *Through which I wandered to eternal truth.*

Humility is the avenue. To be sure, we exaggerate when we represent these two elements as disunited; every man shares them both; but it is true that men generally are marked by a decided predominance of one or of the other element.

In youth and in age we are moralists, and in mature life the moral element steadily rises in the regard of all reasonable men.

'T is a sort of proverbial dying speech of scholars (at least it is attributed to many) that which Anthony Wood reports of Nathaniel Carpenter, an Oxford Fellow. "It did repent him," he said, "that he had formerly so much courted the maid instead of the mistress" (meaning philosophy and mathematics to the neglect of divinity). This, in the language of our time, would be ethics.

And when I say that the world is made up of moral forces, these are not separate. All forces are found in Nature united with that which they move: heat is not separate, light is not massed aloof, nor electricity, nor gravity, but they are always in combination. And so moral powers; they are thirsts for action, and the more you accumulate, the more they mold and form.

It is in the stomach of plants that development begins, and ends in the circles of the universe. 'T is a long scale from the gorilla to the gentlemen—from the gorilla to Plato, Newton, Shakespeare—to the sanctities of religion, the refinements of legislation, the sanctities of science, art and poetry. The beginnings are slow and infirm, but it is an always-accelerated march. The geologic world is chronicled by the growing ripeness of the strata from lower to higher, as it becomes the abode of more highly-organized plants and animals. The civil history of men might be traced by the successive meliorations as marked in higher moral generalizations;—virtue meaning physical courage, then chastity and temperance, then justice and love—bargains of kings with people of certain rights to certain classes, then of rights to masses—then at last came the day when, as the historians rightly tell, the nerves of the world were electrified by the proclamation that all men were born free and equal.

Every truth leads in another. The bud extrudes the old leaf, and every truth brings that which will supplant it. In the court of law the judge sits over the culprit, but in the court of life in the same hour the judge also stands as culprit before a true tribunal. Every judge is a culprit, every law an abuse. Montaigne kills off bigots as cowhage kills worms; but there is a higher muse there sitting where he durst not soar, of eye so keen that it can report of a realm in which all the wit and learning of the Frenchman is no more than the cunning of a fox.

It is the same fact existing as sentiment and as will in the mind, which works in Nature as irresistible law, exerting influence over nations, intelligent beings, or down in the kingdoms of brute or of chemical atoms. Nature is a tropical swamp in sunshine, on whose purlieus we hear the song of summer birds, and see prismatic dewdrops—but her interiors are terrific, full of hydras and crocodiles. In the preadamite she bred valor only; by and by she gets on to man, and adds tenderness, and thus raises virtue piecemeal.

When we trace from the beginning, that ferocity has uses; only so are the conditions of the then world met, and these monsters are the scavengers, executioners, diggers, pioneers and fertilizers, destroying what is more destructive than they, and making better life possible. We see the steady aim of Benefit in view from the first. Melioration is the law. The cruelest foe is a masked benefactor. The wars which make history so dreary have served the cause of truth and virtue. There is always an instinctive sense of right, an obscure idea which animates either party and which in long periods vindicates itself at last. Thus a sublime confidence is fed at the bottom of the heart that, in spite of appearances, in spite of malignity and blind self-interest living for the moment, an eternal, beneficient necessity is always bringing things right; and though we should fold our arms—which we cannot do, for our duty requires us to be the very hands of this guiding sentiment, and work in the present moment—the evils we suffer will at least end themselves through the incessant opposition of Nature to everything hurtful.

The excellence of men consists in the completeness with which the lower system is taken up into the higher—a process of much time and delicacy, but in which no point of the lower should be left untranslated; so that the warfare of beasts should be renewed in a finer field, for more excellent victories. Savage war gives place to that of Turenne and Wellington, which has limitations and a code. This war again gives place to the finer quarrel of property, where the victory is wealth and the defeat poverty.

The inevitabilities are always sapping every seeming prosperity built on a wrong. No matter how you seem to fatten on a crime, that can never be good for the bee which is bad for the hive. See how these things look in the page of history. Nations come and go, cities rise and fall, all the instinct of man, good and bad, work—and every wish, appetite and passion rushes into act and embodies itself in usages, protects itself with laws. Some of them are useful and universally acceptable, hinder none, help all, and these are honored and perpetuated. Others are noxious. Community of property is tried, as when a Tartar horde or an Indian tribe roam over a vast tract for pasturage or hunting; but it is found at last that some establishment of property, allowing each on some distinct terms to fence and cultivate a piece of land, is best for all.

"For my part," said Napoleon, "it is not the mystery of the incarnation which I discover in religion, but the mystery of social order, which associates with heaven that idea of equality which prevents the rich from destroying the poor."

Shall I say then it were truer to see Necessity calm, beautiful, passionless, without a smile, covered with ensigns of woe, stretching her dark warp across the universe? These threads are Nature's pernicious elements, her deluges, miasma, disease, poison; her curdling cold, her hideous reptiles and worse men, cannibals, and the depravities of civilization; the secrets of the prisons of tyranny, the slave and his master, the proud man's scorn, the orphan's tears, the vices of men, lust, cruelty and pitiless avarice. These make the gloomy warp of ages. Humanity sits at the dread loom and throws the shuttle and fills it with joyful rainbows, until the sable ground is flowered all over with a woof of human industry and wisdom, virtuous examples, symbols of useful and generous arts, with beauty and pure love, courage and the victories of the just and wise over malice and wrong.

Nature is not so helpless but it can rid itself at last of every crime. An Eastern poet, in describing the golden age, said that God had made justice so dear to the heart of Nature that, if any injustice lurked anywhere under the sky, the blue vault would shrivel to a snakeskin and cast it out by spasms. But the spasms of Nature are years and centuries, and it will tax the faith of man to wait so long. Man is always throwing his praise or blame on events, and does not see that he only is real, and the world his mirror and echo. He imputes the stroke to fortune, which in reality himself strikes. The student discovers one day that he lives in enchantment: the house, the works, the persons, the days, the weathers—all that he calls Nature, all that he calls institutions, when once his mind is active are visions merely, wonderful allegories, significant pictures of the laws of the mind; and through this enchanted gallery he is led by unseen guides to read and learn the laws of Heaven. This discovery may come early—sometimes in the nursery, to a rare child; later in the school, but oftener when the mind is more mature; and to multitudes of men wanting in mental activity it never comes—any more than poetry or art. But it ought to come; it belongs to the human intellect, and is an insight which we cannot spare.

The idea of right exists in the human mind, and lays itself out in the equilibrium of Nature, in the equalities and periods of our system, in the level of seas, in the action and reaction of forces. Nothing is allowed to exceed or absorb the rest; if it do, it is disease, and is quickly destroyed. It was an early discovery of the mind—this beneficent rule. Strength enters just as much as the moral element prevails. The strength of the animal to eat and to be luxurious and to usurp is rudeness and imbecility. The law is: To each shall be rendered his own. As thou sowest, thou shalt reap. Smite, and thou shalt smart. Serve, and thou shalt be served. It you love and serve men, you cannot, by any hiding or stratagem, escape the remuneration. Secret retributions are always restoring the level, when disturbed, of the Divine Justice. It is impossible to tilt the beam. All the tyrants and proprietors and monopolists of the world in vain set their shoulders to heave the bar. Settles for evermore the ponderous equator to its line, and man and mote and star and sun must range with it, or be pulverized by the recoil.

It is a doctrine of unspeakable comfort. He that plants his foot here passes at once out of the kingdom of illusions. Others may well suffer in the hideous picture of crime with which earth is filled and the life of society threatened, but the habit of respecting that great order which certainly contains and will dispose of our little system, will take all fear from the heart. It did itself create and distribute all that is created and distributed, and trusting to its power, we cease to care for what it will certainly order well. To good men, as we call good men, this doctrine of Trust is an unsounded secret. They use the word, they have accepted the notion of a mechanical supervision of human life, by which that certain wonderful being whom they call God does take up their affairs where their intelligence leaves them, and somehow knits and co-ordinates the issues of them in all that is beyond the reach of private faculty. They do not see the *He*, that *It*, is there, next and within; the thought of the thought; the affair of affairs; that he is existence, and take him from them and they would not be. They do not see that particulars are sacred to him, as well as the scope and outline; that these passages of daily life are his work; that in the moment when they desist from interference, these particulars take sweetness and grandeur, and become the language of mighty principles.

A man should be a guest in his own house, and a guest in his own thought. He is there to speak for truth; but who is he? Some clod the truth has snatched from the ground, and with fire has fashioned to a momentary man. Without the truth, he is a clod again. Let him find his superiority in not wishing superiority; find the riches of love which possesses that which it adores; the riches of poverty; the height of lowliness, the immensity of today; and, in the passing hour, the age of ages. Wondrous state of man! never so happy as when he has lost all private interests and regards, and exists only in obedience and love of the Author.

The fiery soul said: "Let me be a blot on this fair world, the obscurest, the loneliest sufferer, with one proviso—that I know it is his agency. I will love him, though he shed frost and darkness on every way of mine." The emphasis of that blessed doctrine lay in lowliness. The new saint gloried in infirmities. Who or what was he? His rise and his recovery were vicarious. He has fallen in another; he rises in another.

We perish, and perish gladly, if the law remains. I hope it is conceivable that a man may go to ruin gladly, if he see that thereby no shade falls on that he loves and adores. We need not always be stipulating for our clean shirt and roast joint *per diem*. We do not believe the less in astronomy and vegeta-tion, because we are writhing and roaring in our beds with rheumatism. Cripples and invalids, we doubt not there are bounding fawns in the forest, and lilies with graceful, spring-ing stem; so neither do we doubt or fail to love the eternal law, of which we are shabby practicers. Truth gathers itself spotless and unhurt after all our surrenders and concealments and partisanship—never hurt by the treachery or ruin of its best defenders, whether Luther, or William Penn, or St. Paul. We answer, when they tell us of the bad behavior of Luther or Paul: "Well, what if he did? Who was more pained than Luther or Paul?" Shall we attach ourselves violently to our teachers and historical personalities, and think the foundation shaken if any fault is shown in their record? But how is the truth hurt by their falling from it? The law of gravity is not hurt by every accident, though our leg be broken. No more is the law of justice by our departure from it.

We are to know that we are never without a pilot. When we know not how to steer, and dare not hoist a sail, we can drift. The current knows the way, though we do not. When the stars and sun appear, when we have conversed with navigators who know the coast, we may begin to put out an oar and trim a sail. The ship of heaven guides itself, and will not accept a wooden rudder.

Have you said to yourself ever: "I abdicate all choice, I see it is not for me to interfere. I see that I have been one of the crowd; that I have been a pitiful person, because I have wished to be my own master, and to dress and order my whole way and system of living. I thought I managed it very well. I see that my neighbors think so. I have heard prayers, I have prayed even, but I have never until now dreamed that this undertaking the entire management of my own affairs was not commendable. I have never seen, until now, that it dwarfed me. I have not discovered, until this blessed ray flashed just now through my soul, that there dwelt any power in Nature that would relieve me of my load. But now I see."

What is this intoxicating sentiment that allies this scrap of dust to the whole of Nature and the whole of Fate—that makes this doll a dweller in ages, mocker at time, able to spurn all outward advantages, peer and master of the elements? I am taught by it that what touches any thread in the vast web of being touches me. I am representative of the whole; and the good of the whole, or what I call the right, makes me invulnerable.

How came this creation so magically woven that nothing can do me mischief but myself—that an invisible fence surrounds my being which screens me from all harm that I will to resist? If I will stand upright, the creation cannot bend me. But if I violate myself, if I commit a crime, the lightning loiters by the speed of retribution, and every act is not hereafter but instantaneously rewarded according to its quality. Virtue is the adopting of this dictate of the universal mind by the individual will. Character is the habit of this obedience, and Religion is the accompanying emotion, the emotion of reverence which the presence of the universal mind ever excites in the individual.

We go to famous books for our examples of character, just as we send to England for shrubs which grow as well in our own dooryards and cow pastures. Life is always rich, and spontaneous graces and forces elevate it in every domestic circle, which are overlooked while we are reading something less excellent in old authors. From the obscurity and casualty of those which I know, I infer the obscurity and casualty of the like balm and consolation and immortality in a thousand homes which I do not know, all round the world. And I see not why to these simple instincts, simple yet grand, all the heights and transcendencies of virtue and of enthusiasm are not open. There is power enough in them to move the world; and it is not any sterility or defect in ethics, but our negligence of these fine monitors, of these world-embracing sentiments, that makes religion cold and life low.

While the immense energy of the sentiment of duty and the awe of the supernatural exert incomparable influence on the mind, yet it is often perverted, and the tradition received with awe, but without correspondent action of the receiver. Then you find so many men infatuated on that topic! Wise on all other, they lose their head the moment they talk of religion. It is the sturdiest prejudice in the public mind that religion is something by itself; a department distinct from all other experiences, and to which the tests and judgment men are ready enough to show on other things, do not apply. You may sometimes talk with the gravest and best citizen, and the moment the topic of religion is broached, he runs into a childish superstition. His face looks infatuated, and his conversation is. When I talked with an ardent missionary, and pointed out to him that his creed found no support in my experience, he replied, "It is not so in your experience, but is so in the other world." I answer: Other world! there is no other world. God is one and omnipresent; here or nowhere is the whole fact. The one miracle which God works evermore is in Nature, and imparting himself to the mind. When we ask simply, "What is true in thought? what is just in action?" it is the yielding of the private heart to the Divine mind, and all personal preferences, and all requiring of wonders, are profane.

The word miracle, as it is used, only indicates the ignorance of the devotee, staring with wonder to see water turned into wine, and heedless of the stupendous fact of his own personality. Here he stands, a lonely thought harmoniously organized into correspondence with the universe of mind and matter. What narrative of wonders coming down from a thousand years ought to charm his attention like this? Certainly it is human to value a general consent, a fraternity of believers, a crowded church; but as the sentiment purifies and rises, it leaves crowds. It makes churches of two, churches of one. A fatal disservice does this Swedenborg or other who offers to do my thinking for me. It seems as if, when the Spirit of God speaks so plainly to each soul, it were an impiety to be listening to one or another saint. Jesus was better than others, because he refused to listen to others and listened at home.

You are really interested in your thought. You have meditated in silent wonder on your existence in this world! You have perceived in the first fact of your conscious life here a miracle so astounding—a miracle comprehending all the universe of miracles to which your intelligent life gives you access —as to exhaust wonder, and leave you no need of hunting here or there for any particular exhibitions of power. Then up comes a man with a text of I John v. 7, or a knotty sentence from St. Paul, which he considers as the axe at the root of your tree. You cannot bring yourself to care for it. You say: "Cut away; my tree is Ygdrasil—the tree of life." He interrupts for the moment your peaceful trust in the Divine Providence. Let him know by your security that your conviction is clear and sufficient, and if he were Paul himself, you also are here, and with your Creator.

We all give way to superstitions. The house in which we were born is not quite mere timber and stone; is still haunted by parents and progenitors. The creeds into which we are initiated in childhood and youth no longer hold their old place in the minds of thoughtful men, but they are not nothing to us, and we hate to have them treated with contempt. There is so much that we do not know, that we give to these suggestions the benefit of the doubt.

It is a necessity of the human mind that he who looks at one object should look away from all other objects. He may throw himself upon some sharp statement of one fact, some verbal creed, with such concentration as to hide the universe from him: but the stars roll above; the sun warms him. With patience and fidelity to truth he may work his way through, if only by coming against somebody who believes more fables than he does; and in trying to dispel the illusions of his neighbor, he opens his own eyes.

In the Christianity of this country there is wide difference of opinion in regard to inspiration, prophecy, miracles, the future state of the soul; every variety of opinion, and rapid revolution in opinions, in the last half century. It is simply impossible to read the old history of the first century as it was read in the ninth; to do so you must abolish in your mind the lessons of all the centuries from the ninth to the nineteenth.

Shall I make the mistake of baptizing the daylight, and time and space, by the name of John or Joshua, in whose tent I chance to behold daylight, and space, and time? What anthropomorphists we are in this, that we cannot let moral distinctions be, but must mold them into human shape! "Mere morality" means—not put into a personal master of morals. Our religion is geographical, belongs to our time and place; respects and mythologizes some one time and place and person and people. So it is occasional. It visits us only on some exceptional and ceremonial occasion, on a wedding or a baptism, on a sickbed, or at a funeral, or perhaps on a sublime national victory or a peace. But that, be sure, is not the religion of the universal, unsleeping providence, which lurks in trifles, in still, small voices, in the secrets of the heart and our closest thoughts, as efficiently as in our proclamations and successes.

Far be it from me to underrate the men or the churches that have fixed the hearts of men and organized their devout impulses or oracles into good institutions. The Church of Rome had its saints, and inspired the conscience of Europe— St. Augustine, and Thomas à Kempis, and Fénelon; the piety of the English Church in Cranmer, and Herbert, and Taylor; The Reformed Church, Scougal; the mystics, Behmen and Swedenborg; the Quakers, Fox and James Naylor. I confess our later generation appears ungirt, frivolous, compared with the religions of the last or Calvinistic age. There was in the last century a serious habitual reference to the spiritual world, running through diaries, letters and conversation—yes, and into wills and legal instruments also, compared with which our liberation looks a little foppish and dapper.

The religion of seventy years ago was an iron belt to the mind, giving it concentratiön and force. A rude people were kept respectable by the determination of thought on the eternal world. Now men fall abroad—want polarity—suffer in character and intellect. A sleep creeps over the great functions of man. Enthusiasm goes out. In its stead a low prudence seeks to hold society stanch, but its arms are too short, cordage and machinery never supply the place of life.

Luther would cut his hand off sooner than write theses against the pope if he suspected that he was bringing on with all his might the pale negations of Boston Unitarianism. I will not now go into the metaphysics of that reaction by which in history a period of belief is followed by an age of criticism, in which wit takes the place of faith in the leading spirits, and an excessive respect for forms out of which the heart has departed becomes more obvious in the least religious minds. I will not now explore the causes of the result, but the fact must be conceded as of frequent recurrence, and never more evident than in our American church. To a self-denying, ardent church, delighting in rites and ordinances, has succeeded, a cold, intellectual race, who analyze the prayer and psalm of their forefathers, and the more intellectual reject every yoke of authority and custom with a petulance unprecedented. It is a sort of mark of probity and sincerity to declare how little you believe, while the mass of the community indolently follow the old forms with childish scrupulosity, and we have punctuality for faith, and good taste for character.

But I hope the defect of faith with us is only apparent. We shall find that freedom has its own guards, and, as soon as in the vulgar it runs to license, sets all reasonable men on exploring those guards. I do not think the summit of this age truly reached or expressed unless it attain the height which religion and philosophy reached in any former age. If I miss the inspiration of the saints of Calvinism, or of Platonism, or Buddhism, our times are not up to theirs, or, more truly, have not yet their own legitimate force.

Worship is the regard of what is above us. Men are respectable only as they respect. We delight in children because of that religious eye which belongs to them; because of their reverence for their seniors, and for their objects of belief. The poor Irish laborer one sees with respect, because he believes in something, in his church, and in his employers. Superstitious persons we see with respect, because their whole existence is not bounded by their hats and their shoes, but they walk attended by pictures of the imagination, to which they pay homage. You cannot impoverish man by taking away these objects above him without ruin. It is very sad to see men who think their goodness made of themselves; it is very grateful to see those who hold an opinion the reverse of this.

All ages of belief have been great; all of unbelief have been mean. The Orientals believe in Fate. That which shall befall them is written on the iron leaf; they will not turn on their heel to avoid famine, plague or the sword of the enemy. That is great, and gives a great air to the people. We in America are charged with a great deficiency in worship; that reverence does not belong to our character; that our institutions, our politics and our trade have fostered a self-reliance which is small, Lilliputian, full of fuss and bustle; we look at and will bear nothing above us in the state, and do exceedingly applaud and admire ourselves, and believe in our senses and understandings, while our imagination and our moral sentiment are desolated. In religion too we want objects above; we are fast losing or have already lost our old reverence; new views of inspiration, or miracles, of the saints, have supplanted the old opinions, and it is vain to bring them again. Revolutions never go backward, and in all churches a certain decay of ancient piety is lamented, and all threatens to lapse into apathy and indifferentism. It becomes us to consider whether we cannot have a real faith and real objects in lieu of these false ones. The human mind, when it is trusted, is never false to itself. If there be sincerity and good meaning—if there be really in us the wish to seek for our superiors, for that which is lawfully above us, we shall not long look in vain.

Meantime there is great centrality, a centripetence equal to the centrifugence. The mystic or theist is never scared by any startling materialism. He knows the laws of gravitation and of repulsion are deaf to French talkers, be they never so witty. If theology shows that opinions are fast changing, it is not so with the convictions of men with regard to conduct. These remain. The most daring heroism, the most accomplished culture, or rapt holiness, never exhausted the claim of these lowly duties—never penetrated to their origin, or was able to look behind their source. We cannot disenchant, we cannot impoverish ourselves, by obedience; but by humility we rise, by obedience we command, by poverty we are rich, by dying we live.

We are thrown back on rectitude forever and ever, only rectitude—to mend one; that is all we can do. But *that* the zealot stigmatizes as a sterile chimney-corner philosophy. Now the first position I make is that natural religion supplies still all the facts which are disguised under the dogma of popular creeds. The progress of religion is steadily to its identity with morals.

How is the new generation to be edified? How should it not? The life of these once omnipotent traditions was really not in the legend, but in the moral sentiment and the metaphysical fact which the legends enclosed—and these survive. A new Socrates, or Zeno, or Swedenborg, or Pascal, or a new crop of geniuses like those of the Elizabethan age, may be born in this age, and, with happy heart and a bias for theism, bring asceticism, duty and magnanimity into vogue again.

It is true that Stoicism, always attractive to the intellectual and cultivated, has now no temples, no academy, no commanding Zeno or Antoninus. It accuses us that it has none: that pure ethics is not now formulated and concreted into a *cul-*

tus, a fraternity with assemblings and holy-days, with song and book, with brick and stone. Why have not those who believe in it and love it left all for this, and dedicated themselves to write out its scientific scriptures to become its Vulgate for millions? I answer for one that the inspirations we catch of this law are not continuous and technical, but joyful sparkles, and are recorded for their beauty, for the delight they give, not for their obligation; and that is their priceless good to men, that they charm and uplift, not that they are imposed. It has not yet its first hymn. But, that every line and word may be coals of true fire, ages must roll, ere these casual wide-falling cinders can be gathered into broad and steady altar flame.

It does not yet appear what forms the religious feeling will take. It prepares to rise out of all forms to an absolute justice and health perception. Here is now a new feeling of humanity infused into public action. Here is contribution of money on a more extended and systematic scale than ever before to repair public disasters at a distance, and of political support to oppressed parties. Then there are new conventions of social science, before which the questions of the rights of women, the laws of trade, the treatment of crime, regulation of labor, come for a hearing. If these are tokens of the steady currents of thought and will in these directions, one might well anticipate a new nation.

I know how delicate this principle is—how difficult of adaptation to practical and social arrangements. It cannot be profaned; it cannot be forced; to draw it out of its natural current is to lose at once all its power. Such experiments as we recall are those in which some sect or dogma made the tie, and that was an artificial element, which chilled and checked the union. But is it quite impossible to believe that men should be drawn to each other by the simple respect which each man feels for another in whom he discovers absolute honesty; the respect he feels for one who thinks life is quite too coarse and frivolous, and that he should like to lift it a little, should like to be the friend of some man's virtue? for another who underneath his compliances with artificial society, would dearly like to serve somebody—to test his own reality by making himself useful and indispensable?

Man does not live by bread alone, but by faith, by admiration, by sympathy. 'T is very shallow to say that cotton, or iron, or silver and gold are kings of the world; there are rulers that will at any moment make these forgotten. Fear will. Love will. Character will. Men live by their credence. Governments stand by it—by the faith that the people share—whether it comes from the religion in which they were bred, or from an original conscience in themselves, which the popular religion echoes. If government could only stand by force, if the instinct of the people was to resist the government, it is plain the government must be two to one in order to be secure, and then it would not be safe from desperate individuals. But no, the old commandment, "Thou shalt not kill," holds down New York, and London, and Paris, and not a police or horse guards.

The credence of men it is that molds them, and creates at will one or another surface. The mind as it opens transfers very fast its choice from the circumstance to the cause; from courtesy to love, from inventions to science, from London or Washington law, or public opinion, to the self-revealing idea; from all that talent executes to the sentiment that fills the heart and dictates the future of nations. The commanding fact which I never do see is the sufficiency for the moral sentiment. We buttress it up, in shallow hours or ages, with legends, traditions and forms, each good for the one moment in which it was a happy type or symbol of the Power; but the Power sends in the next moment a new lesson, which we lose while our eyes are reverted and striving to perpetuate the old.

America shall introduce a pure religion. Ethics are thought not to satisfy affection. But all the religion we have is the ethics of one or another holy person; as soon as character appears, be sure love will, and veneration, and anecdotes and fables about him, and delight of good men and women in him. And what deeps of grandeur and beauty or insight belongs to it! For innocence is a wonderful electuary for purging the eyes to search the nature of those souls that pass before it. What armor it is to protect the good from outward or inward harm! and with what power it converts evil accidents into benefits; the power of its countenance; the power of its presence! To it alone comes true friendship; to it come grandeur of situation and poetic perception, enriching all it deals with.

Once men thought Spirit divine, and Matter diabolic; one Ormuzd, the other Ahriman. Now science and philosophy recognize the parallelism, the approximation, the unity of the two: how each reflects the other as face answers to face in a glass: nay, how the laws of both are one, or how one is the realization. We are learning not to fear truth.

The man of this age must be matriculated in the university of sciences and tendencies flowing from all past periods. He must not be one who can be surprised and shipwrecked by every bold or subtile word which malignant and acute men may utter in his hearing, but should be taught all skepticisms and unbeliefs, and made the destroyer of all card-houses and paper walls and the sifter of all opinions, by being put face to face from his infancy with Reality.

A man who has accustomed himself to look at all his circumstances as very mutable, to carry his possessions, his relations to persons, and even his opinions, in his hand, and in all these to pierce to the principle and moral law, and everywhere to find that—has put himself out of the reach of all skepticism; and it seems as if whatever is most affecting and sublime in our intercourse, in our happiness, and in our losses, tend steadily to uplift us to a life so extraordinary, and, one might say, superhuman.

From *Lectures and Biographical Sketches*
Volume X

The American Scholar

AN ORATION DELIVERED BEFORE
THE PHI BETA KAPPA SOCIETY, AT CAMBRIDGE,
AUGUST 31, 1837

Mr. President and Gentlemen:

I greet you on the recommencement of our literary year. Our anniversary is one of hope, and, perhaps, not enough of labor. We do not meet for games of strength or skill, for the recitation of histories, tragedies, and odes, like the ancient Greeks; for parliaments of love and poesy, like the Troubadours; nor for the advancement of science, like our contemporaries in the British and European capitals. Thus far, our holiday has been simply a friendly sign of the survival of the love of letters amongst a people too busy to give to letters any more. As such it is precious as the sign of an indestructible instinct. Perhaps the time is already come when it ought to be, and will be, something else; when the sluggard intellect of this continent will look from under its iron lids and fill the postponed expectation of the world with something better than the exertions of mechanical skill. Our day of dependence, our long apprenticeship to the learning of other lands, draws to a close. The millions that around us are rushing into life, cannot always be fed on the sere remains of foreign harvests. Events, actions arise, that must be sung, that will sing themselves. Who can doubt that poetry will revive and lead in a new age, as the star in the constellation Harp, which now flames in our Zenith, astronomers announce, shall one day be the polestar for a thousand years?

In this hope I accept the topic which not only usage but the nature of our association seem to prescribe to this day—the American Scholar. Year by year we come up hither to read one more chapter of his biography. Let us inquire what light new days and events have thrown on his character and his hopes.

It is one of those fables which out of an unknown antiquity convey an unlooked-for wisdom, that the gods, in the beginning, divided Man into men, that he might be more helpful to himself; just as the hand was divided into fingers, the better to answer its end.

The old fable covers a doctrine ever new and sublime; that there is One Man—present to all particular man only partially, or through one faculty; and that you must take the whole society to find the whole man. Man is not a farmer, or a professor, or an engineer, but he is all. Man is priest, and scholar, and statesman, and producer, and soldier. In the *divided* or social state these functions are parceled out to individuals, each of whom aims to do his stint of the joint work, whilst each other performs his. The fable implies that the individual, to possess himself, must sometimes return from his own labor to embrace all the other laborers. But, unfortunately, this original unit, this fountain of power, has been so distributed to multitudes, has been so minutely subdivided and peddled out, that it is spilled into drops, and cannot be gathered. The state of society is one in which the members have suffered amputation from the trunk, and strut about so many walking monsters—a good finger, a neck, a stomach, an elbow, but never a man.

Man is thus metamorphosed into a thing, into many things. The planter, who is Man sent out into the field to gather food, is seldom cheered by any idea of the true dignity of his ministry. He sees his bushel and his cart, and nothing beyond, and sinks into the farmer, instead of Man on the farm. The tradesman scarcely ever gives an ideal worth to his work, but is ridden by the routine of his craft, and the soul is subject to dollars. The priest becomes a form; the attorney a statute-book; the mechanic a machine; the sailor a rope of the ship.

In this distribution of functions the scholar is the delegated intellect. In the right state he is *Man Thinking*. In the degenerate state, when the victim of society, he tends to become a mere thinker, or still worse, the parrot of other men's thinking.

In this view of him, as Man Thinking, the theory of his office is contained. Him Nature solicits with all her placid, all her monitory pictures; him the past instructs; him the future invites. Is not indeed every man a student, and do not all things exist for the student's behoof? And, finally, is not the true scholar the only true master? But the old oracle said, "All things have two handles: beware of the wrong one." In life, too often, the scholar errs with mankind and forfeits his privilege. Let us see him in his school, and consider him in reference to the main influences he receives.

I.   The first in time and the first in importance of the influences upon the mind is that of nature. Every day, the sun; and, after sunset, Night and her stars. Ever the winds blow; ever the grass grows. Every day, men and women, conversing, beholding and beholden. The scholar is he of all men whom this spectacle most engages. He must settle its value in his mind. What is nature to him? There is never a beginning, there is never an end, to the inexplicable continuity of this web of God, but always circular power returning into itself. Therein it resembles his own spirit, whose beginning, whose ending, he never can find—so entire, so boundless. Far too as her splendors shine, system on system shooting like rays, upward, downward, without center, without circumference—in the mass and in the particle, Nature hastens to render account of herself to the mind. Classification begins. To the young mind every thing is individual, stands by itself. By and by, it finds how to join two things and see in them one nature; then three, then three thousand; and so, tyrannized over by its own unifying instinct, it goes on tying things together, diminishing anomalies, discovering roots running under ground whereby contrary and remote things cohere and flower out from one stem. It presently learns that since the dawn of history there has been a constant accumulation and classifying of facts. But what is classification but the perceiving that these objects are not chaotic, and are not foreign, but have a law which is also a law of the human mind? The astronomer discovers that geometry, a pure abstraction of the human mind, is the measure of planetary motion. The chemist finds proportions and intelligible method throughout matter; and science is nothing but the finding of analogy, identity, in the most remote parts. The ambitious soul sits down before each refractory fact; one after another reduces all strange constitutions, all new powers, to their class and their law, and goes on forever to animate the last fiber of organization, the outskirts of nature, by insight.

Thus to him, to this schoolboy under the bending dome of

day, is suggested that he and it proceed from one root; one is leaf and one is flower; relation, sympathy, stirring in every vein. And what is that root? Is not that the soul of his soul? A thought too bold; a dream too wild. Yet when this spiritual light shall have revealed the law of more earthly natures—when he has learned to worship the soul, and to see that the natural philosophy that now is, is only the first gropings of its gigantic hand, he shall look forward to an ever expanding knowledge as to a becoming creator. He shall see that nature is the opposite of the soul, answering to it part for part. One is seal and one is print. Its beauty is the beauty of his own mind. Its laws are the laws of his own mind. Nature then becomes to him the measure of his attainments. So much of nature as he is ignorant of, so much of his own mind does he not yet possess. And, in fine, the ancient precept, "Know thyself," and the modern precept, "Study nature," become at last one maxim.

II.   The next great influence into the spirit of the scholar is the mind of the Past—in whatever form, whether of literature, of art, of institutions, that mind is inscribed. Books are the best type of the influence of the past, and perhaps we shall get at the truth—learn the amount of this influence more conveniently—by considering their value alone.

The theory of books is noble. The scholar of the first age received into him the world around; brooded thereon; gave it the new arrangement of his own mind, and uttered it again. It came into his life; it went out from him truth. It came to him short-lived actions; it went out from him immortal thoughts. It came to him business; it went from him poetry. It was dead fact; now, it is quick thought. It can stand, it can go. It now endures, it now flies, it now inspires. Precisely in proportion to the depth of mind from which it issued, so high does it soar, so long does it sing.

Or, I might say, it depends on how far the process had gone, of transmuting life into truth. In proportion to the completeness of the distillation, so will the purity and imperishableness of the product be. But none is quite perfect. As no air-pump can by any means make a perfect vacuum, so neither can any artist entirely exclude the conventional, the local, the perishable from his book, or write a book of pure thought, that shall be as efficient, in all respects, to a remote posterity, as to contemporaries, or rather to the second age. Each age, it is found, must write its own books; or rather, each generation for the next succeeding. The books of an older period will not fit this.

Yet hence arises a grave mischief. The sacredness which attaches to the act of creation, the act of thought, is transferred to the record. The poet chanting was felt to be a divine man: henceforth the chant is divine also. The writer was a just and wise spirit: henceforward it is settled the book is perfect; as love of the hero corrupts into worship of his statue. Instantly the book becomes noxious: the guide is a tyrant. The sluggish and perverted mind of the multitude, slow to open to the incursions of Reason, having once so opened, having once received this book, stands upon it, and makes an outcry if it is disparaged. Colleges are built on it. Books are written on it by thinkers, not by Man Thinking; by men of talent, that is, who start wrong, who set out from accepted dogmas, not from their own sight of principles. Meek young men grow up in libraries, believing it their duty to accept the views which Cicero, which Locke, which Bacon, have given; forgetful that Cicero, Locke, and Bacon were only young men in libraries when they wrote these books.

Hence, instead of Man Thinking, we have the bookworm. Hence the book-learned class, who value books, as such; not as related to nature and the human constitution, but as making a sort of Third Estate with the world and the soul. Hence the restorers of readings, the emendators, the bibliomaniacs of all degrees.

Books are the best of things, well used; abused, among the worst. What is the right use? What is the one end which all means go to effect? They are for nothing but to inspire. I had better never see a book than to be warped by its attraction clean out of my own orbit, and made a satellite instead of a system. The one thing in the world, of value, is the active soul. This every man is entitled to; this every man contains within him, although in almost all men obstructed and as yet unborn. The soul active sees absolute truth and utters truth, or creates. In this action it is genius; not the privilege of here and there a favorite, but the sound estate of every man. In its essence it is progressive. The books, the college, the school of art, the institution of any kind, stop with some past utterance of genius. This is good, say they—let us hold by this. They pin me down. They look backward and not forward. But genius looks forward: the eyes of man are set in his forehead, not in his hindhead: man hopes: genius creates. Whatever talents may be, if the man create not, the pure efflux of the Deity is not his;—cinders and smoke there may be, but not yet flame. There are creative manners, there are creative actions, and creative words; manners, actions, words, that is, indicative of no custom or authority, but springing spontaneous from the mind's own sense of good and fair.

On the other part, instead of being its own seer, let it receive from another mind its truth, though it was in torrents of light, without periods of solitude, inquest, and self-recovery, and a fatal disservice is done. Genius is always sufficiently the enemy of genius by overinfluence. The literature of every nation bears me witness. The English dramatic poets have Shakespearized now for two hundred years.

Undoubtedly there is a right way of reading, so it be sternly subordinated. Man Thinking must be subdued by his instruments. Books are for the scholar's idle time. When he can read God directly, the hour is too precious to be wasted in other men's transcripts of their readings. But when the intervals of darkness come, as come they must—when the sun is hid and the stars withdraw their shining—we repair to the lamps which were kindled by their ray, to guide our steps to the East again, where the dawn is. We hear, that we may speak. The Arabian proverb says, "A fig tree, looking on a fig tree, becometh fruitful."

It is remarkable, the character of the pleasure we derive from the best books. They impress us with the conviction that one nature wrote and the same reads. We read the verses of one of the great English poets, of Chaucer, of Marvell, of Dryden, with the most modern joy—with a pleasure, I mean, which is in great part caused by the abstraction of all *time* from their verses. There is some awe mixed with the joy of our surprise, when this poet, who lived in some past world, two or three hundred years ago, says that which lies close to my own soul, that which I had also had well-nigh thought and said. But for the evidence thence afforded to the philosophical doctrine of the identity of all minds, we should suppose some preestablished harmony, some foresight of souls that were to be, and some preparation of stores for their future wants, like the fact observed in insects, who lay up food before death for the young grub they shall never see.

I would not be hurried by any love of system, by any exaggeration of instincts, to underrate the Book. We all know, that as the human body can be nourished on any food, though it were boiled grass and the broth of shoes, so the human mind can be fed by any knowledge. And great and heroic men have existed who had almost no other information than by the printed page. I only would say that it needs a strong head to bear that diet. One must be an inventor to read well. As the proverb says, "He that would bring home the wealth of the Indies, must carry out the wealth of the Indies." There is then creative reading as well as creative writing. When the mind is braced by labor and invention, the page of whatever book we read becomes luminous with manifold allusion. Every sentence is doubly significant, and the sense of our author is as broad as the world. We then see, what is always true, that as the seer's hour of vision is short and rare among heavy days and months, so is its record, perchance, the least part of his volume. The discerning will read, in his Plato or Shakespeare, only that least part—only the authentic utterances of the oracle;—all the rest he rejects, were it never so many times Plato's and Shakespeare's.

Of course there is a portion of reading quite indispensable to a wise man. History and exact science he must learn by laborious reading. Colleges, in like manner, have their indispensable office—to teach elements. But they can only highly serve us when they aim not to drill, but to create; when they gather from far every ray of various genius to their hospitable halls and by the concentrated fires, set the hearts of their youth on flame. Thought and knowledge are natures in which apparatus and pretension avail nothing. Gowns and pecuniary foundations, though of towns of gold, can never countervail the least sentence or syllable of wit. Forget this, and our American colleges will recede in their public importance, whilst they grow richer every year.

III. There goes in the world a notion that the scholar should be a recluse, a valetudinarian—as unfit for any handiwork or public labor as a penknife for an axe. The so-called "practical men" sneer at speculative men, as if, because they speculate or *see*, they could do nothing. I have heard it said that the clergy—who are always, more universally than any other class, the scholars of their day—are addressed as women; that the rough, spontaneous conversation of men they do not hear, but only a mincing and diluted speech. They are often virtually disfranchised; and indeed there are advocates for their celibacy. As far as this is true of the studious classes, it is not just and wise. Action is with the scholar subordinate, but it is essential. Without it he is not yet man. Without it thought can never ripen into truth. Whilst the world hangs before the eye as a cloud of beauty, we cannot even see its beauty. Inaction is cowardice, but there can be no scholar without the heroic mind. The preamble of thought, the transition through which it passes from the unconscious to the conscious is action. Only so much do I know, as I have lived. Instantly we know whose words are loaded with life, and whose not.

The world—this shadow of the soul, or *other me*—lies wide around. Its attractions are the keys which unlock my thoughts and make me acquainted with myself. I run eagerly into this resounding tumult. I grasp the hands of those next me, and take my place in the ring to suffer and to work, taught by an instinct that so shall the dumb abyss be vocal with speech.

I pierce its order; I dissipate its fear; I dispose of it within the circuit of my expanding life. So much only of life as I know by experience, so much of the wilderness have I vanquished and planted, or so far have I extended my being, my dominion. I do not see how any man can afford, for the sake of his nerves and his nap, to spare any action in which he can partake. It is pearls and rubies to his discourse. Drudgery, calamity, exasperation, want, are instructors in eloquence and wisdom. The true scholar grudges every opportunity of action past by, as a loss of power. It is the raw material out of which the intellect molds her splendid products. A strange process, too, this by which experience is converted into thought, as a mulberry leaf is converted into satin. The manufacture goes forward at all hours.

The actions and events of our childhood and youth are now matters of calmest observation. They lie like fair pictures in the air. Not so with our recent actions—with the business which we now have in hand. On this we are quite unable to speculate. Our affections as yet circulate through it. We no more feel or know it than we feel the feet, or the hand, or the brain of our body. The new deed is yet a part of life—remains for a time immersed in our unconscious life. In some contemplative hour it detaches itself from the life like a ripe fruit, to become a thought of the mind. Instantly it is raised, transfigured; the corruptible has put on incorruption. Henceforth it is an object of beauty, however base its origin and neighborhood. Observe too the impossibility of antedating this act. In its grub state, it cannot fly, it cannot shine, it is a dull grub. But suddenly, without observation, the selfsame thing unfurls beautiful wings, and is an angel of wisdom. So is there no fact, no event, in our private history, which shall not, sooner or later, lose its adhesive, inert form, and astonish us by soaring from our body into the empyrean. Cradle and infancy, school and playground, the fear of boys, and dogs, and ferules, the love of little maids and berries, and many another fact that once filled the whole sky, are gone already; friend and relative, profession and party, town and country, nation and world, must also soar and sing.

Of course, he who has put forth his total strength in fit action has the richest return of wisdom. I will not shut myself out of this globe of action, and transplant an oak into a flowerpot, there to hunger and pine; nor trust the revenue of some single faculty, and exhaust one vein of thought, much like those Savoyards, who, getting their livelihood by carving shepherds, shepherdesses, and smoking Dutchmen, for all Europe, went out one day to the mountain to find stock, and discovered that they had whittled up the last of their pine trees. Authors we have, in numbers, who have written out their vein, and who, moved by a commendable prudence, sail for Greece or Palestine, follow the trapper into the prairie, or ramble round Algiers, to replenish their merchantable stock.

If it were only for a vocabulary, the scholar would be covetous of action. Life is our dictionary. Years are well spent in country labors; in town; in the insight into trades and manufactures; in frank intercourse with many men and women; in science; in art; to the one end of mastering in all their facts a language by which to illustrate and embody our perceptions. I learn immediately from any speaker how much he has already lived, through the poverty or the splendor of his speech. Life lies behind us as the quarry from whence we get tiles and copestones for the masonry of today. This is the way to learn grammar. Colleges and books only copy the language which the field and the work yard made.

But the final value of action, like that of books, and better than books, is that it is a resource. That great principle of Undulation in nature, that shows itself in the inspiring and expiring of the breath; in desire and satiety; in the ebb and flow of the sea; in day and night; in heat and cold; and, as yet more deeply ingrained in every atom and every fluid, is known to us under the name of Polarity—these "fits of easy transmission and reflection," as Newton called them, are the law of nature because they are the law of spirit.

The mind now thinks, now acts, and each fit reproduces the other. When the artist has exhausted his materials, when the fancy no longer paints, when thoughts are no longer apprehended and books are a weariness—he has always the resource *to live*. Character is higher than intellect. Thinking is the function. Living is the functionary. The stream retreats to its source. A great soul will be strong to live, as well as strong to think. Does he lack organ or medium to impart his truths? He can still fall back on this elemental force of living them. This is a total act. Thinking is a partial act. Let the grandeur of justice shine in his affairs. Let the beauty of affection cheer his lowly roof. Those "far from fame," who dwell and act with him, will feel the force of his constitution in the doings and passages of the day better than it can be measured by any public and designed display. Time shall teach him that the scholar loses no hour which the man lives. Herein he unfolds the sacred germ of his instinct, screened from influence. What is lost in seemliness is gained in strength. Not out of those on whom systems of education have exhausted their culture, comes the helpful giant to destroy the old or to build the new, but out of unhandseled savage nature; out of terrible Druids and Berserkers come at last Alfred and Shakespeare.

I hear therefore with joy whatever is beginning to be said of the dignity and necessity of labor to every citizen. There is virtue yet in the hoe and the spade, for learned as well as for unlearned hands. And labor is everywhere welcome; always we are invited to work; only be this limitation observed, that a man shall not for the sake of wider activity sacrifice any opinion to the popular judgments and modes of action.

I have now spoken of the education of the scholar by nature, by books, and by action. It remains to say somewhat of his duties.

They are such as become Man Thinking. They may all be comprised in self-trust. The office of the scholar is to cheer, to raise, and to guide men by showing them facts amidst appearances. He plies the slow, unhonored, and unpaid task of observation. Flamsteed and Herschel, in their glazed observatories, may catalogue the stars with the praise of all men, and the results being splendid and useful, honor is sure. But he, in his private observatory, cataloguing obscure and nebulous stars of the human mind, which as yet no man has thought of as such —watching days and months sometimes for a few facts; correcting still his old records;—must relinquish display and immediate fame. In the long period of his preparation he must betray often an ignorance and shiftlessness in popular arts, incurring the disdain of the able who shoulder him aside. Long he must stammer in his speech; often forgo the living for the dead. Worse yet, he must accept—how often!—poverty and solitude. For the ease and pleasure of treading the old road, accepting the fashions, the education, the religion of society, he takes the cross of making his own, and, of course, the self-accusation, the faint heart, the frequent uncertainty and loss of time, which are the nettles and tangling vines in the way of the self-relying and self-directed; and the state of virtual hostility in which he seems to stand to society, and especially to educated society. For all this loss and scorn, what offset? He is to find consolation in exercising the highest function of human nature. He is one who raises himself from private considerations and breathes and lives on public and illustrious thoughts. He is the world's eye. He is the world's heart. He is to resist the vulgar prosperity that retrogrades ever to barbarism, by preserving and communicating heroic sentiments, noble biographies, melodious verse, and the conclusions of history. Whatsoever oracles the human heart, in all emergencies, in all solemn hours, has uttered as its commentary on the world of actions—these he shall receive and impart. And whatsoever new verdict Reason from her inviolable seat pronounces on the passing men and events of today—this he shall hear and promulgate.

These being his functions, it becomes him to feel all confidence in himself, and to defer never to the popular cry. He and he only knows the world. The world of any moment is the merest appearance. Some great decorum, some fetish of a government, some ephemeral trade, or war, or man, is cried up by half mankind and cried down by the other half, as if all depended on this particular up or down. The odds are that the whole question is not worth the poorest thought which the scholar has lost in listening to the controversy. Let him not quit his belief that a popgun is a popgun, though the ancient and honorable of the earth affirm it to be the crack of doom. In silence, in steadiness, in severe abstraction, let him hold by himself; add observation to observation, patient of neglect, patient of reproach, and bide his own time—happy enough if he can satisfy himself alone that this day he has seen something truly. Success treads on every right step. For the instinct is sure, that prompts him to tell his brother what he thinks. He then learns that in going down into the secrets of his own mind he has descended into the secrets of all minds. He learns that he who has mastered any law in his private thoughts, is master to that extent of all men whose language he speaks, and of all into whose language his own can be translated. The poet, in utter solitude remembering his spontaneous thoughts and recording them, is found to have recorded that which men in crowded cities find true for them also. The orator distrusts at first the fitness of his frank confessions, his want of knowledge of the persons he addresses, until he finds that he is the complement of his hearers—that they drink his words because he fulfills for them their own nature; the deeper he dives into his privatest, secretest presentiment, to his wonder he finds this is the most acceptable, most public, and universally true. The people delight in it; the better part of every man feels, This is my music; this is myself.

In self-trust all the virtues are comprehended. Free should the scholar be—free and brave. Free even to the definition of freedom, "without any hindrance that does not arise out of his own constitution." Brave; for fear is a thing which a scholar by his very function puts behind him. Fear always springs from ignorance. It is a shame to him if his tranquillity, amid dangerous times, arise from the presumption that like children and women, his is a protected class; or if he seek a temporary peace by the diversion of his thoughts from politics or vexed questions, hiding his head like an ostrich in the flowering bushes, peeping into microscopes, and turning rhymes, as a boy whistles to keep his courage up. So is the danger a danger still; so is the fear worse. Manlike let him turn and face it. Let him look into its eye and search its nature, inspect its origin—see the whelping of this lion—which lies no great way back; he will then find in himself a perfect comprehension of its nature and extent; he will have made his hands meet on the other side, and can henceforth defy it and pass on superior. The world is his who can see through its pretension. What deafness, what stone-blind custom, what overgrown error you behold is there only by sufferance—by your sufferance. See it to be a lie, and you have already dealt it its mortal blow.

Yes, we are the cowed—we the trustless. It is a mischievous notion that we are come late into nature; that the world was finished a long time ago. As the world was plastic and fluid in the hands of God, so it is ever to so much of his attributes as we bring to it. To ignorance and sin, it is flint. They adapt themselves to it as they may; but in proportion as a man has any thing in him divine, the firmament flows before him and takes his signet and form. Not he is great who can alter matter, but he who can alter my state of mind. They are the kings of the world who give the color of their present thought to all nature and all art, and persuade men by the cheerful serenity of their carrying the matter, that this thing which they do is the apple which the ages have desired to pluck, now at last ripe, and inviting nations to the harvest. The great man makes the great thing. Wherever Macdonald sits, there is the head of the table. Linnaeus makes botany the most alluring of studies, and wins it from the farmer and the herbwoman; Davy, chemistry; and Cuvier, fossils. The day is always his who works in it with serenity and great aims. The unstable estimates of men crowd to him whose mind is filled with a truth, as the heaped waves of the Atlantic follow the moon.

For this self-trust, the reason is deeper than can be fathomed—darker than can be enlightened. I might not carry with me the feeling of my audience in stating my own belief. But I have already shown the ground of my hope, in adverting to the doctrine that man is one. I believe man has been wronged; he has wronged himself. He has almost lost the light that can lead him back to his prerogatives. Men are become of no account. Men in history, men in the world of today, are bugs, are spawn, and are called "the mass" and "the herd." In a century, in a millennium, one or two men; that is to say, one or two approximations to the right state of every man. All the rest behold in the hero or the poet their own green and crude being—ripened; yes, and are content to be less, so *that* may attain to its full stature. What a testimony, full of grandeur, full of pity, is borne to the demands of his own nature, by the poor clansman, the poor partisan, who rejoices in the glory of his chief. The poor and the low find some amends to their immense moral capacity, for their acquiescence in a political and social inferiority. They are content to be brushed like flies from the path of a great person, so that justice shall be done by him to that common nature which it is the dearest desire of all to see enlarged and glorified. They sun themselves in the great man's light, and feel it to be their own element. They cast the dignity of man from their downtrod selves upon the shoulders of a hero, and will perish to add one drop of blood to make that great heart beat, those giant sinews combat and conquer. He lives for us, and we live in him.

Men, such as they are, very naturally seek money or power, and power because it is as good as money—the "spoils," so called, "of office." And why not? for they aspire to the highest, and this, in their sleepwalking, they dream is highest. Wake them and they shall quit the false good and leap to the true, and leave governments to clerks and desks. This revolution is to be wrought by the gradual domestication of the idea of Culture. The main enterprise of the world for splendor, for extent, is the upbuilding of a man. Here are the materials strewn along the ground. The private life of one man shall be a more illustrious monarchy, more formidable to its enemy, more sweet and serene in its influence to its friend, than any kingdom in history. For a man, rightly viewed, comprehendeth the particular natures of all men. Each philosopher, each bard, each actor has only done for me, as by a delegate, what one day I can do for myself. The books which once we valued more than the apple of the eye, we have quite exhausted. What is that but saying that we have come up with the point of view which the universal mind took through the eyes of one scribe; we have been that man, and have passed on. First, one, then another, we drain all cisterns, and waxing greater by all these supplies, we crave a better and more abundant food. The man has never lived that can feed us ever. The human mind cannot be enshrined in a person who shall set a barrier on any one side of this unbounded, unboundable empire. It is one central fire, which, flaming now out of the lips of Etna, lightens the capes of Sicily, and now out of the throat of Vesuvius, illuminates the towers and vineyards of Naples. It is one light which beams out of a thousand stars. It is one soul which animates all men.

But I have dwelt perhaps tediously upon this abstraction of the Scholar. I ought not to delay longer to add what I have to say of nearer reference to the time and to this country.

Historically, there is thought to be a difference in the ideas which predominate over successive epochs, and there are data for marking the genius of the Classic, of the Romantic, and now of the Reflective or Philosophical age. With the views I have intimated of the oneness or the identity of the mind through all individuals, I do not much dwell on these differences. In fact, I believe each individual passes through all three. The boy is a Greek; the youth, romantic; the adult reflective. I deny not, however, that a revolution in the leading idea may be distinctly enough traced.

Our age is bewailed as the age of Introversion. Must that needs be evil? We, it seems, are critical; we are embarrassed with second thoughts; we cannot enjoy any thing for hankering to know whereof the pleasure consists; we are lined with eyes; we see with our feet; the time is infected with Hamlet's unhappiness—

"Sicklied o'er with the pale cast of thought."

It is so bad then? Sight is the last thing to be pitied. Would we be blind? Do we fear lest we should outsee nature and God, and drink truth dry? I look upon the discontent of the literary class as a mere announcement of the fact that they find themselves not in the state of mind of their fathers, and regret the coming state as untried; as a boy dreads the water before he has learned that he can swim. If there is any period one would desire to be born in, is it not the age of Revolution; when the old and the new stand side by side and admit of being compared; when the energies of all men are searched by fear and by hope; when the historic glories of the old can be compensated by the rich possibilities of the new era? This time, like all times, is a very good one, if we but know what to do with it.

I read with some joy of the auspicious signs of the coming days, as they glimmer already through poetry and art, through philosophy and science, through church and state.

One of these signs is the fact that the same movement which effected the elevation of what was called the lowest class in the state, assumed in literature a very marked and as benign an aspect. Instead of the sublime and beautiful, the near, the low, the common, was explored and poetized. That which had been negligently trodden under foot by those who were harnessing and provisioning themselves for long journeys into far countries, is suddenly found to be richer than all foreign parts. The literature of the poor, the feelings of the child, the philosophy of the street, the meaning of household life, are the topics of the time. It is a great stride. It is a sign—is it not?—of new vigor when the extremities are made active, when currents of warm life run into the hands and the feet. I ask not for the great, the remote, the romantic; what is doing in Italy or Arabia; what is Greek art, or Provençal minstrelsy; I embrace the common, I explore and sit at the feet of the familiar, the low. Give me insight into today, and you may have the antique and future worlds. What would we really know the meaning of? The meal in the firkin; the milk in the pan; the ballad in the street; the news of the boat; the glance of the eye; the form and the gait of the body;—show me the ultimate reason of these matters; show me the sublime presence of the highest spiritual cause lurking, as always it does lurk, in these suburbs and extremities of nature; let me see every trifle bristling with the polarity that ranges it instantly on an eternal law; and the shop, the plow, and the ledger referred to the like cause by which light undulates and poets sing;—and the world lies no longer a dull miscellany and lumber room, but has form and order; there is no trifle, there is no puzzle, but one design unites and animates the farthest pinnacle and the lowest trench.

This idea has inspired the genius of Goldsmith, Burns, Cowper, and, in a newer time, of Goethe, Wordsworth, and Carlyle. This idea they have differently followed and with various success. In contrast with their writing, the style of Pope, of Johnson, of Gibbon, looks cold and pedantic. This writing is blood-warm. Man is surprised to find that things near are not less beautiful and wondrous than things remote. The near explains the far. The drop is a small ocean. A man is related to all nature. This perception of the worth of the vulgar is fruitful in discoveries. Goethe, in this very thing the most modern of the moderns, has shown us as none ever did, the genius of the ancients.

There is one man of genius who has done much for this philosophy of life, whose literary value has never yet been rightly estimated;—I mean Emanuel Swedenborg. The most imaginative of men, yet writing with the precision of a mathematician, he endeavored to engraft a purely philosophical Ethics on the popular Christianity of his time. Such an attempt of course must have difficulty which no genius could surmount. But he saw and showed the connection between nature and the affections of the soul. He pierced the emblematic or spiritual character of the visible, audible, tangible world. Especially did his shade-loving muse hover over and interpret the lower parts of nature; he showed the mysterious bond that allies moral evil to the foul material forms, and has given in epical parables a theory of insanity, of beasts, of unclean and fearful things.

Another sign of our times, also marked by an analogous political movement, is the new importance given to the single person. Every thing that tends to insulate the individual—to surround him with barriers of natural respect, so that each man shall feel the world is his, and man shall treat with man as a sovereign state with a sovereign state—tends to true union as well as greatness. "I learned," said the melancholy Pestalozzi, "that no man in God's wide earth is either willing or able to help any other man." Help must come from the bosom alone. The scholar is that man who must take up into himself all the ability of the time, all the contributions of the past, all the hopes of the future. He must be an university of knowledges. If there be one lesson more than another which should pierce his ear, it is, The world is nothing, the man is all; in yourself is the law of all nature, and you know not yet how a globule of sap ascends; in yourself slumbers the whole of Reason; it is for you to know all; it is for you to dare all. Mr. President and Gentlemen, this confidence in the unsearched might of man belongs by all motives, by all prophecy, by all preparation, to the American Scholar. We have listened too long to the courtly muses of Europe. The spirit of the American freeman is already suspected to be timid, imitative, tame. Public and private avarice make the air we breathe thick and fat. The scholar is decent, indolent, complaisant. See already the tragic consequence. The mind of this country, taught to aim at low objects, eats upon itself. There is no work for any but the decorous and the complaisant. Young men of the fairest promise, who begin life upon our shores, inflated by the mountain winds, shined upon by all the stars of God, find the earth below not in unison with these, but are hindered from action by the disgust which the principles on which business is managed inspire, and turn drudges, or die of disgust, some of them suicides. What is the remedy? They did not yet see, and thousands of young men as hopeful now crowding to the barriers for the career do not yet see, that if the single man plant himself indomitably on his instincts, and there abide, the huge world will come round to him. Patience—patience; with the shades of all the good and great for company; and for solace and perspective of your own infinite life; and for work the study and the communication of principles, the making those instincts prevalent, the conversion of the world. Is it not the chief disgrace in the world, not to be an unit;—not to be reckoned one character;—not to yield that peculiar fruit which each man was created to bear, but to be reckoned in the gross, in the hundred, or the thousand, of the party, the section, to which we belong; and our opinion predicted geographically as the north, or the south? Not so, brothers and friends—please God, ours shall not be so. We will walk on our own feet; we will work with our own hands; we will speak our own minds. The study of letters shall be no longer a name for pity, for doubt, and for sensual indulgence. The dread of man and the love of man shall be a wall of defense and a wreath of joy around all. A nation of men will for the first time exist, because each believes himself inspired by the Divine Soul which also inspires all men.

From *Nature Addresses and Lectures*
Volume I

Works and Days

Our nineteenth century is the age of tools. They grew out of our structure. "Man is the meter of all things," said Aristotle; "the hand is the instrument of instruments, and the mind is the form of forms." The human body is the magazine of inventions, the patent office, where are the models from which every hint was taken. All the tools and engines on earth are only extensions of its limbs and senses. One definition of man is "an intelligence served by organs." Machines can only second, not supply, his unaided senses. The body is a meter. The eye appreciates finer differences than art can expose. The apprentice clings to his foot rule; a practiced mechanic will measure by his thumb and his arm with equal precision; and a good surveyor will pace sixteen rods more accurately than another man can measure them by tape. The sympathy of eye and hand by which an Indian or a practiced slinger hits his mark with a stone, or a woodchopper or a carpenter swings his axe to a hairline on his log, are examples; and there is no sense or organ which is not capable of exquisite performance.

Men love to wonder, and that is the seed of our science; and such is the mechanical determination of our age, and so recent are our best contrivances, that use has not dulled our joy and pride in them; and we pity our fathers for dying before steam and galvanism, sulphuric ether and ocean telegraphs, photograph and spectroscope arrived, as cheated out of half their human estate. These arts open great gates of a future, promising to make the world plastic and to lift human life out of its beggary to a godlike ease and power.

Our century to be sure had inherited a tolerable apparatus. We had the compass, the printing press, watches, the spiral spring, the barometer, the telescope. Yet so many inventions have been added that life seems almost made over new; and as Leibnitz said of Newton, that "if he reckoned all that had been done by mathematicians from the beginning of the world down to Newton, and what had been done by him, his would be the better half," so one might say that the inventions of the last fifty years counterpoise those of the fifty centuries before them. For the vast production and manifold application of iron is new; and our common and indispensable utensils of house and farm are new; the sewing machine, the power loom, the McCormick reaper, the mowing machines, gaslight, lucifer matches, and the immense productions of the laboratory, are new in this century, and one franc's worth of coal does the work of a laborer for twenty days.

Why need I speak of steam, the enemy of space and time, with its enormous strength and delicate applicability, which is made in hospitals to bring a bowl of gruel to a sick man's bed, and can twist beams of iron like candy-braids, and vies with the forces which upheaved and doubled over the geologic strata? Steam is an apt scholar and a strong-shouldered fellow, but it has not yet done all its work. It already walks about the field like a man, and will do anything required of it. It irrigates crops, and drags away a mountain. It must sew our shirts, it must drive our gigs; taught by Mr. Babbage, it must calculate interest and logarithms. Lord Chancellor Thurlow thought it might be made to draw bills and answers in chancery. If that were satire, it is yet coming to render many higher services of a mechanico-intellectual kind, and will leave the satire short of the fact.

How excellent are the mechanical aids we have applied to the human body, as in dentistry, in vaccination, in the rhinoplastic treatment; in the beautiful aid of ether, like a finer sleep; and in the boldest promiser of all—the transfusion of the blood—which, in Paris, it was claimed, enables a man to change his blood as often as his linen!

What of this dapper caoutchouc and gutta-percha, which make water pipes and stomach pumps, belting for mill wheels, and diving bells, and rainproof coats for all climates, which teach us to defy the wet, and put every man on a footing with the beaver and the crocodile? What of the grand tools with which we engineer, like kobolds and enchanters, tunneling Alps, canaling the American Isthmus, piercing the Arabian desert? In Massachusetts we fight the sea successfully with beach grass and broom, and the blowing sand barrens with pine plantations. The soil of Holland, once the most populous in Europe, is below the level of the sea. Egypt, where no rain fell for three thousand years, now, it is said, thanks Mehemet Ali's irrigations and planted forests for late-returning showers. The old Hebrew king said, "He makes the wrath of man to praise him." And there is no argument of wisdom better than the grandeur of ends brought about by paltry means. The chain of Western railroads from Chicago to the Pacific has planted cities and civilization in less time than it costs to bring an orchard into bearing.

What shall we say of the ocean telegraph, that extension of eye and ear, whose sudden performance astonished mankind as if the intellect were taking the brute earth into training, and shooting the first thrills of life and thought through the unwilling brain?

There does not seem any limit to these new informations of the same Spirit that made the elements at first, and now, through man, works them. Art and power will go on as they have done—will make day out of night, time out of space, and space out of time.

Invention breeds invention. No sooner is the electric telegraph devised than gutta-percha, the very material it requires, is found. The aeronaut is provided with guncotton, the very fuel he wants for his balloon. When commerce is vastly enlarged, California and Australia expose the gold it needs. When Europe is overpopulated, America and Australia crave to be peopled; and so throughout, every chance is timed, as if Nature, who made the lock, knew where to find the key.

Another result of our arts is the new intercourse which is surprising us with new solutions of the embarrassing political problems. The intercourse is not new, but the scale is new. Our selfishness would have held slaves, or would have excluded from a quarter of the planet all that are not born on the soil of that quarter. Our politics are disgusting; but what can they help or hinder when from time to time the primal instincts are impressed on masses of mankind, when the nations are in exodus and flux? Nature loves to cross her stocks—and German, Chinese, Turk, Russ and Kanaka were putting out to sea, and intermarrying race with race; and commerce took the hint, and ships were built capacious enough to carry the people of a county.

This thousand-handed art has introduced a new element into the state. The science of power is forced to remember the power of science. Civilization mounts and climbs. Malthus, when he stated that the mouths went on multiplying geometrically and the food only arithmetically, forgot to say that the human mind was also a factor in political economy, and that the augmenting wants of society would be met by an augmenting power of invention.

Yes, we have a pretty artillery of tools now in our social arrangement: we ride four times as fast as our fathers did; travel, grind, weave, forge, plant, till and excavate better. We have new shoes, gloves, glasses and gimlets; we have the calculus; we have the newspaper, which does its best to make every square acre of land and sea give an account of itself at your breakfast table; we have money, and paper money; we have language—the finest tool of all, and nearest to the mind. Much will have more. Man flatters himself that his command over Nature must increase. Things begin to obey him. We are to have the balloon yet, and the next war will be fought in the air. We may yet find a rose water that will wash the Negro white. He sees the skull of the English race changing from its Saxon type under the exigencies of American life.

Tantalus, who in old times was seen vainly trying to quench his thirst with a flowing stream which ebbed whenever he approached it, has been seen again lately. He is in Paris, in New York, in Boston. He is now in great spirits; thinks he shall reach it yet; thinks he shall bottle the wave. It is however getting a little doubtful. Things have an ugly look still. No matter how many centuries of culture have preceded, the new man always finds himself standing on the brink of chaos, always in a crisis. Can anybody remember when the times were not hard, and money not scarce? Can anybody remember when sensible men, and the right sort of men, and the right sort of women were plentiful? Tantalus begins to think steam a delusion, and galvanism no better than it should be.

Many facts concur to show that we must look deeper for our salvation than to steam, photographs, balloons or astronomy. These tools have some questionable properties. They are reagents. Machinery is aggressive. The weaver becomes a web, the machinist a machine. If you do not use the tools, they use you. All tools are in one sense edge tools, and dangerous. A man builds a fine house; and now he has a master, and a task for life: he is to furnish, watch, show it, and keep it in repair, the rest of his days. A man has a reputation, and is no longer free, but must respect that. A man makes a picture or a book, and, if it succeeds, 't is often the worse for him. I saw a brave man the other day, hitherto as free as the hawk or the fox of the wilderness, constructing his cabinet of drawers for shells, eggs, minerals and mounted birds. It was easy to see that he was amusing himself with making pretty links for his own limbs.

Then the political economist thinks " 't is doubtful if all the mechanical inventions that ever existed have lightened the day's toil of one human being." The machine unmakes the man. Now that the machine is so perfect, the engineer is nobody. Every new step in improving the engine restricts one more act of the engineer—unteaches him. Once it took Archimedes; now it only needs a fireman, and a boy to know the coppers, to pull up the handles or mind the water tank. But when the engine breaks, they can do nothing.

What sickening details in the daily journals! I believe they have ceased to publish the *Newgate Calendar* and the *Pirate's Own Book* since the family newspapers, namely the *New York Tribune* and the London *Times*, have quite superseded them in the freshness as well as the horror of their records of crime. Politics were never more corrupt and brutal; and Trade, that pride and darling of our ocean, that educator of nations, that benefactor in spite of itself, ends in shameful defaulting, bubble and bankruptcy, all over the world.

Of course we resort to the enumeration of his arts and inventions as a measure of the worth of man. But if, with all his arts, he is a felon, we cannot assume the mechanical skill or chemical resources as the measure of worth. Let us try another gauge.

What have these arts done for the character, for the worth of mankind? Are men better? 'T is sometimes questioned whether morals have not declined as the arts have ascended. Here are great arts and little men. Here is greatness begotten of paltriness. We cannot trace the triumphs of civilization to such benefactors as we wish. The greatest meliorator of the world is selfish, huckstering Trade. Every victory over matter ought to recommend to man the worth of his nature. But now one wonders who did all this good. Look up the inventors. Each has his own knack; his genius is in veins and spots. But the great, equal, symmetrical brains, fed from a great heart, you shall not find. Everyone has more to hide than he has to show, or is lamed by his excellence. 'T is too plain that with the material power the moral progress has not kept pace. It appears that we have not made a judicious investment. Works and days were offered us, and we took works.

The new study of the Sanskrit has shown us the origin of the old names of God—Dyaus, Deus, Zeus, Zeu pater, Jupiter—names of the sun, still recognizable through the modifications of our vernacular words, importing that the Day is the Divine Power and Manifestation, and indicating that those ancient men, in their attempts to express the Supreme Power of the universe, called him the Day, and that this name was accepted by all the tribes.

Hesiod wrote a poem which he called "Works and Days," in which he marked the changes of the Greek year, instructing the husbandman at the rising of what constellation he might safely sow, when to reap, when to gather wood, when the sailor might launch his boat in security from storms, and what admonitions of the planets he must heed. It is full of economies for Grecian life, noting the proper age of marriage, the rules of household thrift and of hospitality. The poem is full of piety as well as prudence, and is adapted to all meridians by adding the ethics of work and of days. But he has not pushed his study of days into such inquiry and analysis as they invite.

A farmer said "he should like to have all the land that joined his own." Bonaparte, who had the same appetite, endeavored to make the Mediterranean a French lake. Czar Alexander was more expansive, and wished to call the Pacific *my ocean*; and the Americans were obliged to resist his attempts to make it a close sea. But if he had the earth for his pasture and the sea for his pond, he would be a pauper still. He only is rich who owns the day. There is no king, rich man, fairy or demon who possesses such power as that. The days are ever divine as to the first Aryans. They are of the least pretension and of the greatest capacity of anything that exists. They come and go like muffled and veiled figures, sent from a distant friendly party; but they say nothing, and if we do not use the gifts they bring, they carry them as silently away.

How the day fits itself to the mind, winds itself round it like a fine drapery, clothing all its fancies! Any holiday communicates to us its color. We wear its cockade and favors in our humor. Remember what boys think in the morning of Election Day, of the Fourth of July, of Thanksgiving or Christmas. The very stars in their courses wink to them of nuts and cakes, bonbons, presents and fireworks. Cannot memory still descry the old schoolhouse and its porch, somewhat hacked by jackknives, where you spun tops and snapped marbles and do you not recall that life was then calendared by moments, threw itself into nervous knots of glittering hours, even as now, and not spread itself abroad an equable felicity? In college terms, and in years that followed, the young graduate, when the Commencement anniversary returned, though he were in a swamp, would see a festive light and find the air faintly echoing with plausive academic thunders. In solitude and in the country, what dignity distinguishes the holy time! The old Sabbath, or Seventh Day, white with the religions of unknown thousands of years, when this hallowed hour dawns out of the deep—a clean page, which the wise may inscribe with truth, whilst the savage scrawls it with fetishes—the cathedral music of history breathes through it a psalm to our solitude.

So, in the common experience of the scholar, the weathers fit his moods. A thousand tunes the variable wind plays, a thousand spectacles it brings, and each is the frame or dwelling of a new spirit. I used formerly to choose my time with some nicety for each favorite book. One author is good for winter, and one for the dog days. The scholar must look long for the right hour of Plato's *Timaeus*. At last the elect morning arrives, the early dawn—a few lights conspicuous in the heaven, as of a world just created and still becoming—and in its wide leisures we dare open that book.

There are days when the great are near us, when there is no frown on their brow, no condescension even; when they take us by the hand, and we share their thought. These are days which are the carnival of the year. The angels assume flesh, and repeatedly become visible. The imagination of the gods is excited and rushes on every side into forms. Yesterday not a bird peeped; the world was barren, peaked and pining: today 't is inconceivably populous; creation swarms and meliorates.

The days are made on a loom whereof the warp and woof are past and future time. They are majestically dressed, as if every god brought a thread to the skyey web. 'T is pitiful the things by which we are rich or poor—a matter of coins, coats, and carpets, a little more or less stone, or wood, or paint, the fashion of a cloak or hat; like the luck of naked Indians, of whom one is proud in the possession of a glass bead or a red feather, and the rest miserable in the want of it. But the treasures which Nature spent itself to amass—the secular, refined, composite anatomy of man, which all strata go to form, which the prior races, from infusory and saurian, existed to ripen; the surrounding plastic natures; the earth with its foods; the intellectual, temperamenting air; the sea with its invitations; the heaven deep with worlds; and the answering brain and nervous structure replying to these; the eye that looketh into the deeps, which again look back to the eye, abyss to abyss—these, not like a glass bead, or the coins or carpets, are given immeasurably to all.

This miracle is hurled into every beggar's hands. The blue

sky is a covering for a market and for the cherubim and seraphim. The sky is the varnish or glory with which the Artist
has washed the whole work—the verge or confines of matter
and spirit. Nature could no farther go. Could our happiest
dream come to pass in solid fact—could a power open our eyes
to behold "millions of spiritual creatures walk the earth"—I
believe I should find that mid-plain on which they moved
floored beneath and arched above with the same web of blue
depth which weaves itself over me now, as I trudge the streets
on my affairs.

It is singular that our rich English language should have no
word to denote the face of the world. *Kinde* was the old English term, which, however, filled only half the range of our
fine Latin word, with its delicate future tense—*natura, about
to be born*, or what German philosophy denotes as a *becoming*. But nothing expresses that power which seems to work
for beauty alone. The Greek *Kosmos* did; and therefore, with
great propriety, Humboldt entitles his book, which recounts
the last results of science, *Cosmos*.

Such are the days—the earth is the cup, the sky is the cover,
of the immense bounty of Nature which is offered us for our
daily aliment; but what a force of *illusion* begins life with us
and attends us to the end! We are coaxed, flattered and duped
from morn to eve, from birth to death; and where is the old
eye that never saw through the deception? The Hindus represent Maia, the illusory energy of Vishnu, as one of his princi-
pal attributes. As if, in this gale of warring elements which
life is, it was necessary to bind souls to human life as mariners
in a tempest lash themselves to the mast and bulwarks of a
ship, and Nature employed certain illusions as her ties and
straps—a rattle, a doll, an apple, for a child; skates, a river, a
boat, a horse, a gun, for the growing boy; and I will not begin
to name those of the youth and adult, for they are number-
less. Seldom and slowly the mask falls and the pupil is permitted to see that all is one stuff, cooked and painted under
many counterfeit appearances. Hume's doctrine was that the
circumstances vary, the amount of happiness does not; that
the beggar cracking fleas in the sunshine under a hedge, and
the duke rolling by in his chariot; the girl equipped for her
first ball, and the orator returning triumphant from the debate, had different means, but the same quantity of pleasant
excitement.

This element of illusion lends all its force to hide the values
of present time. Who is he that does not always find himself
doing something less than his best task? "What are you doing?"
"Oh, nothing; I have been doing thus, or I shall do so or so,

but now I am only——" Ah! poor dupe, will you never slip out of the web of the master juggler—never learn that as soon as the irrecoverable years have woven their blue glory between today and us these passing hours shall glitter and draw us as the wildest romance and the homes of beauty and poetry? How difficult to deal erect with them! The events they bring, their trade, entertainments and gossip, their urgent work, all throw dust in the eyes and distract attention. He is a strong man who can look them in the eye, see through this juggle, feel their identity, and keep his own; who can know surely that one will be like another to the end of the world, nor permit love, or death, or politics, or money, war or pleasure to draw him from his task.

The world is always equal to itself, and every man in moments of deeper thought is apprised that he is repeating the experiences of the people in the streets of Thebes or Byzantium. An everlasting Now reigns in Nature, which hangs the same roses on our bushes which charmed the Roman and the Chaldaean in their hanging gardens. "To what end, then," he asks, "should I study languages, and traverse countries, to learn so simple truths?"

History of ancient art, excavated cities, recovery of books and inscriptions—yes, the works were beautiful, and the history worth knowing; and academies convene to settle the claims of the old schools. What journeys and measurements—Niebuhr and Müller and Layard—to identify the plain of Troy and Nimroud town! And your homage to Dante costs you so much sailing; and to ascertain the discoverers of America needs as much voyaging as the discovery cost. Poor child! that flexile clay of which these old brothers molded their admirable symbols was not Persian, nor Memphian, nor Teutonic, nor local at all, but was common lime and silex and water and sunlight, the heat of the blood and the heaving of the lungs; it was that clay which thou heldest but now in thy foolish hands, and threwest away to go and seek in vain in sepulchers, mummy pits and old bookshops of Asia Minor, Egypt and England. It was the deep today which all men scorn; the rich poverty which men hate; the populous, all-loving solitude which men quit for the tattle of towns. HE lurks, *he* hides—*he* who is success, reality, joy and power. One of the illusions is that the present hour is not the critical, decisive hour. Write it on your heart that every day is the best day in the year. No man has learned anything rightly until he knows that every day is Doomsday. 'T is the old secret of the gods that they come in low disguises. 'T is the vulgar great who come dizened with gold and jewels. Real kings hide away their crowns in their wardrobes and affect a plain and poor exterior. In the Norse legend of our ancestors, Odin dwells in a fisher's hut and patches a boat. In the Hindu legends, Hari dwells a peasant among peasants. In the Greek legend, Apollo lodges with the shepherds of Admetus, and Jove liked to rusticate among the poor Ethiopians. So, in our history, Jesus is born in a barn, and his twelve peers are fishermen. 'T is the very principle of science that Nature shows herself best in leasts; it was the maxim of Aristotle and Lucretius; and, in modern times, of Swedenborg and of Hahnemann. The order of changes in the egg determines the age of fossil strata. So it was the rule of our poets, in the legends of fairy lore, that the fairies largest in power were the least in size. In the Christian graces, humility stands highest of all, in the form of the Madonna; and in life, this is the secret of the wise. We owe to genius always the same debt, of lifting the curtain from the common, and showing us that divinities are sitting disguised in the seeming gang of gypsies and peddlers. In daily life, what distinguishes the master is the using those materials he has, instead of looking about for what are more renowned, or what others have used well. "A general," said Bonaparte, "always has troops enough, if he only knows how to employ those he has, and bivouacs with them." Do not refuse the employment which the hour brings you, for one more ambitious. The highest heaven of wisdom is alike near from every point, and thou must find it, if at all, by methods native to thyself alone.

That work is ever the more pleasant to the imagination which is not now required. How wistfully, when we have promised to attend the working committee, we look at the distant hills and their seductions!

The use of history is to give value to the present hour and its duty. That is good which commends to me my country, my climate, my means and materials, my associates. I knew a man in a certain religious exaltation who "thought it an honor to wash his own face." He seemed to me more sane than those who hold themselves cheap.

Zoologists may deny that horsehairs in the water change to worms, but I find that whatever is old corrupts, and the past turns to snakes. The reverence for the deeds of our ancestors is a treacherous sentiment. Their merit was not to reverence the old, but to honor the present moment; and we falsely make them excuses of the very habit which they hated and defied.

Another illusion is that there is not time enough for our work. Yet we might reflect that though many creatures eat from one dish, each, according to its constitution, assimilates from the elements what belongs to it, whether time, or space, or light, or water, or food. A snake converts whatever prey the meadow yields him into snake; a fox, into fox; and Peter and John are working up all existence into Peter and John. A poor Indian chief of the Six Nations of New York made a wiser reply than any philosopher, to someone complaining that he had not enough time. "Well," said Red Jacket, "I suppose you have all there is."

A third illusion haunts us, that a long duration, as a year, a decade, a century, is valuable. But an old French sentence says, "God works in moments"—*"En peu d'heure Dieu labeure."* We ask for long life, but 't is deep life, or grand moments, that signify. Let the measure of time be spiritual, not mechanical. Life is unnecessarily long. Moments of insight, of fine personal relation, a smile, a glance—what ample borrowers of eternity they are! Life culminates and concentrates; and Homer said, "The gods ever give to mortals their apportioned share of reason only on one day."

I am of the opinion of the poet Wordsworth, that "there is no real happiness in this life but in intellect and virtue." I am of the opinion of Pliny that "whilst we are musing on these things, we are adding to the length of our lives." I am of the opinion of Glauco, who said, "The measure of life, O Socrates, is, with the wise, the speaking and hearing such discourses as yours."

He only can enrich me who can recommend to me the space between sun and sun. 'T is the measure of a man—his apprehension of a day. For we do not listen with the best regard to the verses of a man who is only a poet, nor to his problems if he is only an algebraist; but if a man is at once acquainted with the geometric foundations of things and with their festal splendor, his poetry is exact and his arithmetic musical. And him I reckon the most learned scholar, not who can unearth for me the buried dynasties of Sesostris and Ptolemy, the Sothiac era, the Olympiads and consulships, but who can unfold the theory of this particular Wednesday. Can he uncover the ligaments concealed from all but piety, which attach the dull men and things we know to the First Cause? These passing fifteen minutes, men think, are time, not eternity; are low and subaltern, are but hope or memory; that is, the way *to* or the way *from* welfare, but not welfare. Can he show their tie? That interpreter shall guide us from a menial and eleemosynary existence into riches and stability. He dignifies the place where he is. This mendicant America, this curious, peering itinerant, imitative America, studious of Greece and

Rome, of England and Germany, will take off its dusty shoes, will take off its glazed traveler's cap and sit at home with repose and deep joy on its face. The world has no such landscape, the eons of history no such hour, the future no equal second opportunity. Now let poets sing! now let arts unfold!

One more view remains. But life is good only when it is magical and musical, a perfect timing and consent, and when we do not anatomize it. You must treat the days respectfully, you must be a day yourself, and not interrogate it like a college professor. The world is enigmatical—everything said, and everything known or done—and must not be taken literally, but genially. We must be at the top of our condition to understand anything rightly. You must hear the bird's song without attempting to render it into nouns and verbs. Cannot we be a little abstemious and obedient? Cannot we let the morning be?

Everything in the universe goes by indirection. There are no straight lines. I remember well the foreign scholar who made a week of my youth happy by his visit. "The savages in the islands," he said, "delight to play with the surf, coming in on the top of the rollers, then swimming out again, and repeat the delicious maneuver for hours. Well, human life is made up of such transits. There can be no greatness without abandonment. But here your very astronomy is an espionage. I dare not go out of doors and see the moon and stars, but they seem to measure my tasks, to ask how many lines or pages are finished since I saw them last. Not so, as I told you, was it in Belleisle. The days at Belleisle were all different, and only joined by a perfect love of the same object. Just to fill the hour —that is happiness. Fill my hour, ye gods, so that I shall not say, whilst I have done this, 'Behold, also, an hour of my life is gone'—but rather, 'I have lived an hour.'"

We do not want factitious men, who can do any literary or professional feat, as, to write poems, or advocate a cause, or carry a measure, for money; or turn their ability indifferently in any particular direction by the strong effort of will. No, what has been best done in the world—the works of genius— cost nothing. There is no painful effort, but it is the spontaneous flowing of the thought. Shakespeare made his *Hamlet* as a bird weaves its nest. Poems have been written between sleeping and waking, irresponsibly. Fancy defines herself:

> *Forms that men spy*
> *With the half-shut eye*
> *In the beams of the setting sun, am I.*

The masters painted for joy, and knew not that virtue had gone out of them. They could not paint the like in cold blood. The masters of English lyric wrote their songs so. It was a fine efflorescence of fine powers; as was said of the letters of the Frenchwoman—"the charming accident of their more charming existence." Then the poet is never the poorer for his song. A song is no song unless the circumstance is free and fine. If the singer sing from a sense of duty or from seeing no way of escape, I had rather have none. Those only can sleep who do not care to sleep; and those only write or speak best who do not too much respect the writing or the speaking.

The same rule holds in science. The savant is often an amateur. His performance is a memoir to the Academy on fish-worms, tadpoles, or spiders' legs; he observes as other academicians observe; he is on stilts at a microscope, and his memoir finished and read and printed, he retreats into his routinary existence, which is quite separate from his scientific. But in Newton, science was as easy as breathing; he used the same wit to weigh the moon that he had used to buckle his shoes; and all his life was simple, wise and majestic. So was it in Archimedes—always selfsame, like the sky. In Linnaeus, in Franklin, the like sweetness and equality—no stilts, no tiptoe; and their results are wholesome and memorable to all men.

In stripping time of its illusions, in seeking to find out what is the heart of the day, we come to the quality of the moment, and drop the duration altogether. It is the depth at which we live and not at all the surface extension that imports. We pierce to the eternity, of which time is the flitting surface; and, really, the least acceleration of thought and the least increase of power of thought, make life to seem and to be of vast duration. We call it time; but when that acceleration and that deepening take effect, it acquires another and a higher name.

There are people who do not need much experimenting; who, after years of activity, say, We knew all this before; who love at first sight and hate at first sight; discern the affinities and repulsions; who do not care so much for conditions as others, for they are always in one condition and enjoy themselves; who dictate to others and are not dictated to; who in their consciousness of deserving success constantly slight the ordinary means of attaining it; who have self-existence and self-help; who are suffered to be themselves in society; who are great in the present; who have no talents, or care not to have them—being that which was before talent, and shall be after it, and of which talent seems only a tool: this is character, the highest name at which philosophy has arrived.

'T is not important how the hero does this or this, but what he is. What he is will appear in every gesture and syllable. In this way the moment and the character are one.

It is a fine fable for the advantage of character over talent, the Greek legend of the strife of Jove and Phoebus. Phoebus challenged the gods, and said, "Who will outshoot the far-darting Apollo?" Zeus said, "I will." Mars shook the lots in his helmet, and that of Apollo leaped out first. Apollo stretched his bow and shot his arrow into the extreme west. Then Zeus rose, and with one stride cleared the whole distance, and said, "Where shall I shoot? there is no space left." So the bowman's prize was adjudged to him who drew no bow.

And this is the progress of every earnest mind; from the works of man and the activity of the hands to a delight in the faculties which rule them; from a respect to the works to a wise wonder at this mystic element of time in which he is conditioned; from local skills and the economy which reckons the amount of production per hour to the finer economy which respects the quality of what is done, and the right we have to the work, or the fidelity with which it flows from ourselves; then to the depth of thought it betrays, looking to its universality, or that its roots are in eternity, not in time. Then it flows from character, that sublime health which values one moment as another, and makes us great in all conditions, and as the only definition we have of freedom and power.

From *Society and Solitude*
Volume VII

Part II

POEMS

Boston Hymn

READ IN MUSIC HALL, JANUARY 1, 1863

The word of the Lord by night
To the watching Pilgrims came,
As they sat by the seaside,
And filled their hearts with flame.

God said, I am tired of kings,
I suffer them no more;
Up to my ear the morning brings
The outrage of the poor.

Think ye I made this ball
A field of havoc and war,
Where tyrants great and tyrants small
Might harry the weak and poor?

My angel—his name is Freedom—
Choose him to be your king;
He shall cut pathways east and west
And fend you with his wing.

Lo! I uncover the land
Which I hid of old time in the West,
As the sculptor uncovers the statue
When he has wrought his best;

I show Columbia, of the rocks
Which dip their foot in the seas
And soar to the air-borne flocks
Of clouds and the boreal fleece.

I will divide my goods;
Call in the wretch and slave:
None shall rule but the humble,
And none but Toil shall have.

I will have never a noble,
No lineage counted great;
Fishers and choppers and plowmen
Shall constitute a state.

Go, cut down trees in the forest
And trim the straightest boughs;
Cut down trees in the forest
And build me a wooden house.

Call the people together,
The young men and the sires,
The digger in the harvest-field,
Hireling and him that hires;

And here in a pine state-house
They shall choose men to rule
In every needful faculty,
In church and state and school.

Lo, now! if these poor men
Can govern the land and sea
And make just laws below the sun,
As planets faithful be.

And ye shall succor men;
'T is nobleness to serve;
Help them who cannot help again:
Beware from right to swerve.

I break your bonds and masterships,
And I unchain the slave:
Free be his heart and hand henceforth
As wind and wandering wave.

I cause from every creature
His proper good to flow:
As much as he is and doeth,
So much he shall bestow.

But, laying hands on another
To coin his labor and sweat,
He goes in pawn to his victim
For eternal years in debt.

Today unbind the captive,
So only are ye unbound;
Lift up a people from the dust,
Trump of their rescue, sound!

Pay ransom to the owner
And fill the bag to the brim.
Who is the owner? The slave is owner,
And ever was. Pay him.

O North! give him beauty for rags,
And honor, O South! for his shame;
Nevada! coin thy golden crags
With Freedom's image and name.

Up! and the dusky race
That sat in darkness long—
Be swift their feet as antelopes,
And as behemoth strong.

Come, East and West and North,
By races, as snow-flakes,
And carry my purpose forth,
Which neither halts nor shakes.

My will fulfilled shall be,
For, in daylight or in dark,
My thunderbolt has eyes to see
His way home to the mark.

Good-Bye

Good-bye, proud world! I'm going home:
Thou art not my friend, and I'm not thine.
Long through thy weary crowds I roam;
A river-ark on the ocean brine,
Long I've been tossed like the driven foam;
But now, proud world! I'm going home.

Good-bye to Flattery's fawning face;
To Grandeur with his wise grimace;
To upstart Wealth's averted eye;
To supple Office, low and high;
To crowded halls, to court and street;
To frozen hearts and hasting feet;
To those who go, and those who come;
Good-bye, proud world! I'm going home.

I am going to my own hearth-stone,
Bosomed in yon green hills alone—
A secret nook in a pleasant land,
Whose groves the frolic fairies planned;
Where arches green, the livelong day,
Echo the blackbird's roundelay,
And vulgar feet have never trod
A spot that is sacred to thought and God.

O, when I am safe in my sylvan home,
I tread on the pride of Greece and Rome;
And when I am stretched beneath the pines,
Where the evening star so holy shines,
I laugh at the lore and the pride of man,
At the sophist schools and the learned clan;
For what are they all, in their high conceit,
When man in the bush with God may meet?

Ode

INSCRIBED TO W. H. CHANNING

Though loath to grieve
The evil time's sole patriot,
I cannot leave
My honied thought
For the priest's cant,
Or statesman's rant.

If I refuse
My study for their politique,
Which at the best is trick,
The angry Muse
Puts confusion in my brain.

But who is he that prates
Of the culture of mankind,
Of better arts and life?
Go, blindworm, go,
Behold the famous States
Harrying Mexico
With rifle and with knife!

Or who, with accent bolder,
Dare praise the freedom-loving mountaineer?
I found by thee, O rushing Contoocook!
And in thy valleys, Agiochook!
The jackals of the Negro-holder.

The God who made New Hampshire
Taunted the lofty land
With little men;—
Small bat and wren
House in the oak:—
If earth-fire cleave
The upheaved land, and bury the folk,
The southern crocodile would grieve.
Virtue palters; Right is hence;
Freedom praised, but hid;
Funeral eloquence
Rattles the coffin-lid.

What boots thy zeal,
O glowing friend,
That would indignant rend
The northland from the south?
Wherefore? to what good end?
Boston Bay and Bunker Hill
Would serve things still;—
Things are of the snake.

The horseman serves the horse,
The neatherd serves the neat,
The merchant serves the purse,
The eater serves his meat;
'T is the day of the chattel,
Web to weave, and corn to grind;
Things are in the saddle,
And ride mankind.

There are two laws discrete,
Not reconciled—
Law for man, and law for thing;
The last builds town and fleet,
But it runs wild,
And doth the man unking.

'T is fit the forest fall,
The steep be graded,
The mountain tunneled,
The sand shaded,
The orchard planted,
The glebe tilled,
The prairie granted,
The steamer built.

Let man serve law for man;
Live for friendship, live for love,
For truth's and harmony's behoof;
The state may follow how it can,
As Olympus follows Jove.

    Yet do not I implore
The wrinkled shopman to my sounding woods,
Nor bid the unwilling senator
Ask votes of thrushes in the solitudes.
Every one to his chosen work;—
Foolish hands may mix and mar;
Wise and sure the issues are.
Round they roll till dark is light,
Sex to sex, and even to odd;—
The over-god
Who marries Right to Might,
Who peoples, unpeoples—
He who exterminates
Races by stronger races,
Black by white faces—
Knows to bring honey
Out of the lion;
Grafts gentlest scion
On pirate and Turk.

The Cossack eats Poland,
Like stolen fruit;
Her last noble is ruined,
Her last poet mute:
Straight, into double band
The victors divide;
Half for freedom strike and stand—
The astonished Muse finds thousands at her side.

Blight

Give me truths;
For I am weary of the surfaces,
And die of inanition. If I knew
Only the herbs and simples of the wood,
Rue, cinquefoil, gill, vervain and agrimony,
Blue-vetch and trillium, hawkweed, sassafras,
Milkweeds, and murky brakes, quaint pipes and sundew,

And rare and virtuous roots, which in these woods
Draw untold juices from the common earth,
Untold, unknown, and I could surely spell
Their fragrance, and their chemistry apply
By sweet affinities of human flesh,
Driving the foe and stablishing the friend—
O, that were much, and I could be a part
Of the round day, related to the sun
And planted world, and full executor
Of their imperfect functions.
But these young scholars, who invade our hills,
Bold as the engineer who fells the wood,
And traveling often in the cut he makes,
Love not the flower they pluck, and know it not,
And all their botany is Latin names.
The old men studied magic in the flowers,
And human fortunes in astronomy,
And an omnipotence in chemistry,
Preferring things to names, for these were men,
Were unitarians of the united world,
And, wheresoever their clear eye-beams fell,
They caught the footsteps of the SAME. Our eyes
Are armed, but we are strangers to the stars,
And strangers to the mystic beast and bird,
And strangers to the plant and to the mine.
The injured elements say, "Not in us";
And night and day, ocean and continent,
Fire, plant and mineral say, "Not in us";
And haughtily return us stare for stare.
For we invade them impiously for gain;
We devastate them unreligiously,
And coldly ask their pottage, not their love.
Therefore they shove us from them, yield to us
Only what to our griping toil is due;
But the sweet affluence of love and song,
The rich results of the divine consents
Of man and earth, of world beloved and lover,
The nectar and ambrosia, are withheld;
And in the midst of spoils and slaves, we thieves
And pirates of the universe, shut out
Daily to a more thin and outward rind,
Turn pale and starve. Therefore, to our sick eyes,
The stunted trees look sick, the summer short,
Clouds shade the sun, which will not tan our hay,
And nothing thrives to reach its natural term;
And life, shorn of its venerable length,

Even at its greatest space is a defeat,
And dies in anger that it was a dupe;
And, in its highest noon and wantonness,
Is early frugal, like a beggar's child;
Even in the hot pursuit of the best aims
And prizes of ambition, checks its hand,
Like Alpine cataracts frozen as they leaped,
Chilled with a miserly comparison
Of the toy's purchase with the length of life.

Concord Hymn

SUNG AT THE COMPLETION OF THE BATTLE MONUMENT, JULY 4, 1837

By the rude bridge that arched the flood,
  Their flag to April's breeze unfurled,
Here once the embattled farmers stood
  And fired the shot heard round the world.

The foe long since in silence slept;
  Alike the conqueror silent sleeps;
And Time the ruined bridge has swept
  Down the dark stream which seaward creeps.

On this green bank, by this soft stream,
  We set today a votive stone;
That memory may their deed redeem,
  When, like our sires, our sons are gone.

Spirit, that made those heroes dare
  To die, and leave their children free,
Bid Time and Nature gently spare
  The shaft we raise to them and thee.

Ode

SUNG IN THE TOWN HALL, CONCORD, JULY 4, 1857

O tenderly the haughty day
  Fills his blue urn with fire;
One morn is in the mighty heaven,
  And one in our desire.

The cannon booms from town to town,
    Our pulses beat not less,
The joy-bells chime their tidings down,
    Which children's voices bless.

For He that flung the broad blue fold
    O'er-mantling land and sea,
One third part of the sky unrolled
    For the banner of the free.

The men are ripe of Saxon kind
    To build an equal state—
To take the statute from the mind
    And make of duty fate.

United States! the ages plead—
    Present and Past in under-song—
Go put your creed into your deed,
    Nor speak with double tongue.

For sea and land don't understand,
    Nor skies without a frown
See rights for which the one hand fights
    See the other cloven down.

Be just at home; then write your scroll
    Of honor o'er the sea,
And bid the broad Atlantic roll,
    A ferry of the free.

And henceforth there shall be no chain,
    Save underneath the sea
The wires shall murmur through the main
    Sweet songs of liberty.

The conscious stars accord above,
    The waters wild below,
And under, through the cable wove,
    Her fiery errands go.

For He that worketh high and wise,
    Nor pauses in his plan,
Will take the sun out of the skies
    Ere freedom out of man.

Terminus

It is time to be old,
To take in sail:—
The god of bounds,
Who sets to seas a shore,
Came to me in his fatal rounds,
And said: "No more!
No farther shoot
Thy broad ambitious branches, and thy root.
Fancy departs: no more invent;
Contract thy firmament
To compass of a tent.
There's not enough for this and that,
Make thy option which of two;
Economize the falling river,
Not the less revere the Giver,
Leave the many and hold the few.
Timely wise accept the terms,
Soften the fall with wary foot;
A little while
Still plan and smile,
And—fault of novel germs—
Mature the unfallen fruit.
Curse, if thou wilt, thy sires,
Bad husbands of their fires,
Who, when they gave thee breath,
Failed to bequeath
The needful sinew stark as once,
The Baresark marrow to thy bones,
But left a legacy of ebbing veins,
Inconstant heat and nerveless reins—
Amid the Muses, left thee deaf and dumb,
Amid the gladiators, halt and numb."

As the bird trims her to the gale,
I trim myself to the storm of time,
I man the rudder, reef the sail,
Obey the voice at eve obeyed at prime:
"Lowly faithful, banish fear,
Right onward drive unharmed;
The port, well worth the cruise, is near,
And every wave is charmed."

The Past

The debt is paid,
The verdict said,
The Furies laid,
The plague is stayed.
All fortunes made;
Turn the key and bolt the door,
Sweet is death forevermore.
Nor haughty hope, nor swart chagrin,
Nor murdering hate, can enter in.
All is now secure and fast;
Not the gods can shake the Past;
Flies-to the adamantine door
Bolted down forevermore.
None can re-enter there—
No thief so politic,
No Satan with a royal trick
Steal in by window, chink, or hole,
To bind or unbind, add what lacked,
Insert a leaf, or forge a name,
New-face or finish what is packed,
Alter or mend eternal Fact.

Compensation

The wings of Time are black and white,
Pied with morning and with night.
Mountain tall and ocean deep
Trembling balance duly keep.
In changing moon and tidal wave
Glows the feud of Want and Have.
Gauge of more and less through space,
Electric star or pencil plays,
The lonely Earth amid the balls
That hurry through the eternal halls,
A makeweight flying to the void,
Supplemental asteroid,
Or compensatory spark,
Shoots across the neutral Dark.

Man's the elm, and Wealth the vine;
Stanch and strong the tendrils twine:
Though the frail ringlets thee deceive,
None from its stock that vine can reave.

Fear not, then, thou child infirm,
There's no god dare wrong a worm;
Laurel crowns cleave to deserts,
And power to him who power exerts.
Hast not thy share? On winged feet,
Lo! it rushes thee to meet;
And all that Nature made thy own,
Floating in air or pent in stone,
Will rive the hills and swim the sea,
And, like thy shadow, follow thee.

Nature

I

A subtle chain of countless rings
The next unto the farthest brings;
The eye reads omens where it goes,
And speaks all languages the rose;
And, striving to be man, the worm
Mounts through all the spires of form.

II

The rounded world is fair to see,
Nine times folded in mystery:
Though baffled seers cannot impart
The secret of its laboring heart,
Throb thine with Nature's throbbing breast,
And all is clear from east to west.
Spirit that lurks each form within
Beckons to spirit of its kin;
Self-kindled every atom glows
And hints the future which it owes.

Quatrains

Orator

He who has no hands
Perforce must use his tongue;
Foxes are so cunning
Because they are not strong.

Climacteric

I am not wiser for my age,
Nor skillful by my grief;
Life loiters at the book's first page—
Ah! could we turn the leaf.

from Life

Of all wit's uses the main one
Is to live well with who has none.

Music

Let me go where'er I will,
I hear a sky-born music still:
It sounds from all things old,
It sounds from all things young,
From all that's fair, from all that's foul,
Peals out a cheerful song.

It is not only in the rose,
It is not only in the bird,
Nor only where the rainbow glows,
Nor in the song of woman heard,
But in the darkest, meanest things
There alway, alway something sings.

'T is not in the high stars alone,
Nor in the cup of budding flowers,
Nor in the redbreast's mellow tone,
Nor in the bow that smiles in showers,
But in the mud and scum of things
There alway, alway something sings.

Fame

Ah Fate, cannot a man
   Be wise without a beard?
East, West, from Beer to Dan,
   Say, was it never heard
That wisdom might in youth be gotten,
Or wit be ripe before 't was rotten?

He pays too high a price
   For knowledge and for fame
Who sells his sinews to be wise,
   His teeth and bones to buy a name,
And crawls through life a paralytic
To earn the praise of bard and critic.

Were it not better done,
   To dine and sleep through forty years;
Be loved by few; be feared by none;
   Laugh life away; have wine for tears;
And take the mortal leap undaunted,
Content that all we asked was granted?

But Fate will not permit
   The seed of gods to die,
Nor suffer sense to win from wit
   Its guerdon in the sky,
Nor let us hide, whate'er our pleasure,
The world's light underneath a measure.

Go then, sad youth, and shine;
   Go, sacrifice to Fame;
Put youth, joy, health upon the shrine,
   And life to fan the flame;
Being for Seeming bravely barter
And die to Fame a happy martyr.

Good Hope

The cup of life is not so shallow
That we have drained the best,
That all the wine at once we swallow
And lees make all the rest.

Maids of as soft a bloom shall marry
As Hymen yet hath blessed,
And fairer forms are in the quarry
Than Phidias released.

Part III

APOTHEGMS

Excerpts from the Journals

(The numbers following each quotation indicate [1] the year in the 1800s in which the item was entered in Emerson's journal, [2] his age at the time, [3] the number of the volume in which it appears and [4] the page number.)

Great actions, from their nature, are not done in the closet; they are performed in the face of the sun, and in behalf of the world. ('22-18-I 118)

Greatness is a property for which no man gets credit too soon; it must be possessed long before it is acknowledged. ('22-18-I 122)

He rejoices in the birthright of a country where the freedom of opinion and action is so perfect that every man enjoys exactly that consideration to which he is entitled, and each mind, as in the bosom of a family, institutes and settles a comparison of its powers with those of its fellow, and quietly takes that stand which nature intended for it. ('22-19-I 161)

Men's minds visit heaven as they visit earth, and hence the Turkish heaven is a Harem; the Scandinavian, a hunting field; the Arabian, a place of wheaten cakes and murmuring fountains. We've supple understandings and so it comes that a new religion ever suits itself to the state in which 't is born, whether despotism or democracy, as Montesquieu has remarked. ('22-19-I 191)

Of Professor N., Shakespeare long ago wrote the good and bad character:

> *Oh it is excellent*
> *To have a giant's strength, but it is tyrannous*
> *To use it like a giant.*

('22-19-I 195)

It is often alleged, with a great mass of instances to support the assertion, that the spirit of philosophy and a liberal mind is at discord with the principles of religion, so far, at least, as to imply that hoary error that religion is a prejudice which statesmen cherish in the vulgar as a wholesome terror. ('23-19-I 238, 239)

Alas! The wildest dreams of poetry have uttered no such thing. There *is* a huge and disproportionate abundance of *evil* on earth. Indeed the good that is here is but a little island of light amidst the unbounded ocean. ('23-19-I 246)

But the vast rapidity with which the deserts and forests of the interior of this country are peopled have led patriots to fear lest the nation grow *too fast* for its virtue and its peace.
('23-19-I 247)

I thought how History has a twofold effect, viz., intellectual pleasure and moral pain. ('23-20-I 268)

But the quiet wisdom of History, as she winds along her way through sixty centuries, speaks of no wonders, and of little glory. ('23-20-I 300)

Keep the moral fountains pure. Open schools. ('24-20-I 315)

We were not made to breathe oxygen, or to talk poetry, or to be always wise. We are sorry habitants of an imperfect world, and it will not do for such beings to take admiration by storm. ('24-20-I 315)

The kingdom of thought is a proud aristocracy.
('24-20-I 317)

Franklin was political economist, a natural philosopher, a moral philosopher, and a statesman; invests and dismisses subtle theories (e.g. of the Earth) with extraordinary ease. Unconscious of any mental effort in detailing the profoundest solutions of phenomena, and therefore makes no parade. He writes to a friend when [aged] 80, "I feel as if I was intruding among posterity when I ought to be abed and asleep. I look upon death to be as necessary to the constitution as sleep. We shall rise refreshed in the morning." ('23-20-I 320)

Agriculture is the venerable Mother of all the arts, and compared with the pastoral or the hunting life is certainly friendly to the mind; it is next to commerce in this respect, but must necessarily precede commerce in the growth of society. Virtue and good sense and a contemplative turn are universally characteristic of an agricultural people. In the city, "those who think must govern those who toil"; in the country, the laborers both toil and govern. ('23-20-I 322)

But why are the askers of praise ridiculous, and not the askers of silver? ('24-20-I 339)

Teach us no more arts, but how those which are already should be learned. ('24-20-I 344)

Material beauty perishes or palls. Intellectual beauty limits admiration to seasons and ages; hath its ebbs and flows of delight. . . . But moral beauty is lovely, imperishable, perfect. ('24-20-I 345)

> *Goodbye, proud world, I'm going home:*
> *Thou'rt not my friend and I'm not thine.*
> *Long I've been tossed like the salt sea foam,*
> *All day mid weary crowds I roam—*
> *And O my home, O holy home!*
> *Goodbye to Flattery's fawning face,*
> *To Grandeur with his wise grimace,*
> *To upstart Wealth's averted eye,*
> *To supple Office, low and high,*
> *To frozen hearts and hasting feet,*
> *To noisy Toil, to Court and Street,*
> *To those who go, and those who come;*
> *Goodbye, proud World! I'm going home.*
>   *I'm going to my own hearthstone,*
> *Bosomed in yon green hills alone;*
> *Sweet summer birds are warbling there.*

('24-20-I 347, 348)

I fear the progress of metaphysical philosophy may be found to consist in nothing else than the progressive introduction of opposite metaphors. ('24-20-I 348, 349)

For men graduate their respect, not by the secret wealth, but by the outward use; not by the power to understand, but by the power to act. ('24 20-I 360)

But you have no literature. It is admitted we have none. But we have what is better. We have a government and a national spirit that is better than poems or histories, and these have a premature ripeness that is incompatible with the rapid production of the latter. We should take shame to ourselves as sluggish and Bœotian if it were righteously said that we had done nothing for ourselves, neither in learning, nor arts, nor government, nor political economy. But we see and feel that in the space of two generations this nation has taken such a start as already to outstrip the bold freedom of modern speculation which ordinarily (universally, but for this case) is considerably in advance of practice. ('24-21-I 388, 389)

Why has my motley diary no jokes? Because it is a soliloquy and every man is grave alone. ('24-21-I 393)

The two chief differences among men (touching the talents) consist, 1, in the different degrees of *attention* they are able to command; 2, in the unlike expression they give to the same ideas. ('24-21-I 393)

I confess I am a little cynical on some topics, and when a whole nation is roaring Patriotism at the top of its voice, I am fain to explore the cleanness of its hands and purity of its heart. I have generally found the gravest and most useful citizens are not the easiest provoked to swell the noise, though they may be punctual at the polls. ('24-21-II 21, 22)

Faith is a telescope. ('24-21-II 27)

But the dead sleep in their moonless night; my business is with the living. ('25-21-II 41, 42)

Since it is not truth, but bread, that men seek, and when bread is procured, the exercise of their faculties delights them not so much as love and pride, it follows that very different agents enter into the offices of life from those of which wise men would compose their ideal Commonwealths.

('25-21-II 43)

It is the part of wisdom, therefore, to choose that safe middle path which shall avail itself of the good and escape as much of the evil as is possible. . . . ('25-21-II 60)

There is reason in Action. ('25-21-II 62)

Choose a sensible man to a responsible place rather than a man versed in the particular art which is to be taught, inasmuch as a method of acquiring truth is better than the truth it has already ascertained. Let your discipline liberalize the mind of a boy rather than teach him sciences, that he may have means, more than results.

The Indian will give his bow for the knife with which it was made. ('25-21-II 67)

I say that sin is ignorance, that the thief steals from himself; that he who practices fraud is himself the dupe of the fraud he practices, those whoso borrows runs in his own debt; and whoso gives to another benefits himself to the same amount. ('26-22-II 75)

> *He pays too high a price*
> *For knowledge and for fame*
> *Who sells his sinews to be wise,*
> *His teeth and bones to buy a name,*
> *And crawls half-dead, a paralytic,*
> *To earn the praise of bard and critick.*

> *Is it not better done*
> *To dine and sleep through forty years,*
> *Be loved by few, be feared by none,*
> *Laugh life away, have wine for tears,*
> *And take the mortal leap undaunted,*
> *Content that all we asked was granted?*
> ('26-22-II 81)

Ballads, *bon mots,* anecdotes, give us better insight into the depths of past centuries than grave and voluminous chronicles. "A Straw," says Selden, "thrown up into the air will show how the wind sits, which cannot be learned by casting up a stone." ('26-23-II 97)

There is no thought which is not seed as well as fruit. It spawns like fish. ('26-23-II 97)

A man may propose a course of exercises designed to strengthen his arm with such indiscreet zeal as to paralyze it. ('26-23-II 106)

Others laugh, weep, sell or proselyte. I admire.
('26-23-II 111)

Yesterday I attended the funeral solemnities in Faneuil Hall in honor of John Adams and Thomas Jefferson. The oration of Mr. Webster was worthy of his fame, and what is much more, was worthy of the august occasion. Never, I think, were the awful charms of person, manners and voice outdone. For though in the beginning unpromising, and in other parts imperfect, in what was truly grand he fully realized the boldest conception of eloquence. ('26-23-II 113)

It is melancholy to suffer on account of others without any appeal to our own self-devotion as the cause. ('26-23-II 115)

Few things need more philosophy than the study of history. For it is not easy or safe to look long on these turning wheels, lest we grow giddy. ('26-23-II 127)

If the string cannot be made to accord, it must be broken. ('27-23-II 145)

Politeness ruins conversation. ('27-23-II 171)

What set me forth on this odd declamation was the curious moral quality we call patriotism, which seems to flourish best, like flowers, in lowest grounds. ('27-23-II 174)

To believe too much is dangerous, because it is the near neighbor of unbelief. Pantheism leads to Atheism.
('27-23-II 178)

He has seen but half the Universe who never has been shown the house of Pain. ('27-23-II 180)

"A necessary preliminary, however, is to ascertain how far we can have an *absolute* notion of truth. This is paramount to all subsequent indignations." ('27-23-II 188)

"Age gives good advice when it is no longer able to give a bad example." ('28-24-II 228)

There's a great difference between good poetry and ever-lasting poetry. ('28-24-II 233)

I am always uneasy when the conversation turns in my presence upon popular ignorance and the duty of adapting our public harangues and writings to the mind of the people. 'T is all pedantry and ignorance. The people know as much and reason as well as we do. None so quick as they to discern brilliant genius or solid parts. And I observe that all those who use this cant most, are such as do not rise above mediocrity of understanding. ('28-25-II 243)

But the only evil I find in idleness is unhappiness.
('28-25-II 244)

I like a man who likes to see a fine barn as well as a good tragedy. ('28-25-II 246)

Sir Henry Wotton says of the institutions of Education, that they are more important than the laws, because, if young trees were at first well fastened at the root, they would little want any props and fence afterwards. ('28-25-II 246)

The way for us to be wise is to foresee the great tendencies and currents of the universe in the leanings and motions of the little straws which our eyes can see. ('29-26-II 269)

A man is known by the books he reads, by the company he keeps, by the praise he gives, by his dress, by his tastes, by his distastes, by the stories he tells, by his gait, by the motion of his eye, by the look of his house, of his chamber; for nothing on earth is solitary, but everything hath affinities infinite. . . . ('30-27-II 300)

There are two kinds of pertinence. One to the circumstances, and one to the thing itself. ('30-27-II 305)

I would have a man trust himself, believe that he has all the endowments necessary to balance each other in a perfect character, if only he will allow them all fair play. ('30-27-II 309)

A great deal may be learned from studying the history of Enthusiasts. ('30-27-II 318)

Means and ends. Goodness consists in seeking goodness for its own sake. Heaven is not something else than virtue. Truth must be sought, not for farther ends, but must be the ultimate end. ('30-27-II 322)

Trust to that prompting within you. ('31-27-II 368)

It is a luxury to be understood. ('31-27-II 368)

Persist, only persist in seeking the truth. Persist in saying you do not know what you do not know, and you do not care for what you do not care. . . . ('31-27-II 379)

It is remarkable that we cannot be willing to say, *I do not know*. ('31-28-II 393)

No man can write well who thinks there is any choice of words for him. ('31-28-II 401)

The effect of a fanciful word misplaced, is like that of a horn of exquisite polish growing on a human head.

('31-28-II 401)

In good writing, words become one with things.

('31-28-II 401)

The things taught in colleges and schools are not an education, but the means of education. ('31-28-II 404)

Books are to be read, and every library should be a circulating library. ('31-28-II 407)

"Some minds think about things; others think the things themselves." SCHELLING. ('31-28-II 422)

Our very defects are thus shadows of our virtues.

('31-28-II 436)

I do not fear death. I believe those who fear it have borrowed the terrors through which they see it from vulgar opinion, and not from their own minds. My own mind is the direct revelation which I have from God and far least liable to mistake in telling his will of any revelation. ('31-28-II 438)

Books are apt to turn reason out of doors. ('31-28-II 441)

The bubble of the Present is every moment hardening into the flint of the Past. ('32-28-II 485)

I know very well that it is a bad sign in a man to be too conscientious, and stick at gnats. The most desperate scoundrels have been the over-refiners. ('32-29-II 497)

> I will not live out of me.
> I will not see with others' eyes;
> My good is good, my evil ill.
> I would be free; I cannot be
> While I take things as others please to rate them.
> I dare attempt to lay out my own road.

('32-29-II 518)

To live in a field of pumpkins, yet eat no pie!

('32-29-II 525)

Let us insist on having our say. ('33-29-III 14)

And how men can toil and scratch so hard for things so dry, lifeless, unsightly, as these famous dogmas, when the divine beauty of the truths to which they are related lies behind them; how they can make such a fuss about the case, and never open it to see the jewel, is strange, pitiful.

('33-30-III 160)

God save a great man from a little circle of flatterers.

('33-30-III 187)

I wrote above something concerning the golden mean wherein grace and safety lies. ('33-30-III 195)

The purpose of life seems to be to acquaint man with himself. He is not to live to the future as described to him, but to live to the real future by living to the real present.

('33-30-III 201)

The teacher of the coming age must occupy himself in the study and explanation of the moral constitution of man more than in the elucidation of difficult texts. ('33-30-III 225)

"It is not permitted to a man to corrupt himself for the sake of mankind." ROUSSEAU. ('33-30-III 230)

I will not refer, defer, confer, prefer, differ. I renounce the whole family of *fero*. I embrace absolute life. ('33-30-III 232)

It is very seldom that a man is truly alone. He needs to retire as much from his solitude as he does from society, into very loneliness. While I am reading and writing in my chamber I am not alone, though there is nobody there. There is one means of procuring solitude which to me, and I apprehend to all men, is effectual, and that is to go to the window and look at the stars. If they do not startle you and call you off from vulgar matters I know not what will. ('34-30-III 263, 264)

I count no man much because he cows or silences me. Any fool can do that. But if his conversation enriches or rejoices me, I must reckon him wise. ('34-30-III 265)

Wherever the truth is injured, defend it. You are there on that spot within hearing of that word, within sight of that action, as a Witness, to the end that you should speak for it.

> *My Heritage how long and wide—*
> *Time is my heritage, my field is Time.*
>
> ('34-30-III 269)

Write solid sentences, and you can even spare punctuation.
('34-30-III 272)

All the mistakes I make arise from forsaking my own station and trying to see the object from another person's point
of view. I read so absolute a self-thinker as Carlyle, and am
convinced of the riches of wisdom that ever belong to the man
who utters his own thought with a divine confidence that it
must be true if he heard it there. ('34-30-III 272, 273)

I had observed long since that, to give the thought a just and
full expression, I must not prematurely utter it. Better not talk
of the matter you are writing out. It was as if you had let the
spring snap too soon. I was glad to find Goethe say to the
same point, that "he who seeks a hidden treasure must not
speak." ('34-30-III 273)

He must feel and teach that the best wisdom cannot be
communicated; must be acquired by every soul for itself.
('34-30-III 280)

Literature is the conversion of action into thought for the
delight of the Intellect. It is the turning into thought what
was done without thought.
It aims at ideal truth. But it is only approximation. The
word can never cover the thing. You don't expect to describe
a sunrise. ('34-30-III 286)

Intellectual courage, intellectual duty says we must not
blink the question, we must march up to it and sit down before
it and watch there, incessantly getting as close as we can to
the black wall, and watch and watch, until slowly lines and
handles and characters shall appear on its surface and we
shall learn to open the gate and enter the fortress, unroof it
and lay bare its ground-plan to the day. ('34-30-III 295)

I will not affect to suffer. Be my life then a long gratitude. I
will trust my instincts. ('34-30-III 299)

The solitary bird that sung in the pine tree reminded me of
one talker who has nothing to say alone, but when friends
come, and the conversation grows loud, is forthwith set into

intense activity, mechanically echoing and strengthening everything that is said, without any regard to the subject or to truth. ('34-31-III 304)

Everything teaches, even dilettantism. The dilettante does not, to be sure, learn anything of botany by playing with his microscope, and with the terminology of plants, but he learns what dilettantism is; he distinguishes between what he knows and what he affects to know, and through some pain and self-accusation he is attaining to things themselves.

('34-31-III 307, 308)

Webster's speeches seem to be the utmost that the unpoetic West has accomplished or can. We all lean on England; scarce a verse, a page, a newspaper, but is writ in imitation of English forms; our very manners and conversation are traditional, and sometimes the life seems dying out of all literature, and this enormous paper currency of Words is accepted instead. ('34-31-III 308)

But Goethe was a person who hated words that did not stand for things, and had a sympathy with everything that existed, and therefore never writes without saying something. ('34-31-III 313, 314)

I wish to be a true and free man. . . . ('34-31-III 319)

We sit down with intent to write truly, and end with making a book that contains no thought of ours, but merely the tune of the time. ('34-31-III 333)

Man is great, not in his goals, but in his transition from state to state. Great in act, but instantly dwarfed by self-indulgence. ('34-31-III 349)

The root and seed of democracy is the doctrine, Judge for yourself. Reverence thyself. It is the inevitable effect of that doctrine, where it has any effect (which is rare), to insulate the partisan, to make each man a state. At the same time it replaces the dead with a living check in a true, delicate reverence for superior, congenial minds. "How is the king greater than I, if he is not more just?" ('34-31-III 369, 370)

Nature keeps much on her table, but more in her closet. ('34-31-III 411)

It is a great happiness when two good minds meet, both culti-vated and with such difference of learning as to excite each the other's curiosity, and such similarity as to understand each other's allusions in the Touch-and-go of conversation. They make each other strong and confident. . . . The unspoken part of this conversation is the most valuable. ('35-31-III 440)

Never utter the truism, but live it among men and by your fireside.

This rebellious Understanding is the incorrigible liar; con-vict him of perfidy, and he answers you with a new fib. No man speaks the truth or lives a true life two minutes together. ('35-31-III 455)

The *Quarterly Review* toils to prove that there is no selfish aristocracy in America, but that every man shakes hands heart-ily with every other man, and the chancellor says, "My brother, the grocer." And to fix this fact will be to stamp us with desired infamy. I earnestly wish it could be proved. I wish it could be shown that no distinctions created by a con-temptible pride existed here, and none but the natural ones of talent and virtue. But I fear we do not deserve the praise of this Reviewer's ill opinion. The only ambition which truth allows is to be the servant of all. The last shall be first.
('35-32-III 509)

A fact is only a fulcrum of the spirit. It is the terminus of a past thought, but only a means now to new sallies of the imagination and new progress of wisdom. . . . ('36-33-IV 71)

When I spoke or speak of the democratic element, I do not mean that ill thing, vain and loud, which writes newspapers, spouts at caucuses, and sells its lies for gold, but that spirit of love for the general good whose name this assumes. There is nothing of the true democratic element in what is called De-mocracy; it must fall, being wholly commercial. I beg I may not be understood to praise anything which the soul in you does not honor, however grateful may be names to your ear and your pocket. ('36-33-IV 95)

The house praises the carpenter. ('36-33-IV 111)

A man knows no more to any purpose than he practices. "He that despises little things shall perish by little and little." ('36-33-IV 125)

Otherism. I see plainly the charm which belongs to alienation or otherism. "What wine do you like best, O Diogenes?" "Another's," replied the sage. What fact, thought, word, like we best? Another's. The very sentiment I expressed yesterday without heed, shall sound memorable to me tomorrow if I hear it from another. My own book I read with new eyes when a stranger has praised it. ('36-33-IV 155)

Do you not see that a man is a bundle of relations, that his entire strength consists not in his properties, but in his innumerable relations? ('36-33-IV 167)

The only aristocracy in this country is—the editors of newspapers. ('37-33-IV 187)

Economy does not consist in saving the coal, but in using the time whilst it burns. ('37-33-IV 225)

Courage consists in the conviction that they with whom you contend are no more than you. If we believed in the existence of strict individuals, natures, that is, not radically identical but unknown, immeasurable, we should never dare to fight.
('37-34-IV 257)

The two most noble things in the world are Learning and Virtue. The latter is health, the former is power. The latter is Being, the former is Action. But let them go erect evermore and strike sail to none. ('37-34-IV 261)

A man should behave himself as a guest of nature but not as a drone. ('37-34-IV 266)

We need nature, and cities give the human senses not room enough. I go out daily and nightly to feed my eyes on the horizon and the sky, and come to feel the want of this scope as I do of water for my washing. ('37-34-IV 288)

It is very hard to be simple enough to be good.
('37-34-IV 337)

Proportion certainly is a great end of Culture.
('37-34-IV 368)

The unbelief of the age is attested by the loud condemnation of trifles. ('38-35-IV 479)

I hate goodies. I hate goodness that preaches. Goodness that preaches undoes itself. A little electricity of virtue lurks here and there in kitchens and among the obscure, chiefly women, that flashes out occasional light and makes the existence of the thing still credible. But one had as lief curse and swear as be guilty of this odious religion that watches the beef and watches the cider in the pitcher at table, that shuts the mouth hard at any remark it cannot twist nor wrench into a sermon, and preaches as long as itself and its hearer is awake. Goodies make us very bad. We should, if the race should increase, be scarce restrained from calling for bowl and dagger. We will almost sin to spite them. ('38-35-IV 491, 492)

God is our name for the last generalization to which we can arrive, and, of course, its sense differs today and tomorrow. But never compare your generalization with your neighbor's. Speak now, and let him hear you and go his way. Tomorrow, or next year, let him speak, and answer thou not. So shall you both speak truth and be of one mind; but insist on comparing your two thoughts; or insist on hearing in order of battle, and instantly you are struck with blindness, and will grope and stagger like a drunken man. ('38-35-V 5)

How much a fine picture seems to say! It knows the whole world. How good an office it performs! What authentic messengers are there of a wise soul, which thus stamped its thought, and sends it out distinct, undecayed, unadulterated to me, at the end of centuries, and at the ends of the earth. ('38-35-V 16)

Life is a pretty tragedy, especially for women.
                                        ('38-35-V 16)

With all my ears I cannot detect unity or plan in a strain of Beethoven. Here is a man who draws from it a frank delight. So much is he more a man than I. ('38-35-V 19)

I decline invitations to evening parties chiefly because, besides the time spent, commonly ill, in the party, the hours preceding and succeeding the visit are lost for any solid use, as I am put out of tune for writing or reading. ('38-35-V 23)

The great difference between educated men is that one class acknowledge an ideal standard and the other class do not. We demand of an intellectual man, be his defects what they may, and his practice what it may, faith in the possible improvement of man. ('38-35-V 24)

Put three or four educated people together who have not seen each other for years, and perhaps they shall be unable to converse aloud without force. Each predicts the opinion of the other, so that talking becomes tedious. All know what each would say. Why should I officiously and emphatically offer a pail of water to my neighbor Minot? He has a well of his own that sucks the same springs at the same level that mine does. Why should I drum on his tympanum with my words to convey thoughts to which he has access equally with me? ('38-35-V 25)

How expressive is form! I see by night the shadow of a poor woman against a window curtain that instantly tells a story of so much meekness, affection, and labor, as almost to draw tears. ('38-35-V 25)

The whole History of the Negro is tragedy. By what accursed violation did they first exist that they should suffer always. . . . I think they are more pitiable when rich than when poor. Of what use are riches to them? They never go out without being insulted. Yesterday I saw a family of Negroes riding in a coach. How pathetic! ('38-35-V 26, 27)

I am convinced that if a man will be a true scholar, he shall have perfect freedom. The young people and the mature hint at odium, and aversion of faces to be presently encountered in society. I say, No: I fear it not. No scholar need fear it.
('38-35-V 30)

Who are these murmurers, these haters, these revilers? Men of no knowledge, and therefore no stability. ('38-35-V 31)

Is it not better to live in Revolution than to live in dead times? Are we not little and low out of good nature now, when, if our companions were noble, or the crisis fit for heroes, we should be great also? ('38-35-V 34)

Fancy relates to color; imagination to form. ('38-35-V 37)

Stetson, talking of Webster this morning, says, "He commits great sins sometimes, but without any guilt."
('38-35-V 37)

Not the fact avails, but the use you make of it.
('38-35-V 44)

A Stranger. What is the meaning of that? The fork falling sticks upright in the floor, and the children say, a stranger is coming. A stranger is expected or announced, and an uneasiness betwixt pleasure and pain invades all the hearts of a household. . . . ('38-35-V 49)

Is not the beauty that piques us in every object, in a straw, an old nail, a cobblestone in the road, the announcement that always our road lies *out* into nature, and not inward to the wearisome, odious anatomy of ourselves and comparison of me with thee, and accusation of me, and ambition to take this from thee and add it to me? ('38-35-V 50, 51)

A new degree is taken in scholarship as soon as a man has learned to read in the wood as well as he reads in the study. ('38-35-V 51)

We are by nature observers, and so learners. ('38-35-V 53)

The greater is the man, the less are books to him. Day by day he lessens the distance between him and his authors, and soon finds very few to whom he can pay so high a compliment as to read them. ('38-35-V 54)

I said above, Cause and Effect forever! . . . ('38-35-V 67)

Censure and Praise. I hate to be defended in a newspaper. As long as all that is said is said *against* me, I feel a certain sublime assurance of success, but as soon as honied words of praise are spoken for me, I feel as one that lies unprotected before his enemies. ('38-35-V 69)

It seems as if a man should learn to fish, to plant, or to hunt, that he might secure his subsistence if he were cast out from society and not be painful to his friends and fellow men. ('38-35-V 70)

Every vice is only an exaggeration of a necessary and virtuous function. ('38-35-V 71)

. . . for, every man's idea of God is the last or most comprehensive generalization at which he has arrived.
('38-35-V 73)

Once I thought it a defect peculiar to me, that I was confounded by interrogatories and when put on my wits for a definition was unable to reply without injuring my own truth: but now, I believe it proper to man to be unable to answer in terms the great problems put by his fellow: it is enough if he can live his own definitions. A problem appears to me. I cannot solve it with all my wits: but leave it there; let it lie awhile: I can by patient, faithful truth live at last its uttermost darkness into light. ('38-35-V 74)

It is strange how superficial are our views of these matters, seeing we are all writers and philosophers. ('38-35-V 75)

Any single fact considered by itself confounds, misleads us. Let it lie awhile. It will find its place, by and by, in God's chain; its golden brothers will come, one on the right hand and one on the left, and in an instant it will be the simplest, gladdest, friendliest of things. ('38-35-V 79)

It is not true that educated men desire truth. ('38-35-V 80)

But now I am not sure that the educated class ever ascend to the idea of virtue; or that they desire truth: they want safety, utility, decorum. ('38-35-V 81)

Succession, division, parts, particles—this is the condition, this the tragedy of man. All things cohere and unite. Man studies the parts, strives to tear the part from its connection, to magnify it, and make it whole. ('38-35-V 83, 84)

The physician tends always to invert man, to look upon the body as the cause of the soul, to look upon man as tyrannized over by his members. ('38-35-V 85)

The devil can quote texts. ('38-35-V 89)

I call an Idol anything which a man honors, which the constitution of his mind does not necessitate him to honor. ('38-35-V 95)

As soon as we hear a new vocabulary from our own, at once we exaggerate the alarming differences—account the man suspicious, a thief, a pagan, and set no bounds to our disgust or hatred, and, late in life, perhaps too late, we find he was loving and hating, doing and thinking the same *things* as we, under his own vocabulary. ('38-35-V 99, 100)

Do not even look behind. Leave that bone for them to pick, and welcome. ('38-35-V 100)

Let me study and work contentedly and faithfully; I do not remember my critics. I forget them—I depart from them by every step I take. If I think of them, it is a bad sign.

('38-35-V 100)

Literature is a heap of verbs and nouns enclosing an intuition or two, a few ideas and a few fables.

Literature is a subterfuge.

One man might have writ all the first-rate pieces we call English literature.

Literature is eavesdropping. ('38-35-V 102)

Sincerity is the highest compliment you can pay. Jones Very charmed us all by telling us he hated us all. ('38-35-V 106)

I should not dare to tell all my story. A great deal of it I do not yet understand. How much of it is incomplete. In my strait and decorous way of living, native to my family and to my country, and more strictly proper to me, is nothing extravagant or flowing. ('38-35-V 113, 114)

A woman should always challenge our respect, and never move our compassion. ('38-35-V 115)

If you cannot be free, be as free as you can. ('38-35-V 120)

So is music an asylum. It takes us out of the actual and whispers to us dim secrets that startle our wonder as to who we are, and for what, whence, and whereto. All the great interrogatories, like questioning angels, float in on its waves of sound. "Away, away," said Richter to it, "thou speakest to me of things which in all my endless being I have not and shall not find."

So is Beauty an asylum. ('38-35-V 121)

Let me never fall into the vulgar mistake of dreaming that I am persecuted whenever I am contradicted. No man, I think, had ever a greater well-being with a less desert than I. I can very well afford to be accounted bad or foolish by a few dozen or a few hundred persons—I who see myself greeted by the good expectations of so many friends far beyond any power of thought or communication of thought residing in me. Besides, I own, I am often inclined to take part with those who say I am bad or foolish, for fear I am both. I believe and know there must be a perfect compensation. I know too well my own dark spots. Not having myself attained, not satisfied myself, far from a holy obedience—how can I expect to satisfy others, to command their love? A few sour faces, a few biting paragraphs—is but a cheap expiation for all these short-comings of mine. ('38-35-V 123)

I find no good lives. I would live well, I seem to be free to do so, yet I think with very little respect of my way of living; it is weak, partial, not full and not progressive. But I do not see any other that suits me better. The scholars are shiftless and the merchants are dull. ('38-35-V 126)

I acceded and confessed that this was the tragedy of Art that the artist was at the expense of the man. . . .

('38-35-V 129)

The great facts of history are four or five names: Homer, Phidias, Jesus, Shakespeare—one or two names more I will not add, but see what these names stand for. All civil history and all philosophy consist of endeavors more or less vain to explain these persons. ('38-35-V 133)

I can do well for weeks with no other society than the partridge and the jay, my daily company. ('38-35-V 134)

Proportion is not. Every man is lobsided, and even hold-ing in his hands some authentic token and gift of God, holds it awry. ('38-35-V 135)

Would you know if the man is just, ask of the taxgatherer. ('39-35-V 166)

No Age in Talk. I make no allowance for youth in talking with my friends. If a youth or maiden converses with me I forget they are not as old as I am. ('39-35-V 168)

Isolation must precede society. I like the silent church be-fore the service begins better than any preaching. . . .

('38-35-V 172, 173)

Conversation. The office of conversation is to give me self-possession. I lie torpid as a clod. ('39-35-V 173)

Institutions are optical illusions. ('39-35-V 175)

Painting seems to be to the eye what dancing is to the body. . . . ('39-35-V 175)

Popularity is for dolls; a hero cannot be popular.
('39-35-V 176)

A man must consider what a rich realm he abdicates when he becomes a conformist. . . . ('39-35-V 177)

Whatever we travel to see was domestic, and not the product of traveling; as the Pyramids, the Parthenon, its marbles; Raphael's and Michael Angelo's pictures; Venice, and the residence of Dante, Shakespeare, Burns. We shall never find God out there in the world. Always he abides fast at home. ('39-35-V 182)

It is the best part of each writer which has nothing private in it. That is the best part of each which he does not know; that which flowed out of his constitution. . . . ('39-35-V 183)

Philosophy teaches how to be personal without being unparliamentary. ('39-35-V 193)

If you visit your friend, why need you apologize for not having visited him and waste his time and deface your own act? Visit him now. . . . ('39-35-V 193, 194)

The best conversation equally, I think, with the worst, makes me say, I will not seek society. At least I wish to hear the thoughts of men which differ widely in some important respect from my own. I would hear an artist, or a wise mechanic, or agriculturist, or statesman, or historian, or wit, or poet, or scholar, great in a peculiar department of learning, but not one who only gives me in a varied garb my own daily thoughts. I think it is better to sever and scatter men of kindred genius than to unite them. ('39-35-V 196, 197)

Our aim in our writings ought to be to make daylight shine through them. ('39-35-V 198)

Add the *humanity* of the great writers and their spontaneity. ('39-35-V 199)

I think I gain more from one picture than from a gallery. One picture gives me, in the first place, all the agreeable stimulus of color—itself a tonic—that a gallery can. This makes me brisk, gay, and thoughtful. Then, I see freely the forms, and dream pleasantly of what they would say—I carry the picture out far and wide on every side, and I highly enjoy the unity of the hour: for the picture, of course, excludes all other things; and for a long time afterwards I can well remember the day. I conspire with the painter, lend myself willingly to him, see more than he has done, see what he meant to do. But the gallery will not permit this. The eye glances from picture to picture. Each interferes with the other. Each can only now stand for what it really is, no more. And the artist is lowered, not exalted, by the beholder. At least thus thought I at Allston's gallery, where I recognized in almost all the pictures that they gained nothing by Juxtaposition.

It is somewhat so with men. They are less together than they are apart. They are somewhat wronged, discrowned and disgraced by being put many together in one apartment.

('39-35-V 199, 200)

Fear is an instructor who has a great talent. You may learn one thing of him passing well, this, namely, that there is certainly rottenness where he appears. . . . If you do not feel pleasantly toward your workman or workwoman, your kinsman or townsman, you have not dealt justly. ('39-35-V 202)

And this it does not seem unreasonable or ungrateful to demand, that the artist should pierce the soul; should command; should not sit aloof and circumambient merely, but should come and take me by the hand and lead me somewhither. . . .
('39-35-V 205)

Be thyself too great for enmity and faultfinding.

('39-36-V 206)

Now let a stern preacher arise who shall reveal the resources of man, and tell men they are not leaning willows. . . .
('39-36-V 208)

There is no history. There is only Biography. The attempt to perpetrate, to fix a thought or principle, fails continually.

('39-36-V 208)

The finite is the foam of the infinite. ('39-36-V 209)

How can I hope for a friend to me who have never been one? ('39-36-V 210)

I think we ought to have manual labor, each man.

('39-36-V 210)

'T is pity we should leave with the children all the romance, all that is daintiest in life, and reserve for ourselves as we grow old only the prose. Goethe fell in love in his old age, and I would never lose the capacity of delicate and noble sentiments. ('39-36-V 211)

Language is made up of the spoils of all actions, trades, arts, games, of men. ('39-36-V 213)

The Sabbath is painfully consecrated because the other days are not, and we make prayers in the morning because we sin all day. And if we pray not aloud and in form, we are constrained to excuse ourselves to others with words. O son of man, thou should'st not excuse thyself with words. Thy doing or thy abstaining should preclude words, and make every contrary act from thine show false and ugly. ('39-36-V 214)

My life is a May game, I will live as I like. I defy your straitlaced, weary, social ways and modes. Blue is the sky, green the fields and groves, fresh the springs, glad the rivers, and hospitable the splendor of sun and star. I will play my game out. And if any shall say me nay, shall come out with swords and staves against me to prick me to death for their foolish laws—come and welcome. I will not look grave for such a fool's matter. I cannot lose my cheer for such trumpery. Life is a May game still. ('39-36-V 215, 216)

I wish my house to be a college, open as the air to all to whom I spiritually belong, and who belong to me.
('39-36-V 239)

I have no right of nomination in the choice of my friends. Sir, I should be happy to oblige you, but my friends must elect themselves. ('39-36-V 241)

Education. Sad it was to see the death-cold convention yesterday morning, as they sat shivering, a handful of pale men and women in a large church, for it seems the Law has touched the business of Education with the point of its pen, and instantly it has frozen stiff in the universal congelation of society. An education in things is not. We all are involved in the condemnation of words, an age of words. We are shut up in schools and college recitation rooms for ten or fifteen years, and come out at last with a bellyful of words and do not know a thing. We cannot use our hands, or our legs, or our eyes, or our arms. We do not know an edible root in the woods. We cannot tell our course by the stars, nor the hour of the day by the sun. It is well if we can swim and skate. We are afraid of a horse, of a cow, of a dog, of a cat, of a spider. Far better was the Roman rule to teach a boy nothing that he could not learn standing. ('39-36-V 250, 251)

It seems as if the present age of words should naturally be followed by an age of silence, when men shall speak only through facts, and so regain their health. We die of words. We are hanged, drawn and quartered by dictionaries. We walk in the vale of shadows. It is an age of hobgoblins. . . .
('39-36-V 254)

With the Past, as past, I have nothing to do; nor with the Future, as future. I live now, and will verify all past history in my own moments. ('39-36-V 255)

All conversation among literary men is muddy.
('39-36-V 256)

Temperance that knows itself is not temperance.
('39-36-V 258)

In every house there is a good deal of false hospitality.
('39-36-V 270)

Once more I must renew my work, and I think only once in the same form, though I see that he who thinks he does something for the last time ought not to do it at all. ('39-36-V 288)

Fact is better than fiction if only we could get pure fact. ('39-36-V 298)

Temperance when it is only the sign of intrinsic virtue is graceful as the bloom on the cheek that betokens health, but temperance that is nothing else but temperance is phlegm or conceit. Is it not better they should do bad offices and be intemperate so long as that is their ruling love? ('39-36-V 300)

The world can never be learned by learning all its details. ('39-36-V 306)

We ought never to lose our youth. In all natural and necessary labors, as in the work of a farm, in digging, in splitting, rowing, drawing water, a man always appears young—is still a boy. So in doing anything which is still above him—which asks all his strength and more; somewhat commensurate with his ability, so that he works up to it, not down upon it—he is still a youth. But if his work is unseasonable, as botany and shells or the Greek verbs at eighty years of age, or playing Blindman's Buff, we say, Go up, thou baldhead!

('39-36-V 307)

The City delights the Understanding. It is made up of finites: short, sharp, mathematical lines, all calculable. It is full of varieties, of successions, of contrivances. The Country, on the contrary, offers an unbroken horizon, the monotony of an endless road, of vast uniform plains, of distant mountains, the melancholy of uniform and infinite vegetation; the objects on the road are few and worthless, the eye is invited ever to the horizon and the clouds. It is the school of Reason.

('39-36-V 310, 311)

Generosity does not consist in giving money or money's worth.

The poor therefore are only they who *feel poor*, and poverty consists in feeling poor. . . . ('39-36-V 324)

You teach your boy to walk, but he learns to run himself. ('39-36-V 340)

We are misled by an ambiguity in the use of the term Subjective. It is made to cover two things, a good and a bad. The great always introduce us to facts; small men introduce us always to themselves. . . . ('39-36-V 347)

All life is a compromise. We are haunted by an ambition of a celestial greatness, and balked of it by all manner of paltry impediments. ('39-36-V 360)

I have read Plato's Dialogue, "The Politicians," in Cousin. He seems to me, as before, to owe his fame to the fact that he is a great Average Man. . . . ('40-36-V 369)

The aim of art is always at somewhat better than nature, but the work of art is always inferior to nature. ('40-36-V 376)

In all my lectures, I have taught one doctrine, namely, the infinitude of the private man. This the people accept readily enough, and even with loud commendation, as long as I call the lecture Art, or Politics, or Literature, or the Household; but the moment I call it Religion, they are shocked, though it be only the application of the same truth which they receive everywhere else, to a new class of facts. ('40-36-V 380, 381)

To stand in true relations with men in a false age is worth a fit of insanity, is it not? ('40-36-V 383)

Every man supposes himself not to be fully understood or appreciated. . . . ('40-36-V 388)

If a man knows the law, he may settle himself in a shanty in the pine forest, and men will and must find their way to him as readily as if he lived in the City Hall. ('40-36-V 392)

All spontaneous thought is irrespective of all else.
('40-36-V 392, 393)

Wordsworth has done as much as any living man to restore sanity to cultivated society. ('40-36-V 393)

Beware when the great God lets loose a new thinker on this planet. . . . ('40-36-V 393)

The great man will not be prudent in the popular sense. . . .
('40-37-V 412)

We love to paint those qualities which we do not possess. . . . I, who suffer from excess of sympathy, proclaim always the merits of self-reliance. ('40-37-V 417)

We are never so fit for friendship as when we cease to seek for it, and take ourselves to friend. ('40-37-V 417)

Montaigne. The language of the street is always strong. What can describe the folly and emptiness of scolding like the word *jawing*? I feel too the force of the double negative, though clean contrary to our grammar rules. And I confess to some pleasure from the stinging rhetoric of a rattling oath in the mouth of truckmen and teamsters. How laconic and brisk it is by the side of a page of the *North American Review*. Cut these words and they would bleed; they are vascular and alive; they walk and run. Moreover, they who speak them have this elegancy, that they do not trip in their speech. It is a shower of bullets, whilst Cambridge men and Yale men correct themselves and begin again at every half sentence.
('40-37-V 419, 420)

The simplest things are always better than curiosities.
('40-37-V 425)

Our expense is almost all for conformity. It is for cake that we all run in debt—not the intellect, not the heart, not beauty, not worship, that costs us so much. . . . ('40-37-V 429)

Whenever I read Plutarch or look at a Greek vase I am inclined to accept the common opinion of the learned that the Greeks had cleaner wits than any other people in the Universe. ('40-37-V 434)

Education aims to make the man prevail over the circumstance. ('40-37-V 441)

But genius is the power to labor better and more availably than others. ('40-37-V 443)

I cannot . . . travel with parties of pleasure or with parties of business. The frivolous make me lonely. Neither can I well go to see those whom I esteem, unless they also esteem me, for I can bestow my time well at home. I have thus found that I cannot visit anyone with advantage for a longer time than one or two hours. ('40-37-V 445)

The discovery and the planting of America and the American Revolution and mechanic arts are Greek, Attic, Antique, in this sense, as much as the Parthenon or the *Prometheus Chained*. I can easily see in our periodical literature, for example, a diffused and weakened Athens. ('40-37-V 449)

Do not *say* things. What you *are* stands over you the while and thunders so that I cannot hear what you say to the contrary. ('40-37-V 451)

If we, dear friends, shall arrive at speaking the truth to each other we shall not come away as we went. ('40-37-V 455)

There is so much to be done that we ought to begin quickly to bestir ourselves. ('40-37-V 459)

I am only an experimenter. Do not, I pray you, set the least value on what I do, or the least discredit on what I do not, as if I had settled anything as true or false. I unsettle all things. No facts are to me sacred, none are profane; I simply experiment, an endless seeker, with no past at my back.

('40-37-V 460, 461)

I value the poet. I think all the argument and all the learning is not in the Encyclopedia, or the Treatise on Metaphysics, or the Body of Divinity, but in the sonnet and the tragedy. ('40-37-V 483)

My page about "Consistency" would be better written thus: Damn Consistency! ('40-37-V 484)

When I go into my garden with the spade and dig . . . I discover that I have been defrauding myself all this time in letting others do for me what I should have done with my own hands. . . . ('40-37-V 486)

I have a pen and learned eyes and acute ears, yet am ashamed before my woodchopper, my plowman and my cook, for they have some sort of self-sufficiency. They can contrive without my aid to make a whole day and whole year; but I depend on them. ('40-37-V 486)

I make my own temptations. ('40-37-V 491)

Beauty can never be clutched; in persons and in nature is equally inaccessible. . . . Glory is not for hands to handle. ('40-37-V 494)

No great man ever complains of want of opportunity. . . . ('41-37-V 534)

You will then see that, though I am full of tenderness, and born with as large hunger to love and to be loved as any man can be, yet its demonstrations are not active and bold, but are passive and tenacious. My love has no flood and no ebb, but is always there under my silence, under displeasure, under cold, arid, and even weak behavior. ('41-38-V 565)

I think that only is real which men love and rejoice in. . . . ('41-38-V 565)

Yet we care for individuals, not for the waste universality. ('41-38-VI 13)

When I was praised I lost my time, for instantly I turned round to look at the work I had thought slightly of, and that day I made nothing new. ('41-38-VI 20)

Scholar. We all know enough to be endless writers. Those who have written best are not those who have known most, but those to whom writing was natural and necessary.

('41-38-VI 21)

He said, of one thing he was persuaded, that wisdom and berries grew on the same bushes, but that only one could ever be plucked at one time. ('41-38-VI 49)

The reason of all idleness and of all crime is the same. Whilst we are waiting, we beguile the time, one with jokes, one with sleep, one with eating, one with crimes. ('41-38-VI 50)

Temperament. Every man, no doubt, is eloquent once in his life. The only difference betwixt us is that we boil at different degrees of the thermometer. This man is brought to the boiling point by the excitement of conversation in the parlor; that man requires the additional caloric of a large meeting, a public debate; and a third needs an antagonist, or a great indignation; a fourth must have a revolution; and a fifth nothing less than the grandeur of absolute Ideas, the splendors of Heaven and Hell, the vastness of truth and love.

('41-38-VI 55, 56)

No great cause is ever defended on its merits. ('41-38-VI 58)

The head and the tail are called in the language of philosophy *Finite* and *Infinite*. Visible and Spiritual, Relative and Absolute, Apparent and Eternal, and many more fine names. ('41-38-VI 61)

Every sentence hath some falsehood of exaggeration in it. ('41-38-VI 65)

The philosopher sat with his face to the East until cobwebs were spun over the brim of his pot of porridge. Intemperance is the only vulgarity. ('41-38-VI 69)

Wine and honey are good, but so are rice and meal. Perhaps all that is not performance is preparation, or performance that shall be. ('41-38-VI 81)

Riches. People say law, but they mean wealth.

('41-38-VI 86)

Hope. We sit chatting here in the dark, but do we not all know that the sun will yet again shine, and we shall depart each to our work? God will resolve all doubts, fill all measures. ('41-38-VI 86)

I neither wish to be hated and defied by such as I startle, nor to be kissed and hugged by the young whose thoughts I stimulate. ('41-38-VI 87)

The sum of life ought to be valuable when the fractions and particles are so sweet. ('41-38-VI 87)

It is a great satisfaction to see the best in each kind, and as a good student of the world, I desire to let pass nothing that is excellent in its own kind unseen, unheard. ('41-38-VI 91)

The aim of aristocracy is to secure the ends of good sense and beauty without vulgarity, or deformity of any kind, but they use a very operose method. What an apparatus of means to secure a little conversation. . . . ('41-38-VI 93)

We read either for antagonism or for confirmation. It matters not which way the book works on us, whether to contradict or enrage, or to edify and inspire. *Bubb Dodington* is of the first class, which I read today. A good indignation brings out all one's powers. ('41-38-VI 99)

Make love a crime, and we shall have lust. ('41-38-VI 102)

There is a terrific skepticism at the bottom of the determined conservers. ('41-38-VI 103)

It seems to me sometimes that we get our education ended a little too quick in this country. ('41-38-VI 105)

Good not to let the Conscience sleep, but to keep it irritated by the presence and reiterated action of reforms and ideas. ('41-38-VI 107)

. . . but we think evil arises from disproportion, interruption, mistake of means for end. ('41-38-VI 109)

There are three wants which can never be satisfied: that of the traveler, who says, *"Anywhere but here"*; that of the rich who wants *something more*; and that of the sick who wants *something different*. ('41-38-VI 112)

The willing or acquiescent are certainly better candidates for that idea which is creating the new world than the recalcitrating. ('41-38-VI 112)

Scholars should not carry their memories to balls.
('41-38-VI 113)

To believe in luck, if it were not a solecism so to use the word *believe,* is skepticism. ('41-38-VI 116)

Our contemporaries do not always contemporize us. . . .
('41-38-VI 116)

A man with a truth to express is caught by the beauty of his own words and ends with being a rhymester or critic. And Genius is sacrificed to talent every day. ('41-38-VI 121)

Originality. All originality is relative. ('41-38-VI 122)

No man can write anything who does not think that what he writes is for the time the history of the world . . . or do anything well who does not suppose his work to be of greatest importance. My work may be of none, but I must not think it of none, or I shall not do it with impunity.
Whoso does what he thinks mean, is mean. ('41-38-VI 126)

All writing is by the grace of God. People do not deserve to have good writing, they are so pleased with bad. In these sentences that you show me, I can find no beauty, for I see death in every clause and every word. There is a fossil or a mummy character which pervades this book. The best sepulchers, the vastest catacombs, Thebes and Cairo, Pyramids, are sepulchers to me. I like gardens and nurseries. Give me initiative, spermatic, prophesying, man-making words.
('41-38-VI 132,133)

It is never worth while to worry people with your contritions. ('41-38-VI 133)

We ask to be self-sustained, nothing less. ('41-38-VI 134)

Who is up so high as to receive a gift well? We are either glad or sorry at a gift. . . . ('41-38-VI 135)

We lose time in trying to be like others, accusing ourselves because we are not like others. ('41-38-VI 136)

I told him he was like the good man of Noah's neighbors who said, "Go to thunder with your old ark! I don't think there'll be much of a shower." ('41-38-VI 137)

Historians of reform are not necessarily lovers of reform among their contemporaries. ('41-38-VI 138)

I like the spontaneous persons of both classes: and those on the Conservative side have as much truth and progressive force as those on the Liberal. ('41-38-VI 142)

Sorrow makes us all children again—destroys all differences of intellect. The wisest knows nothing. ('42-38-VI 153)

The scholar is a man of no more account in the street than another man; as the sound of a flute is not louder than the noise of a saw. But as the tone of the flute is heard at a greater distance than any noise, so the fame of the scholar reaches farther than the credit of the banker. ('42-38-VI 166)

The most Indian thing about the Indian is surely not his moccasins or his calumet, his wampum or his stone hatchet, but traits of character and sagacity, skill or passion which would be intelligible to all men and which Scipio or Sidney or Colonel Worth or Lord Clive would be as likely to exhibit as Osceola and Black Hawk. As Johnson remarked that there was a middle style in English above vulgarity and below pedantry, which never became obsolete and in which the plays of Shakespeare were written, so is there in human language a middle style, proper to all nations and spoken by Indians and by Frenchmen, so they be men of personal force. ('42-38-VI 167)

Instead of wondering that there is a Bible, I wonder that there are not a thousand. ('42-38-VI 168)

. . . for he stood brooding on the edge of discovery of the Absolute from month to month. . . . ('42-38-VI 176)

Very soon the Reformers whom he had joined would disappoint him; they were pitiful persons, and, in their coarseness and ignorance, he began to pine again for literary society. In these oscillations from the Scholars to the Reformers, and back again, he spent his days. ('42-38-VI 177)

Truth; Realism. Are you not scared by seeing that the Gypsies are more attractive to us than the Apostles? For though we love goodness and not stealing, yet also we love freedom and not preaching. ('42-38-VI 184)

. . . the majestic and beautiful Necessity. . . .
                                              ('42-38-VI 185)

You should never ask me what I can do. If you do not find my gift without asking, I have none for you. Would you ask a woman wherein her loveliness consists? Those to whom she is lovely will not discover it so. Such questions are but curiosity and gossip. Besides, I cannot tell you what my gift is unless you can find it without my description. ('42-38-VI 186,187)

In short, there ought to be no such thing as Fate.
                                              ('42-38-VI 189)

That is to say, I believe in Fate. As long as I am weak, I shall talk to Fate; whenever the God fills me with his fullness, I shall see the disappearance of Fate. ('42-38-VI 189)

The gates of thought—how slow and late they discover themselves! Yet when they appear, we see that they were always there, always open. ('42-38-VI 196)

Goodness is not enough, unless it has insight, universal insights, results that are of universal application.
                                              ('42-38-VI 198)

Dull, cheerless business this of playing lion and talking down to people. Rather let me be scourged and humiliated; then the exaltation is sure and speedy. ('42-38-VI 200)

In the fields, this lovely day, I was ashamed of the inhospitality of disputing. Very hoarsely sounds the parlor debate on theology from the lonely, sunny hill, or the meadow where the children play. ('42-38-VI 202, 203)

Our poetry reminds me of the catbird, who sings so affectedly and vaingloriously to me near Walden. Very sweet and musical! very various! fine execution! but so conscious, and *such a performer!* not a note is his own, except at last, *Miou, miou.* ('42-38-VI 208, 209)

A highly endowed man with good intellect and good conscience is a Man-woman and does not so much need the complement of woman to his being as another. Hence his relations to the sex are somewhat dislocated and unsatisfactory. He asks in woman sometimes the woman, sometimes the man. ('42-39-VI 210)

None longs for a church so much as he who stays at home. ('42-39-VI 216)

"It is not so in your experience, but is so in the other world." —Other world? I reply, there is no other world; here or nowhere is the whole fact. . . . ('42-39-VI 219)

Three Classes. I had occasion to say the other day to Elizabeth Hoar that I like best the strong and worthy persons like her father, who support the social order without hesitation or misgiving. I like these: they never incommode us by exciting grief, pity, or perturbation of any sort. But by conscience, my unhappy conscience, respects that hapless class who see the faults and stains of our social order and who pray and strive incessantly to right the wrong. This annoying class of men and women commonly find the work altogether beyond their faculty, and though their honesty is commendable, their results are for this present distressing. But there is a third class who are born into a new heaven and earth with organs for the new element, and who from that Better behold this bad world in which the million gropes and suffers. By their life and happiness in the new, I am assured of the doom of the old, and these, therefore, I love and worship. ('42-39-VI 220, 221)

It is sad to outgrow our preachers, our friends, and our books, and find them no longer potent. Proclus and Plato last me still, yet I do not read them in a manner to honor the writer. . . . ('42-39-VI 221)

Some play at chess, some at cards, some at the Stock Exchange. I prefer to play at Cause and Effect. ('42-39-VI 229)

Rings and jewels are not gifts, but apologies for gifts. The only gift is a portion of thyself. . . . ('42-39-VI 247)

Men are so gregarious that they have no solitary merits. They all—the reputed leaders and all—lean on some other— and this superstitiously, and not from insight of his merit. They follow a fact, they follow success, and not skill.

('42-39-VI 250)

The sons of great men should be great; if they are little, it is because they eat too much pound cake, which is an accident; or, because their fathers married dolls. ('42-39-VI 267)

The worst times that ever fell were good times to somebody. There is always someone in the gap. ('42-39-VI 269)

Pecunia est alter Sanguis.
> *The seamstress' wax,*
> *The woodman's axe—*
> *These pay the tax.*

('42-39-VI 271)

I think I will never read any but the commonest of all books: the Bible, Shakespeare, Milton, Dante, Homer.

('42-39-VI 273)

We learn with joy and wonder this new and flattering art of language, deceived by the exhilaration which accompanies the attainment of each new word. We fancy we gain somewhat. We gain nothing. It seemed to men that words come nearer to the thing; described the fact; were the fact. They learn later that they only suggest it. ('42-39-VI 274)

But he is a good vagabond and knows how to take a walk. ('42-39-VI 277, 278)

Rabelais is not to be skipped in literary history, as he is the source of so much proverb, story, and joke which are derived from him into all modern books in all languages. He is the Joe Miller of modern literature. ('42-39-VI 281, 282)

Do not let us meet to argue; let us meet to rest.

('42-39-VI 282)

You shall have joy, or you shall have power, said God; you shall not have both. ('42-39-VI 282)

These things became stereotyped as *Education.*

('42-39-VI 289)

Life is so much greater than thought, that when we talk on an affair of grave personal interest with one with whom hitherto we have had only intellectual discourse, we use lower tones, much less oratory, but we come much nearer and are quickly acquainted. ('42-39-VI 289)

Today I think the common people very right, and literary justice to be certain. ('42-39-VI 292)

Men of aim must always rule the aimless. And yet there will always be singing birds. ('42-39-VI 297)

If a man will kick a fact out of the window, when he comes back he finds it again in the chimney corner. ('42-39-VI 298)

Do not be too timid and squeamish about your actions. ^ life is an experiment. The more experiments you make th better. What if they are a little coarse, and you get your coat soiled or torn? What if you do fail, and get fairly rolled in the dirt once or twice? Up again you shall never be so afraid of a tumble. ('42-39-VI 302)

But do not require of me, sitting out here, to say what he, within there, ought to do. I can never meddle with other people's facts, I have enough of my own. But this one thing I know, that, if I do not clear myself, I am in fault, and that my condition is matched, point for point, with every other man's. I can only dispose of my own facts. ('42-39-VI 304)

You never can hurt us by new ideas. God speed you, gentlemen reformers. ('42-39-VI 314)

W. H. Channing thinks that, not in solitude, but in love, in the actual society of beloved persons, have been his highest intuitions. To me it sounds like shallow verbs and nouns; for in closest society a man is by thought wrapt into remotest isolation. ('42-39-VI 315)

History is a foolish, pragmatic misstatement.

('42-39-VI 323)

Heroes are the lucky individuals who stand at the pole and are the largest and ripest. ('42-39-VI 323)

Life would not be worth taking or keeping, if it were not full of surprises. I wake in the morning, and go to my window, and see the day break, and receive from the spectacle a new secret of Nature that goes to compromise all my past manner of living, and invite me to a new. ('42-39-VI 324)

Elizabeth Hoar affirms that religion bestows a refinement which she misses in the best-bred people not religious, and she considers it essential therefore to the flower of gentleness.

('42-39-VI 328)

Everything is good which a man does naturally. . . .
                                            ('43-39-VI 337)

It makes men very bad to talk good. ('43-39-VI 337)

"It is true that he sometimes commits crimes, but without
any guilt." ('43-39-VI 344)

Poet. It is true that when a man writes poetry, he appears
to assume the high feminine part of his nature. We clothe the
poet, therefore, in robes and garlands, which are proper to
woman. The Muse is feminine. But action is male. And a king
is draped almost in feminine attire. ('43-39-VI 361)

I think we are not quite yet fit for Flying Machines, and
therefore there will be none. . . . ('43-39-VI 409)

The Chinese are as wonderful for their etiquette as the
Hebrews for their piety. ('43-40-VI 418)

Tragedy and comedy always go hand in hand.
                                            ('43-40-VI 419)

These people know so well how to live, and have such perfect adjustment in their tastes and their power to gratify them,
that the ideal life is necessarily thrown into the shade, and I
have never seen a strong conservatism appear so amiable and
wise. We saw their well-built houses which an equal and generous economy warmed and animated; and their good neighborhood was never surpassed: the use of the doorbell and
knocker seems unknown. And the fine children who played in
the yards and piazzas appeared to come of a more amiable
and gentle stock ('43-40-VI 428, 429)

Perhaps it was this, perhaps it was a mark of having out-
lived some of my once finest pleasures, that I found no appetite to return to the Court in the afternoon and hear the con-
clusion of his argument. The green fields on my way home
were too fresh and fair, and forbade me to go again.
                                            ('43-40-VI 431)

I only wish he would never truckle; I do not care how much
he spends. ('43-40-VI 434)

Confide in your power, whether it be to be a wet nurse or a wood sawyer, lion-taming Van Amburgh, or Stewart maker of steam candy, keep your shop, magnify your office. Fear smears our work, and ignorance gilds our neighbor's, but the sure years punish our faintheartedness. ('43-40-VI 437)

There is nothing in history to parallel the influence of Jesus Christ. ('43-40-VI 438)

I respect cats, they seem to have so much else in t heads besides their mess. . . . I prefer a tendency to sta liness to an excess of fellowship. ('43-40-VI 439)

If you ask the former for his definition of God, he would answer, "My possibility"; for his definition of Man, "My actuality." ('43-40-VI 441)

The day laborer is popularly reckoned as standing at the foot of the social scale: yet, talk with him, he is saturated with the beautiful laws of the world. . . . ('43-40-VI 446)

The capital defect of my nature for society (as it is of so many others) is the want of animal spirits. ('43-40-VI 447)

The Reformer (after the Chinese). There is a class whom I call the thieves of virtue. They are those who mock the simple and sincere endeavorers after a better way of life, and say, These are pompous talkers; but when they come to act they are weak, nor do they regard what they have said. These mockers are continually appealing to the ancients, and they say. Why make ourselves singular? Let those who are born in this age, act as men of this age. Thus they secretly obtain the flattery of the age. . . . The multitude all delight in them and they confuse virtue. ('43-40-VI 458, 459)

It seems to me that he has learned its lesson who has come to feel so assured of his well-being as to hold lightly all particulars of today and tomorrow, and to count death amongst the particulars. He must have such a grasp of the whole as to be willing to be ridiculous and unfortunate. ('43-40-VI 467)

Very painful is the discovery we are always making that we can only give to each other a rare and partial sympathy; for as much time as we have spent in looking over into our neighbor's field and chatting with him is lost to our own, and must be made up by haste and renewed solitude.
"L'esprit est une sorte de luxe qui détruit le bon sens, comme le luxe détruit la fortune." ('43-40-VI 471, 472)

The moment we quote a man to prove our sanity, we give up all. No authority can establish it, and if I have lost confidence in myself I have the Universe against me.
('43-40-VI 477)

We love morals until they come to us with mountainous melancholy and grim overcharged rebuke: then we so gladly for intellect, the lightmaker. ('43-40-VI 480)

ends, and how much the years teach which the know! . . . but the individual is always mistaken. 480)

We rail at trade, but the historian of the world will see that it was the principle of liberty; that it settled America, and destroyed feudalism, and made peace and keeps peace; that it will abolish slavery. ('43-40-VI 481)

The unbeliever supports the church, education, the fine arts, etc., as *amusements*. ('43-40-VI 482)

I approve every wild action of the experimenters. I say what they say concerning celibacy, or money, or community of goods, and my only apology for not doing their work is preoccupation of mind. I have a work of my own which I know I can do with some success. It would leave that undone if I should undertake with them, and I do not see in myself any vigor equal to such an enterprise. ('43-40-VI 482)

Why should we have only two or three ways of life, and not thousands and millions? ('44-40-VI 491)

Then I discovered the Secret of the World; that all things subsist, and do not die, but only retire a little from sight and afterwards return again. ('44-40-VI 494)

Somebody said of me after the lecture at Amory Hall, within hearing of A.W., "The secret of his popularity is, that he has a *damn* for everybody." ('44-40-VI 497)

It is curious that intellectual men should be most attractive to women. But women are magnetic; intellectual men are magnetic: therefore, as soon as they meet, communication is found difficult or impossible. ('44-40-VI 500)

By acting rashly, we buy the power of talking wisely. People who know how to act are never preachers. ('44-40-VI 500)

The Oriental behave well, but who cannot behave well who has nothing else to do? The poor Yankees who are doing the work are all wrinkled and vexed. ('44-40-VI 502)

I am always environed by myself: what I am, all thing[s] flect to me. ('44-40-VI 503)

I wish to have rural strength and religion for my children[,] and I wish city facility and polish. I find with chagrin that I cannot have both. ('44-40-VI 506)

Able men do not care in what work a man is able so only he is able. . . . ('44-40-VI 506)

Our people are slow to learn the wisdom of sending character instead of talent to Congress. Again and again they have sent a man of great acuteness, a fine scholar, a fine forensic orator, and some master of the brawls has crunched him up in his hand like a bit of paper. ('44-40-VI 507, 508)

Theory and Practice in Life. In our recipe, the ingredients are separately named, but in the cup which we drink, the elements are exquisitely mixed; the heart and head are both nourished, and without fumes or repentance.

('44-40-VI 518, 519)

If two or three persons should come with a high spiritual aim and with great powers, the world would fall into their hands like a ripe peach. ('44-40-VI 521)

I think the best argument of the conservative is this bad one: that he is convinced that the angry democrat, who wishes him to divide his park and château with him, will, on entering into the possession, instantly become conservative, and hold the property and spend it as selfishly as himself. For a better man, I might dare to renounce my estate; for a worse man, or for as bad a man as I, why should I? All the history of man with unbroken sequence of examples establishes this inference. Yet it is very low and degrading ground to stand upon. We must never reason from history, but plant ourselves on the ideal. ('44-40-VI 522, 523)

Be an opener of doors for such as come after thee, and do not try to make the universe a blind alley. ('44-41-VI 525)

Government. A fire breaking out in a village makes immediately a natural government. The most able and energetic take the command, and are gladly obeyed by the rest. The feeble individuals take their place in the line to hand buckets, the boys pass the empty ones. ('44-41-VI 527)

... to bawl "constitution" and "patriotism"; those ... once too often have a most ironical hoarseness. ...31)

... is the Anti-Slave: here is Man; and if you have men, ...ck or white is an insignificance. Why, at night all men are black. ('44-41-VI 533)

. . . great anthem of the world which we call history. . . . ('44-41-VI 533)

There are many topics which ought not to be approached except in the plentitude of health and playfully.
('44-41-VI 538)

She knows her own worth, and that she cannot be soiled by a plain dress, or by the hardest household drudgery.
('44-41-VI 549)

Poetry must be as new as foam, and as old as the rock. ('45-41-VII 36)

Our virtue runs in a narrow rill: we have never a freshet. We ought to be subject to enthusiasms. One would like to see Boston and Massachusetts agitated like a wave with some generosity, mad for learning, for music, for philosophy, for association, for freedom, for art; but now it goes like a peddler with its hand ever on its pocket, cautious, calculating.
('45-41-VII 49, 50)

Society is a great boardinghouse in which people of all characters and habits meet for their dinner and eat harmoniously together; but, the meal once over, they separate to the most unlike and opposite employments. ('45-42-VII 60)

Adaptiveness. The philosophy we want is one of fluctions and mobility; not a house but a ship in these billows we inhabit. . . . ('45-42-VII 61)

One who wishes to refresh himself by contact with the bone and sinew of society must avoid what is called the respectable portion of his city or neighborhood with as much care as in Europe a good traveler avoids American and English people. ('45-42-VII 66)

Shall I say that I am driven to express my faith by a series of skepticisms? . . . ('45-42-VII 67)

An orator is a thief of belief.
Garrison is a virile speaker; he lacks the feminine element which we find in men of genius. He has great body to his discourse, so that he can well afford occasional flourishes and eloquence. He is a man in his place. He brings his whole history with him, wherever he goes, and there is no falsehood or patchwork, but sincerity and unity. ('45-42-VII 97)

The poetic gift we want, but not the poetic profession. . . . ('45-42-VII 98)

Henry Thoreau says "that philosophers are broken-down poets"; and "that universal assertions should never allow any remarks of the individual to stand in their neighborhood, for the broadest philosophy is narrower than the worst poetry." ('45-42-VII 99)

Eloquence. The eloquent man is he who is no beautiful speaker, but who is inwardly and desperately drunk with a certain belief. . . . ('45-42-VII 105)

The scholar's is a position of present immunity. The vulgar think he would found a sect; he knows better. Society has no bribe for him. ('45-42-VII 105)

Knowledge is the straight Line; *Wisdom* is the power of the straight line, or the Square; *Virtue* is the power of the Square; or the Solid. ('45-42-VII 114)

He has knowledge, he has wisdom, but he has missed Virtue, which he only acquires who endures routine and sweat and postponement of fancy to the achievement of a worthy end. ('45-42-VII 115)

Every man who would do anything well must come to it from a higher ground, and a philosopher must be much more than a philosopher. Plato is a Poet. ('45-42-VII 119)

Wisdom consists in keeping the soul liquid, or, in resisting the tendency to too rapid petrification. ('45-42-VII 130)

The *Five Evils* which proceed from our *Three Errors,* and which make the misery of life, are, (1) religious perplexities; (2) disappointment in affections; (3) pecuniary difficulties; (4) intemperance; (5) anxiety for offspring. He also requires a Transitional State. *Fourier* he saw in his old age. Fourier learned of him all the truth he had, and the rest of his system was imagination, and the imagination of a banker.

('45-42-VII 133, 134)

You are very external with your evils, Mr. Owen: let me give you some real mischiefs: Living for show; losing the whole in the particular; indigence of vital power. I am afraid these will appear in a phalanstery, or in a tub.

('45-42-VII 134)

Greeley surprises by playing all the parts. Only possible in America. ('45-42-VII 136)

The one good in life is concentration, the one evil is dissipation. . . . ('46-42-VII 157)

Nobody is entitled to travel but such as have done their work. Whilst this world is in chaos, we shall not be allowed to leave it. ('46-42-VII 161)

Companions. Men of thought who live in the same sphere are poor company for each other. ('46-42-VI 166)

. . . the faults of his speech increased my respect for his character. ('46-42-VII 168)

Is not the mystic like a rogue who comes to an honest man and says, "By your accumulated character you could deal an immense stroke at counterfeiting?" ('46-42-VII 171)

The best is accessible, is cheap. Every man cannot get land or jewels, but every man can get what land and money and rank are valued for—namely, substantial manhood, thoughts self-realizing and prophetic of the farthest future, thoughts of which poetry and music are the necessary expression.

('46-42-VII 174)

"A new commandment," archly said the Muse: "Thou shalt not preach, my dismal one. . . ." ('46-42-VII 179)

But, on the instant when we rise so high as to see and affirm the ethical law in relation to our business, no apology is needed. ('46-42-VII 189)

Nature never draws the moral, but leaves it for the spectator. Neither does the sculptor, nor the painter, nor the poet. ('46-42-VII 190)

Nobody is profoundly good or bad. Were they profound, they would satisfy. ('46-42-VII 191)

If I were a member of the Massachusetts legislature, I should propose to exempt all colored citizens from taxation because of the inability of the government to protect them by passport out of its territory. It does not give the value for which they pay the tax. ('46-42-VII 192)

Democracy becomes a government of bullies tempered by editors. ('46-42-VII 193)

One thing we have, though it is not of us, continuity.
('46-42-VII 194)

The mania takes a milder form. People go a-fishing, and know the taste of their meat. They cut their own whippletree in the woodlot, they know something practically of the sun and the east wind, of the underpinning and the roofing of the house, of the pan and the mixture of the soils.
('46-42-VII 195)

. . . but you cannot escape the demand for courage. . . .
('46-42-VII 201)

Is not America more than ever wanting in the male principle? A good many village attorneys we have, saucy village talents, preferred to Congress, and the Cabinet—Marcys, Buchanans, Walkers, etc.—but no great Captains. Webster is a man by himself of the great mold, but he also underlies the American blight, and wants the power of the initiative, the affirmative talent, and remains, like the literary class, only a commentator, his great proportions only exposing his defect. America seems to have immense resources, land, men, milk, butter, cheese, timber, and iron, but it is a village littleness— village squabble and rapacity characterize its policy. It is a great strength on a basis of weakness. ('46-43-VII 218)

Teachers. The teacher should be the complement of the pupil; now, for the most part, they are Earth's diameters wide of each other. A college professor should be elected by setting all the candidates loose on a miscellaneous gang of young men taken at large from the street. He who could get the ear of these youths after a certain number of hours, or of the greatest number of these youths, should be professor. Let him see if he could interest these rowdy boys in the meaning of a list of words. ('46-43-VII 224)

Affirmative. Set down nothing but what will help somebody.
('47-43-VII 245)

But if he is not well mixed and averaged, then he needs to achieve something, build a railroad, make a fortune, write an ~~iad~~, as a compensation to himself for his abnormal position.
('47-43-VII 246)

Purpose, tendency, I have learned to value and nothing else. Have you made the life of man clearer of any snag or sawyer?
('47-43-VII 250)

. . . if only I could be set aglow. ('47-43-VII 252)

The name of Washington City in the newspapers is every day of blacker shade. All the news from that quarter being of a sadder type, more malignant. It seems to be settled that no act of honor or benevolence or justice is to be expected from the American government, but only this, that they will be as wicked as they dare. No man now can have any sort of success in politics without a streak of infamy crossing his name.
('47-43-VII 253, 254)

Nonsense is only sense deranged, chaos is paradise dislocated, poverty is wealth decomposed; spite, apathy, bad blood, frivolity, only dispersed matter and light.
('47-43-VII 261)

When I see my friend after a long time, my first question is, Has anything become clear to you? ('47-43-VII 278)

Criticism should not be querulous and wasting, all knife and root-puller, but guiding, instructive, inspiring, a south wind, not an east wind. ('47-44-VII 291)

The one event which never loses its romance is the alighting of superior persons at my gate. ('47-44-VII 300)

The idler is a diseased person and is to be treated by the state as a diseased person. ('48-44-VII 463)

Nature is regardless of the individual. . . . ('48-44-VII 466)

I was accustomed to characterize Alcott, in England, by saying that he was the one man I had met who could read Plato without surprise. ('48-45-VII 493)

The English habit of betting makes them much more accurate than we are in their knowledge of particulars.
('48-45-VII 495)

Alcott declares that a teacher is one who can assist the child in obeying his own mind, and who can remove all unfavorable circumstances. He believes that from a circle of twenty well-selected children he could draw in their conversation everything that is in Plato, and as much better in form than it is in Plato. . . . ('48-45-VII 499)

I say I will not dispute against the sun, but beware of taking any one thing out of its connections, for that way folly lies.
('48-45-VII 509)

Great cities, enormous populations, are disgusting, like the population of cheese, like hills of ants, or swarms of fleas— the more the worse. ('48-45-VII 514)

The world is a glass dictionary. ('48-45-VII 515)

Nature uniformly does one thing at a time: if she will have a perfect hand, she makes head and feet pay for it. So now, as she is making railroad and telegraph ages, she starves the *spirituel,* to stuff the *matériel* and *industriel.* ('48-45-VII 518)

Accommodation. Did you give Athens the best laws?
Solon. No, but the best it would receive. ('48-45-VII 519)

I think it is indispensable that we should converse both with our superiors and our inferiors in intellect. With the first, for new aim and corrections; and, with the last, for self-possession and talent. ('48-45-VII 527)

It is necessary that you should know the people's facts. If you have no place for them, the people absolutely have no place for you. You may prove your theory by all syllogisms and all symbols, but heaven and earth, the constitution of things, is on the people's side, and that is a reason not liable to a fallacy. ('48-45-VII 533)

Every man is entitled to be measured or characterized by his best influence. ('48-45-VII 541)

Our poetry is an affectation, but read Chaucer, and the old lays in which Merlin and Arthur are celebrated, and you will find it as simple as the speech of children. ('48-45-VII 545)

Laws. I see no security in laws, but only in the nature of men; and in the reactive force which develops all kinds of energy at the same time; energy of good with energy of evil; the ecstasies of devotion with the exasperations of debauchery. The sons of Democrats will be Whigs, and the fury of republicanism in the father is only the immense effort of Nature to engender an intolerable tyrant in the next age.

('48-45-VII 547)

"He is the best-natured man I ever met. The rats and mice make their nests in him." ('48-45-VII 552)

What all men think, he thinks better. ('48-45-VII 561)

If a man is going to California, he announces it with some hesitation; because it is a confession that he has failed at home. ('49-45-VIII 4)

If you have sharp eyes, use them, not brag of them.

('49-45-VIII 19)

"Things that are natural are never without a certain grace and excellence." ('49-45-VIII 19)

One sad reflection arises on all the course of the narrative, of wonder, namely, at the depravity of men in power, and at the shocking tameness with which it is endured.

('49-46-VIII 29)

He is unmistakably able, and might have ruled America, but he was cowardly, and has spent his life on specialties.

('49-46-VIII 46)

But it is plain that the adults' education should be undertaken. When our Republic, O Plato! shall begin, the education shall not end with the youth, but shall be as vigorously continued in maturity. ('49-46-VIII 57)

Life. Some of the sweetest hours of life, on retrospect, will be found to have been spent with books. ('49-46-VIII 58)

Natural Aristocracy. It is a vulgar error to suppose that a gentleman must be ready to fight. The utmost that can be demanded of the gentleman is that he is incapable of a lie.
('49-46-VIII 75)

They have never admitted the claims of either of them. The fate of my books is like the impression of my face. My acquaintances, as long back as I can remember, have always said, "Seems to me you look a little thinner than when I saw you last." ('50-46-VIII 88)

I have made no note of these long weary absences at New York and Philadelphia. I am a bad traveler, and the hotels are mortifications to all sense of well-being in me. The people who fill them oppress me with their excessive virility, and would soon become intolerable if it were not for a few friends, who, like women, tempered the acrid mass. Henry James was true comfort—wise, gentle, polished, with heroic manners, and a serenity like the sun. ('50-46-VIII 109)

The badness of the times is making death attractive.
('50-46-VIII 112)

She could (and she was alone in this) talk of persons and never gossip, for she had a fine instinct that kept her from any reality and from any effect of treachery. The fact is she had large sympathies. ('50-47-VIII 118)

Men as naturally make a state as caterpillars a web. . . .
('50-47-VIII 120)

Amount and Quality. Schelling's distinction, "Some minds speak about things, and some minds speak the things themselves," remains by far the most important intellectual distinction, as the quality is the important moral distinction.
('50-47-VIII 126)

Democracy. The objection of practical men to free institutions is that responsibility is shirked. Every power is exerted by a committee, which is every moment composed of new persons. If you should take an Irishman out of the street, and make him despotic in your town, he would try to rule it well, because it was his own. But these rotating governors and legislators go for their own interests, which is the only permanency they know. They go for their party, which is much more permanent than their office, and for their contract, or claim, or whatever private interest. ('50-47-VIII 140)

We are wasted with our versatility; with the eagerness to grasp on every possible side, we all run to nothing. I cannot open an agricultural paper without finding objects enough for Methusalem. I jilt twenty books whenever I fix on one. I stay away from Boston, only because I cannot begin there to see those whom I should wish, the men and the things. I wish to know France. I wish to study art. I wish to read laws.
('50-47-VIII 155)

Rotation. What an excellent principle our favorite rule of rotation in office would be if applied in industrial matters. You have been watchmaker long enough, now it is my turn to make watches, and you can bake muffins. The carpenter is to make glasses this year, and the glass blower staircases. The blacksmith is to cut me a coat, and the tailor to take charge of the machine shop. Mr. Benton has served an apprenticeship of thirty years to the Federal Senate, has learned the routine, has opened his views to a national scope, and must now retire to give place to Johnny Raw. ('51-47-VIII 165, 166)

I found when I had finished my new lecture that it was a very good house, only the architect had unfortunately omitted the stairs. ('51-47-VIII 167)

Union is a delectable thing, and so is wealth, and so is life, but they may all cost too much, if they cost honor.
('51-47-VIII 199)

One way certainly the Nemesis is seen. Here is a measure of pacification and union. What is its effect?—that it has made one subject, one only subject for conversation and painful thought throughout the Union, Slavery. We eat it, we drink it, we breathe it, we trade, we study, we wear it. We are all poisoned with it, and after the fortnight the symptoms appear, purulent, making frenzy in the head and rabidness.
('51-47-VIII 201)

. . . This Slavery shall not be, it poisons and depraves everything it touches. ('51-47-VIII 202)

A man who is always behind time is careworn and painful. ('51-48-VIII 208)

The young minister did very well, but one day he married a wife, and after that, he noticed, that, though he planted corn never so often, it was sure to come up tulips, contrary to all the laws of botany. ('51-48-VIII 213)

In each town you visit, there is some man who is in his brain and performance an explanation of all that meets the eye there. . . . If you see him, all will become plain. Mr. Erastus Bigelow, Mr. McElrath, Mr. Lawrence, Mr. Crocker, Mr. Vanderbilt, the old Rotch and Rodman, Jackson and Lowell, the Dwights at Springfield, Mr. Mills, Mr. Forbes, are each a walking city, and, wherever you put them, will build one.

Also, I believe that nothing can be done except by inspiration. . . . ('51-48-VIII 222, 223)

It did not seem that he was enamored of his thoughts, as all good thinkers ought to be. A fair ample house with excellent windows, but no fireplace. ('51-48-VIII 225)

Is it not a convenience to have a person in town who knows where pennyroyal grows, or sassafras, or punk for a slow match; or Celtis—the false elm; or cats-o'-nine-tails; or wild cherries; or wild pears; where is the best apple tree, where is the Norway pine, where the beech, or Epigaea, or Linnaea, or sanguinaria, or Orchis pulcherrima, or Drosera, or Laurus benzoin, or pink huckleberry, or shagbarks; where is the best chestnut grove, hazelnuts; where are trout, where woodcocks, where wild bees, where pigeons; or who can tell where the stake driver (bittern) can be heard; who has seen and can show you the Wilson's plover? ('51-48-VIII 227)

I don't like linear, but spheral people; but discontent merely shows incompleteness as you measure yourself by times and events; as soon as you express yourself, you will round.
                                                   ('51-48-VIII 230)

All the drops of his blood have eyes that look downward.
                                                   ('51-48-VIII 231)

Economy. Nature says thou shalt keep the air, skate, swim, walk, ride, run. When you have worn out your shoes, the strength of the sole leather has passed into the fiber of your body. I measure your health by the number of shoes and hats and clothes you have worn out. He is the richest man who pays the largest debt to his shoemaker. ('51-48-VIII 232)

There must come an end of this too much prosperity of ours, or it would go on to madness. ('51-48-VIII 235)

It is as bad as going to Congress; none comes back innocent. ('51-48-VIII 240)

And who is truly wanted, the railroad engineer or the philosopher? It is a mere question of time. ('51-48-VIII 240)

Autobiography. I am never beaten until I know that I am beaten. I meet powerful people to whom I have no skill to reply. . . . ('51-48-VIII 241, 242)

We are not such pedants as to suppose a king comes only with a crown on his head. The moment a man says, "Give up your rights, here is money," there is tyranny. It comes masquerading in monks' cowls and in citizens' coats; comes savagely or comes politely. But it is tyranny.

('51-48-VIII 242, 243)

I looked through the first part of *Faust* today, and find it a little too modern and intelligible. ('51-48-VIII 245)

Prudence. Half measures fail. Don't be leaky.

('51-48-VIII 248)

Goethe is the pivotal man of the old and new times with us. He shuts up the old, he opens the new. No matter that you were born since Goethe died—if you have not read Goethe, or the Goetheans, you are an old fogy, and belong with the antediluvians. ('51-48-VIII 249)

What do we know of his own life? The courage which is grand, the courage to feel that Nature who made me may be trusted, and one's self painted as also a piece of Nature, he has not. ('51-48-VIII 251)

Edith's opinion. Edith, when a little girl, whimpered when her mother described the joys of Heaven. She did not want to go there, she "wanted to stay" (and she looked around the room) "where there was folks, and *things, and a door.*"

('51-48-VIII 256)

Faith shall be justified. Live for the year, not for the day. Let logic, let character rule the hour. That is never vulgar.

('51-48-VIII 261)

But I think we shall never understand political economy until we get Béranger or Burns or some poet to teach it in songs. ('51-48-VIII 265)

'T is said, a man can't be aught in politics without some cordial support in his own district; nor can a man dupe others long, who has not duped himself first. ('51-48-VIII 273)

The misfortune of scholars is that people are nonconductors. ('52-48-VIII 273)

Which was the best age of philosophy? That in which there were yet no philosophers. ('52-48-VIII 274)

Few know how to read. Women read to find a hero whom they can love; men, for amusement; editors, for something to crib; authors, for something that supports their view; and hardly one reads comprehensively and wisely.

('52-48-VIII 277)

He must be inestimable to us to whom we can say what we cannot say to ourselves. ('52-49-VIII 292)

Eloquence. Who could convince X of any truth which he does not see (and what truth does he see?) must be a master of his art. And eloquence is the power to translate a truth into language perfectly intelligible to the persons to whom you speak. Is this a vulgar power? Declamation is common; but such possession of thought as is here required, such practical chemistry as the conversion of a truth written in God's language, into a truth in X's language, is one of the most beautiful and cogent weapons ever forged in the shop of the Divine artificer. ('52-49-VIII 313)

Good Neighborhood. Neighborhood is of great importance, and you buy much with given prices that is not rightly rendered in the bill. ('52-49-VIII 315)

I find that the Americans have no passions, they have appetites. ('52-49-VIII 321)

Are we always to be the victims of the meanest of mankind, who kill off as sentimental and visionary every generous and just design? ('52-49-VIII 343)

Sphinx. 'T is said that the age ends with the poet or successful man who knots up into himself the genius or idea of his nation; and that when the Jews have at last flowered perfectly into Jesus, there is the end of the nation. When Greece is complete in Plato, Phidias, Pericles, the race is spent and rapidly takes itself away. When Rome has arrived at Caesar and Cicero, it has no more that it can do, and retreats. When Italy has got out Dante, all the rest will be rubbish. So that we ought rather to be thankful that our hero or poet does not hasten to be born in America, but still allows us others to live a little and warm ourselves at the fire of the sun, for, when he comes, we others must pack our petty trunks and be gone. ('52-49-VIII 345)

He has taste for realities. ('52-49-VIII 347)

The English genius never parts with its materialistic tendency, and even in its inspirations is materialistic.
('53-49-VIII 360)

The want of elevation, the absence of ideas, the sovereignty of the abdomen, reduces all to the same poorness.
('53-49-VIII 364)

Channing told Mr. Edmund Hosmer "that he did not see but trouble was as good as anything else, if you only have enough of it." ('53-49-VIII 373)

When you talk with people in this country, the climate stimulates them to talk, but you soon come to the end of all they know. ('53-50-VIII 377)

He said, "An obelisk says but one word, *Here!* but it speaks very loud." ('53-50-VIII 391)

It is her glory that she takes her life in her hand, and is ready for a new world. ('53-50-VIII 393)

"On ne se dégage pas les voies où les siècles vous ont engagés." (DE NOAILLES.) You cannot free yourself from your times. ('53-50-VIII 402)

Mirabeau said of Robespierre, "That man will go far, he believes what he says." ('53-50-VIII 419)

And thus are politics the school of the people, the game which every one of them learns to play. ('53-50-VIII 420)

. . . that terrible gift of familiarity. ('53-50-VIII 430)

Bonaparte said, "In twenty-five years the United States will write the treaties of Europe. . . ." ('53-50-VIII 433)

He had only a *platform*-existence, and no personality.
('53-50-VIII 434)

Whenever a noble soul comes, the audience awaits. And he is not judged by his performance, but by the spirit of his performance. . . . ('54-50-VIII 445)

There are no finalities in Nature. ('54-50-VIII 446)

Culture teaches to omit the unnecessary word and to say the greatest things in the simplest way. *"Le secret d'ennuyer est celui de tout dire."* ('54-50-VIII 449)

. . . give me continuity. I am tired of scraps.
('54-50-VIII 463)

I am here to represent humanity: it is by no means necessary that I should live, but it is by all means that I should act rightly. If there is danger, I must face it. I tremble. What of that? so did he who said, "It is my body trembles, out of knowing into what dangers my spirit will carry it."
('54-50-VIII 469)

I, too, am an American and value practical ability. I delight in people who can do things, I prize talent—perhaps no man more. But I think of the wind, and not of the weathercocks.
('54-50-VIII 473)

. . . marry the means, and defeat the ends.
('54-50-VIII 479)

Universities are, of course, hostile to geniuses. . . .
('54-51-VIII 500)

The art of conversation, or the qualification for a good companion, is a certain self-control, which now holds the subject, now lets it go, with a respect to the emergencies of the moment. ('54-51-VIII 501)

But the English believe that by mountains of fact they can climb into the heaven of thought and truth. . . .
('54-51-VIII 505)

Don't attempt too many things. Unlimited activity is bankruptcy. ('55-51-VIII 516)

Beauty is the quality which makes to endure. . . .

('55-51-VIII 525)

But these fine young wits who write exquisite verses now, "the brain of a purple mountain," etc.—their poetry has no legs. ('55-51-VIII 527)

Common Fame. I trust a good deal to common fame, as we all must. If a man has good corn, or wood, or boards, or pigs, to sell, or can make better chairs or knives, crucibles or church organs, than anybody else, you will find a broad hard-beaten road to his house, though it be in the woods. And if a man knows the law, people find it out, though he live in a pine shanty, and resort to him. And if a man can pipe or sing, so as to wrap the prisoned soul in an elysium; or can paint landscape, and convey into oils and ochers all the enchantments of Spring or Autumn; or can liberate or intoxicate all people who hear him with delicious songs and verses; 't is certain that the secret cannot be kept: the first witness tells it to a second, and men go by fives and tens and fifties to his door. What a signal convenience is fame.

Well, it is still so with a thinker. If he proposes to show me any high secret, if he profess to have found the profoundly secret pass that leads from Fate to Freedom, all good heads and all mankind aspiringly and religiously wish to know it, and, though it sorely and unusually taxes their poor brain, they find out at last whether they have made the transit or no. If they have, they will know it; and his fame will surely be bruited abroad. ('55-51-VIII 528, 529)

Out upon scholars with their pale, sickly, etiolated indoor thoughts. Give me the out-of-door thoughts of sound men— the thoughts, all fresh, blooming. ('55-51-VIII 532)

A scholar is a man with this inconvenience, that, when you ask him his opinion of any matter, he must go home and look up his manuscripts to know. ('55-52-VIII 557)

It seems impossible to hold governments to the belief that the use of dishonest partnerships is as ruinous for nations as for private men. ('55-52-VIII 563)

I dread autobiography which usurps the largest part, sometimes the whole, of the discourse of very worthy persons whom I know. ('55-52-VIII 565)

You must not look at fireflies by daylight. ('59-56-IX 212)

The imagination enters into all the details and ennobles life.
('59-56-IX 234)

If Ellery Channing tells me, "Here is a good book," I know
I have a day longer to live. ('59-56-IX 238)

Then what a debt is ours to books. How much we owe to
imaginative books! ('59-56-IX 252)

The man who can make hard things easy is the educator.
('61-58-IX 342)

Cannot we let people be themselves, and enjoy life in their
own way? You are trying to make that man another *you*.
One's enough. ('62-58-IX 355)

We will not against disparage America, now that we have
seen what men it will bear. ('62-58-IX 359)

This world belongs to the energetical. ('62-58-IX 367)

Wherever snow falls, man is free. Where the orange blooms,
man is the foe of man. ('62-58-IX 368)

It is impossible to extricate oneself from the questions in
which your age is involved. You can no more keep out of
politics than you can keep out of the frost. ('62-58-IX 369)

Let us work rather for those interests which the gods honor
and promote: justice, love, utility, freedom, knowledge.
('62-58-IX 371)

Everything good is the result of antagonisms. . . .
('62-58-IX 400)

Resources or feats. I like people who can do things.
('62-59-IX 421)

If I receive good news every day, and give none of myself,
I am in false position, and a consumer and not a producer.
('62-59-IX 422)

He had no talent for wealth, and knew how to be poor
without the least hint of squalor or inelegance. Perhaps he fell
—all of us do—into his way of living, without forecasting it
much, but approved and confirmed it with later wisdom.
('62-59-IX 425)

I wish only to read that which it would be a serious disaster to have missed. ('62-59-IX 429)

"What other liberty is there worth having, if we have no freedom and peace in our minds, if our inmost and most private man is but a sour and turbid pool?"

('62-59-IX 430, 431)

When I bought my farm, I did not know what a bargain I had in the bluebirds, bobolinks, and thrushes; as little did I know what sublime mornings and sunsets I was buying.

('62-59-IX 447, 448)

[A lawyer says] I am a teacher of youth, and by taste a religionist, but I defy you to put your hand on any act or word of mine in behalf of what was unpopular. So far has Slavery poisoned the air of America, that an assertion of Freedom marks vulgarity. ('62-59-IX 448)

But ideas and their slow massive might are irresistible at last. ('62-59-IX 456)

But in a Democracy, every movement has a deep-seated cause. ('62-59-IX 460)

. . . war is not the greatest calamity. ('63-59-IX 493)

When we quarrel, how we wish we had been blameless!

('63-59-IX 497)

But the scholar must keep faith with himself. His sheet anchor is sincerity, and when he loses this, he loses really the talent of his talent. ('63-60-IX 528)

Time is short, but always long enough for the finest trait of courtesy. ('63-60-IX 562)

Men are good where they have experience, but not off their beat. ('64-61-X 47)

The test of civilization is the power of drawing the most benefit out of cities. ('64-61-X 54)

> Though Love recoil, and Reason chafe,
> There came a voice without reply,
> 'T is man's perdition to be safe,
> When for the Truth he ought to die.

('64-41-X 62)

Agassiz is perfectly accessible, has a brave manliness which can meet a peasant, a mechanic, or a fine gentleman with equal fullness. ('64-61-X 64, 65)

We read often with as much talent as we write.
('64-61-X 67)

The retrospective value of a new thought is immense. 'T is like a torch applied to a long train of powder. ('64-61-X 67)

How often I have to say that every man has material enough in his experience to exhaust the sagacity of Newton in working it out. We have more than we use. We know vastly more than we digest. I never read poetry, or hear a good speech at a caucus, or a cattle show, but it adds less stock to my knowledge than it apprises me of admirable uses to which what I knew can be turned. ('64-61-X 70)

[One] point would seem to be absolute—Emancipation—establishing the fact that the United States henceforward knows no color, no race, in its law, but legislates for all alike—one law for all men. . . . ('64-61-X 71)

The Age, and the Hour. The party of virility rules the hour, the party of ideas and sentiments rules the age. ('64-61-X 76)

America makes its own precedents. ('64-61-X 78)

Home from Chicago and Milwaukee. Chicago grows so fast that one ceases to respect civic growth: as if all these solid and stately squares which we are wont to see as the slow growth of a century had come to be done by machinery as cloth and hardware are made, and were therefore shoddy architecture without honor.

'T was tedious, the squalor and obstructions of travel; the advantage of their offers at Chicago made it necessary to go; in short, this dragging of a decorous old gentleman out of home and out of position to this juvenile career was tantamount to this—"I'll bet you fifty dollars a day that you will not leave your library, and wade and ride and run and suffer all manner of indignities and stand up for an hour each night reading in a hall"; and I answered, "I'll bet I will." I do it and win the $900. ('65-61-X 91, 92)

I should say of Samuel Hoar, Senior, what Clarendon writes of Sir Thomas Coventry, that "he had a strange power of making himself believed, the only justifiable design of eloquence." ('65-61-X 95)

There is no police so effective as a good hill and wide pasture in the neighborhood of a village, where the boys can run and play and dispose of their superfluous strength and spirits, to their own delight and the annoyance of nobody.

('65-61-X 95)

Criticism. Illusion of words. There are really few people who distinguish, on reading, a page full of words from a page full of new experience. They are satisfied with the first, if it is in harmony with their habitual opinions. ('65-61-X 95)

It is becoming to the Americans to dare in religion to be simple, as they have in government, in trade, in social life; and they have rightly pronounced Toleration—that no religious test shall be put. They are to abolish laws against atheism. ('65-61-X 99)

America. The difference between writers is that one counts forms, and the other counts powers. ('65-62-X 109)

. . . that this country belonged to the men of the most liberal persuasion. ('65-62-X 114)

Slowly they advanced towards each other as they could, and at last met, said nothing, but shook hands long and cordially. At last Cass said, "Any light, Tracy?" "None," answered Tracy; and then said, "Any light, Cass?" "None," replied he. They looked in each other's eye, gave one shake more each to the hand he held, and thus parted for the last time.

('65-62-X 121)

The Past will not sleep. It works still. With every new fact a ray of light shoots up from the long-buried years.

('65-62-X 124)

When I read a good book, say, one which opens a literary question, I wish that life were 3000 years long. ('66-62-X 140)

Bias. Seven men went through a field, one after another. One was a farmer, he saw only the grass; the next was an astronomer, he saw the horizon and the stars; the physician noticed the standing water and suspected miasma; he was followed by a soldier, who glanced over the ground, found it easy to hold, and saw in a moment how the troops could be disposed; then came the geologist, who noticed the boulders and the sandy loam; after him came the real-estate broker, who bethought him how the line of the house lots should run, where would be the driveway, and the stables. The poet admired the shadows cast by some trees, and still more the music of some thrushes and a meadow lark.

('66-63-X 146, 147)

I see with joy the Irish emigrants landing at Boston, at New York, and say to myself, There they go—to school.

('66-63-X 153)

I can find my biography in every fable that I read.

('66-63-X 162)

Every word in the language has once been used happily.

('66-63-X 174)

I don't know but I value the name of a thing, that is, the true poet's name for it, more than the thing. If I can set the right word for the moon, or about it—the word that suggests to me and to all men its humane and universal beauty and significance—then I have what I want of it, and shall not desire that a road may be made from my garden to the moon, or that the gift of this elephant be made over to me.

('66-63-X 175, 176)

Cunning egotism. If I cannot brag of knowing something, then I brag of not knowing it. At any rate, Brag.

('66-63-X 176)

The office of America is to liberate, to abolish kingcraft, priestcraft, caste, monopoly, to pull down the gallows, to burn up the bloody statute book, to take in the immigrant, to open the doors of the sea and the fields of the earth—to extemporize government in Texas, in California, in Oregon—to make provisional law where statute law is not ready. This liberation appears in the power of invention, the freedom of thinking, in readiness for reforms. . . . ('67-63-X 195)

The good writer seems to be writing about himself, but has his eye always on that thread of the universe which runs through himself, and all things. ('67-63-X 198)

For good quoting, then, there must be originality in the quoter—bent, bias, delight in the truth, and only valuing the author in the measure of his agreement with the truth, which we see, and which he had the luck to see first. . . .

('67-64-X 221)

Tax opium, tax poisons, tax brandy, gin, wine, hashish, to-bacco, and whatever articles of pure luxury, but not healthy and delicious food. ('68-64-X 229)

Extremes meet, and there is no better example than the haughtiness of humility. ('68-64-X 231)

Revolutions. In my youth, Spinoza was a hobgoblin; now he is a saint. ('68-64-X 237)

Beauty is in great part a moral effect. It comes to serenity, to cheerfulness, to benignity, to innocence, to settled noble purpose. It flees from the perplexed, the self-seeking, the cowardly, the mean, the despairing, the frivolous, and the stupid. Self-respect, how indispensable to it! A free and con-tented air. ('68-65-X 246, 247)

For my report on the Greek Committee I must not forget to insert my opinion on examinations—that whenever one is on trial, two are on trial; the examiner is instructed whenever the pupil is examined. ('68-65-X 259)

The only place where I feel the joy of eminent domain is in my woodlot. My spirits rise whenever I enter it. I can spend the entire day there with hatchet or pruning shears making paths, without a remorse of wasting time. I fancy the birds know me, and even the trees make little speeches or hint them. Then Allah does not count the time which the Arab spends in the chase. ('68-65-X 261)

"Don't ask me," he said to his pupils, "what I thought a year ago on this or that; ask me what I think today." He, Hunter, first used the expression *"arrested development,"* which plays so important a part in modern science.

('68-65-X 265)

Culture is one thing, and varnish another. There can be no high culture without pure morals. With the truly cultivated man—the maiden, the orphan, the poor man, and the hunted slave feel safe. ('68-65-X 269)

In the matter of religion, men eagerly fasten their eyes on the differences between their own creed and yours; whilst the charm of the study is in finding the agreements and identities in all the religions of men. ('69-65-X 278)

Alcott came, and talked Plato and Socrates, extolling them with gravity. I bore it long, and then said, that was a song for others, not for him. He should find what was the equivalent for these masters in our times; for surely the world was always equal to itself, and it was for him to detect what was the counterweight and compensation to us. ('69-65-X 287)

Reality, however has a sliding floor. ('71-68-X 365)

I thought today, in these rare seaside woods, that if absolute leisure were offered me, I should run to the college or the scientific school which offered best lectures on Geology, Chemistry, Minerals, Botany, and seek to make the alphabets of those sciences clear to me. How could leisure to labor be better employed? ('72-69-X 393)

His last words (except to say "Sit down" to Mr. Hooper, who came to his bedside, but had gone out before his death) were these: "Judge, tell Emerson how much I love and revere him." I replied, "He said of you once that he never knew so *white* a soul."

During the morning, he had repeated to several persons, to me among the rest, "You must take care of The Civil Rights Bill." That was his last public thought. ('74-70-X 430)

A man's style is his mind's voice. Wooden minds, wooden voices. Truth is shrill as a fife, various as a panharmonium. ('62-'72, 59-69-X 457)

Philosophy is called the homesickness of the soul.

('62-'72, 59-69-X 469)

MENTOR Books of Special Interest

EIGHT GREAT TRAGEDIES
  edited by Sylvan Barnet, Morton Berman and William Burto

  The great dramatic literature of the ages, and essays on the tragic form. (#MT195—75¢)

EIGHT GREAT COMEDIES
  edited by Sylvan Barnet, Morton Berman and William Burto

  A companion volume to **Eight Great Tragedies**, containing plays and essays. (#MD216—50¢)

THE GOLDEN TREASURY OF F. T. PALGRAVE
  enlarged and up-dated by Oscar Williams

  Great lyric poems of the English language from 1526 to the present. (#MT245—75¢)

THE SILVER TREASURY OF LIGHT VERSE
  edited by Oscar Williams

  Over 600 sparkling poems, from Chaucer to Ogden Nash and Gertrude Stein. (#MD201—50¢)

ENJOYING MODERN ART   **by Sarah Newmeyer**

  The unconventional lives of the great modern painters, from early French rebels to today. Illustrated.
  (#MD211—50¢)

THE PAINTER'S EYE   **by Maurice Grosser**

  A brilliant examination of conventions, principles, and techniques of painting, with 32 reproductions of masterpieces. (#MD159—50¢)

BOOKS THAT CHANGED THE WORLD
  by Robert B. Downs

  Histories of sixteen epoch-making books, from **The Prince** to **Theories of Relativity**. (#MD229—50¢)